ANCIENT HAWAIIAN CIVILIZATION

Cover design: Hawaiian tapa, courtesy of Bishop Museum, Honolulu

ANCIENT HAWAIIAN CIVILIZATION

A series of lectures delivered at
THE KAMEHAMEHA SCHOOLS

REVISED EDITION

by
E. S. CRAIGHILL HANDY
KENNETH P. EMORY
EDWIN H. BRYAN
PETER H. BUCK
JOHN H. WISE
and Others

CHARLES E. TUTTLE CO.: PUBLISHERS
Rutland, Vermont & Tokyo, Japan

Representatives

For Continental Europe:
BOXERBOOKS, INC., Zurich

For the British Isles:
PRENTICE-HALL INTERNATIONAL, INC., London

For Australasia:
PAUL FLESCH & CO., PTY. LTD., Melbourne

Published by the Charles E. Tuttle Company, Inc.
of Rutland, Vermont & Tokyo, Japan
with editorial offices at
Suido 1-chome, 2-6, Bunkyo-ku, Tokyo

Library of Congress
Catalog Card No. 65-23709

First printing, 1965

Printed in Japan

TABLE OF CONTENTS

INTRODUCTION

The second edition of *Ancient Hawaiian Civilization* is published with the generous permission of Frank E. Midkiff, who was President of The Kamehameha Schools at the time the first edition was published in 1933 and who was responsible for the organization of the lecture series comprising the contents of the book. Since 1939, Dr. Midkiff has been a member and president of the Board of Trustees of the Bernice P. Bishop Estate (foundation of The Kamehameha Schools) and the Bernice Pauahi Bishop Museum. He has also held membership on the Pacific War Memorial Commission and was United States High Commissioner of the Trust Territory of the Pacific Islands. The King of Denmark decorated him Knight of Danneborg.

There has been a scattered but steady demand for the first edition of *Ancient Hawaiian Civilization* to the point that the book has become a "collector's item." In preparation of the book for republication, fresh prints of the illustrations have been utilized and have been supplied through the courtesy of Margaret Titcomb, librarian of the Bishop Museum. The biographies have been updated with the assistance of the living authors. Certain deceased authors also made significant achievements in their respective fields following publication of the first edition of this book and their biographies have been amended accordingly.

Important discoveries have been made in several of the subject fields treated in *Ancient Hawaiian Civilization.* Through the courtesy of Roland Force, Director of the Bishop Museum, comments on such discoveries have been prepared and are included in this book. One comment involving religion and education is considered appropriate for this introduction. Since it was stated in the chapter on *Religion and Education* that the Polynesians had a conception of a supreme being, a creator god, knowlege of whom was so sacred that his priests were under oath not to divulge his name to any but the initiated, it has been revealed that the prayer to this god, given as an example, came from a Maori who had been a Christian convert and under the influence of biblical teachings. This and other evidence makes it appear doubtful that an esoteric cult of a supreme being was ancient or widespread in Polynesia as Dr. Peter H. Buck has explained in his book *The Coming of the Maori,* (Wellington,1949), pp. 533-36.

Kenneth Emory, chairman of the Department of Anthropology, and Marian Kelly, assistant in Anthropology of the Bishop Museum, have prepared summaries of certain of the chapters and these will be found at the end of the book following Chapter 29.

Harold W. Kent
President Emeritus
The Kamehameha Schools

PREFACE

The title of this book "Ancient Hawaiian Civilization" was selected with considerable care. Many people, including indeed many of the Hawaiian people themselves, are not aware that there existed in Hawaii a very thorough and, in many respects, adequate civilization a hundred years ago and more. Civilization in Hawaii a century and more ago was the civilization of the Stone Age, for the Hawaiians had no metals which would enable them to apply the principles of science to their living; and, whereas the Hawaiians of those days had no alphabet, no system of numbers such as the one we have adopted from the Arabs, no wheels such as came to Western civilization from the Orient, and lacked in other "distinctions" of modern Western civilization, nevertheless they had rules of living, modes, and customs which permitted them to live happily and healthfully in these islands in very large numbers.

The book itself, like other similar projects in The Kamehameha Schools, was conceived with a very definite purpose: it is intended to acquaint the Hawaiian people and others who come to Hawaii with the many fine things and social adaptations that existed in Ancient Hawaii, so that all concerned may have a respect for the achievements and customs of the Ancient Hawaiians, and so that the Hawaiians may have a justifiable and beneficial satisfaction and pride in their heritage.

There is growing up in Hawaii what has been significantly called a new Pacific race. This race is a composite of many of the best things from the many races that interact and fuse here in these Mid-Pacific islands. The Hawaiians were here first and although the present character of Hawaii is not that of Ancient Hawaii but is more that of a Western culture pattern, nevertheless the characteristics of Hawaii that are probably the most significant today are those that are coming to this new Pacific race from the Ancient Hawaiians. I refer to such characteristics as gentleness, happiness, hospitality, friendliness, and cooperativeness. These things are understood to be particularly needed in the world today and any source of such characteristics is to be looked upon with very great respect and consideration. The Hawaiians were never a savage people; in no case were strangers visiting their shores treated with other than hospitality and friendliness. Although they had not developed some of the characteristics that are regarded as so necessary in modern industrial society, they did have, to a large degree, the other characteristics that we are beginning to recognize as more important than the characteristics that make for successful individual competition.

The Hawaiians, then, had a significant civilization of their own and the chapters of this book bring out in a very interesting fashion various phases of this civilization.

This material has been compiled from lectures given at The Kamehameha Schools. Many of the lecturers are scientists who are widely known. They adapted their scientific knowledge to their audience of boys and girls, and in no case should the reader regard any of the lectures as being complete statements of these scientists on the subjects they presented. The lectures given by people who are not scientists were read and authenticated by members of the Bishop Museum staff. The material is authentic, but not exhaustive. It is intended for the boys and girls of Hawaii, not for the critical eye of other scientists or students.

We are very greatly indebted to each one who has contributed of his experience and thinking in the preparation of these lectures and especially to Dr. E. S. C. Handy, who advised generously in planning the course, to Mr. John Wise, who acted as chairman and arranged details of each meeting, and to Miss Helen Pratt, who has very carefully edited this book.

Frank E. Midkiff

President,
The Kamehameha Schools.

Honolulu, Hawaii.
May 1, 1933.

ANCIENT HAWAIIAN CIVILIZATION

CHAPTER 1

RACE*

E. S. C. HANDY

In Hawaii are found peoples of different races. It is very important that all of us who live in the islands have an understanding of just what race means, so that we may live together in friendship and yet continue to prize those things which are the best part of our own racial heritage. We are going to consider together many of those things which went to make up the civilization of ancient Hawaii. We shall begin with discussing race. Race is being talked about a great deal at the present time. Everyone is becoming race-concious. Nearly everyone is proud of his race. Some people, unfortunately, instead of being proud, are self-conscious about their racial descent. We cannot ignore race, whether we are of European blood, or of Polynesian or Asiatic descent, or of the mixed racial types growing up in Hawaii today. What we do need to do is to think intelligently about what race means.

Science attempts to measure race in certain very definite ways. The scientist makes certain measurements of the human body and of the remains of dead people found in caves and such places. These measurements give indications of the difference between such races as, for instance, the Chinese, the haole, and the Hawaiian. Some of these measurements are very accurate. Among these are head length, breadth, and height from ear hole to top, or height of the face from the chin to the top of the nose and from the bottom of the upper gum to the top of the nose; the nose length and the width of the face; the body stature, breadth of shoulders, length of arms, the proportion of the body, and all of these things. Races differ in bodily proportions. For instance, the old Hawaiian type has a much longer body from the waist up in comparison with the length

* This chapter is arranged from stenographic notes of an extemporaneous lecture delivered by Dr. Handy, who read and corrected the notes.

of the legs, than the northern European or haole type. The blond haole has long legs and a short trunk. The Hawaiian has a long trunk and short legs.

In addition to the measurements described, observations are taken of the color of the skin where it is not sunburned, and of the color and shape of the hair. Hair has various shapes. A cross-section of perfectly straight hair, such hair as Chinese have, is, under the microscope, perfectly round. On the other hand very curly hair studied under the microscope, appears flat. Other observations are made—of the teeth, of eye color, of eye form. On the basis of all these measurements and observations, the scientist attempts to define the different racial types. When these racial characteristics are analyzed, it is found that every race is really a complex type made up of mixtures and is not by any means a separate and distinct division of the human race. Even the Chinese who appear more or less alike are a very mixed type. The same thing is true of the Japanese, of the Portuguese, and of all the people living in Hawaii. Haoles are mixtures of three distinct European races. Anthropologists have established the fact that all modern races of the sort that have come to Hawaii—the haole, the Oriental, the old Hawaiians—are all mixed races. The process that is going on today in Hawaii in the intermarrying of the different races is nothing but a continuation of what has gone on for thousands of years in the Pacific and all over the world.

When measurements and observations are made, most of the traits and characteristics are found to be variable. The height of people changes with their diet, with the place of abode, and with the amount of exercise they take; height is not a permanent unchanging characteristic. Skin color is very variable, affected as it is by the sun. The proportions of the body are more fixed than stature and color. But the most permanent thing about the human body apparently is the shape of the head. The skull seems to be a thing that has crystallized, so to speak, and which maintains its shape generation after generation regardless of where people live. The shape of the skull remains the same, in spite of migrations from cold climates to warm ones, in spite of changes in diet, customs, and ways of living. The skull may be regarded as a permanent sign of what is behind a particular racial type. When we are interested in determining the nature of the Hawaiian racial type, we take Hawaiian skulls and measure them. We measure the heads of living Hawaiians. We study these measurements and compare them with measurements of skulls of other peoples in the world. In this manner we attempt to find out just what other races the Hawaiians most closely resemble, and from this, to determine just where the ancestors of the Hawaiian people came from.

We may think of the process that is going on here in Hawaii, and which has gone on for thousands of years, as one in which different streams of racial stock flow into Hawaii just as streams flow into a lake. We may think of the Pacific as land, of Hawaii as a lake; then the people coming in from all directions are just like streams flowing into one central lake. And these streams of peoples have brought with them different head forms and different characteristics. They have poured in here and formed the Hawaiian type. So far as scientists have been able to discover, there was an old and very early stream which came into all the islands of the Pacific and into Hawaii, which seems to have been closely related to the northern European type. It was a tall long-headed type with reddish tinge in skin and hair. It is preserved in the ehu type in Hawaii and in all the other island groups. So far as is known, it is the oldest Polynesian type. That old type probably came in out of central Asia and very likely it came down through the islands east of China into Polynesia. It is a type found all through central Asia. Some of these people probably moved out into Europe where they became the north European type. Others moved through Asia and into the islands of the Pacific. When we say that this type is like the north European type, we do not mean that it is just the same. It was, rather, the common ancestor from which the north Europeans and the early Polynesian types derived. In India there is a type belonging to the same race. Here it has the brown skin of the Polynesian, while in the cold climate of Europe the type is blond. But wherever that racial type is found today, it is tall and long-headed, with a tendency toward reddish hair and ruddy skin.

A second type, which seems to be Mongolian, entered Hawaii later. Probably it came in by a more southerly route through the islands to the south. This type is closely related to the south Chinese or Malay type. It is shorter in stature than this earlier type, it has straight black hair, and it has a tendency to have eyes like the Chinese. The face and skull closely resemble those of the south Chinese, though the skin color is much darker. A third type which seems to have come in still later is hard to describe exactly. It seems to be strongly represented in the Alii type and is related apparently most closely to another European type, the central European or Alpine, which is also found in various parts of Asia. In the ancient Hawaiian, there are then two European types and one Asiatic type. There was also in old Polynesia a dash of negroid blood acquired probably in passing through the islands of the western Pacific which are inhabited by blacks.

For the last century and a half, since the discovery of Hawaii, Europeans of both the tall long-headed type and the tall short-headed type have been coming in again, and another European type, the south European, represented by the Portuguese, has also come in. Meanwhile, from Asia the Mongolians have come again, and mixed here with the Hawaiians and the Europeans. In the racial process going on today there is, in this mixing of Asiatic and European types, a continuation of the process which began a thousand or two thousand years ago when the original ancestors of the Hawaiians began coming to the islands. What does this mean for the future? It means that in this same group of islands there are now, again, streams of the same racial elements which came some two thousand years ago to create the old type, and that these new streams are combining with the old type to create a new Hawaiian type for the future. This new type will be a stronger type, because it is known in biology that the incoming of new blood always strengthens the species.

We speak in anthropology of the influence of environment. What we mean by environment is all of the things in climate and in the food that we eat, in the sun, the sea, the wind, which influence the form of the human body and the mode of living. Because we live so close to nature in Hawaii, environment has a strong influence on us. When people live shut up in houses, when they have to put on heavy clothing, as they do in Europe; then the sun, the sea, the wind, and the soil cannot work as directly on them as they do on the people of Hawaii. Environment works both directly and indirectly.The sun is always at work on us here in the islands. It is tanning people with dark skins and burning people with light skins; it is creating vitamins in the blood; it is affecting the nervous system. The sea and the fresh water, the swimming, influence people here all the time. The food that is eaten is building the body. The very bones of the body are built out of the poi, the fish, the vegetables, and the other foods eaten. These foods are largely the products of this environment. They come from the soil and the sea. Everyone born and living in Hawaii is to a great extent built out of the soil of Hawaii, out of its sunshine, its air, and its water. There is always a constant process of the direct working of the local environment on the body. Then there is also the powerful process of selecting traits and characteristics in bodies, and selecting bodies suitable to the local environment. This process of selection may be explained if we imagine two families living in some very hot part of Hawaii. One of these families, let us suppose, is dark-skinned with dark hair while the other is light-skinned and light-haired. In the intense sun of the region in which they live, the brown-skinned people are better off than the light-skinned people. The children of the light-skinned people will not be as well adjusted as the children of the other family. If the two families continue to live in this locality for half a dozen generations, and breed independently, at the end of that time the dark-skinned persons will be healthier than the others. This power of the environment to select the types and the traits suitable for a particular region is called natural selection. When we consider the influence of environment on people, we must bear in mind the double process always going on—the process of building the body, and the process of choosing physical traits suitable for the climate. That process has been going on here all the time through a thousand or two thousand years. That process selected those traits most suitable to Hawaii and it is these traits which are represented by the old Hawaiian stock.

The Hawaiian sun and soil and sea, which are exactly the same as they were when the first Hawaiian came to the islands, are slowly and irresistably at work selecting the same traits out of the new racial streams coming here. Very likely the Hawaiian type of a thousand years hence will be something like the Hawaiian type of the present, since the whole process at work will probably select the same type again and bring out the same characteristics. Of course, life is not so simple here now as it was a few hundred years ago, and even in Hawaii environment cannot continue to act so powerfully on the individual as it did in the past. Also, civilization is improving and becoming more refined, so the entire Hawaiian environment will probably produce in the course of the coming generations, a much higher type, a stronger type, a more intense type, and a more refined type than it produced in the past.

Hawaii is often spoken of as a melting pot. The United States is called a melting pot. In each case, the melting pot refers to the process of racial assimilation which is going on in these countries. Some people say we ought not to talk about race at all because this intensifies the differences which exist, and that if we are going to be melted up together the best thing we can do is to forget race. It might be a good thing if we could do that but we cannot. It is not the racial studies of the scientist which make people conscious of racial differences. Race consciousness is a thing which has been slowly developing and becoming stronger over the world, especially during the last twenty or thirty years with the newly awakened self-consciousness of people of different nationalities. Different nations of the world and the different races of the world are gradually becoming conscious of themselves and of their characteristics. No one can avoid this race consciousness. Is it not better that we take hold of it and make it intelligent, refusing to allow it to degenerate into stupid race prejudice? The value of making racial studies and observations, the value of considering the topic of race, lies in the possibility of developing through these means an intelligent attitude toward the subject. When anyone takes these observations, these studies, these discussions, and looks at them impersonally, he gets a different feeling about the whole matter and knows there is no reason to be hilahila about race. Some races are very race proud. Northern Europeans are very race proud. The Chinese in China are perhaps the most race proud people known, for they think all foreigners are devils. Such a feeling comes from prejudice and from ignorance. The only way to get rid of such false race pride is to obtain an intelligent understanding of the meaning and composition of race.

At the present time, there is a very strong and definite tendency on the part of Hawaiians to draw apart and feel, as a group, separate from the rest of the community. If any such thing as the isolation and the drawing aside of the Hawaiians results from this tendency, it will be the most unfortunate thing that could happen to them. No reason, however strong, could justify this withdrawal, because the whole destiny of the place here is a common one and all the people here must work things out together. Any group which pulls aside and stands off alone against the others is bound in the long run to lose out. It will be a very unfortunate thing for the Hawaiian people if they allow anything to get hold of them, take them out of the community, and intensify their race consciousness so that they want to stand apart from the other races.

There is another side to race, besides the physical side which has been described. That is the matter of personality. What really is meant by being Hawaiian? Some people of Hawaiian blood do not know about Hawaiian life or Hawaiian history. They do not know about the Hawaiian race, and they do not think as Hawaiians do. Are these people really Hawaiian? On the other hand, there are haoles in the islands who are so Hawaiian in everything they think and do that they are Hawaiian in this matter of personality. What is meant when anyone says, "I am a Hawaiian?" Does he mean that he happens to have some blood of the old Hawaiian race? That is probably what he means, but it is not enough, if we are to think of race in terms of human behavior. The important thing about race is really the point of view of the people. The Hawaiian point of view is extremely valuable and important to the community as a whole. For example, all of us here in Hawaii, whether we have Hawaiian blood or not, are proud of the fact that we have aloha for each other and for strangers. This feeling of aloha is one of the things we consider Hawaiian. Any such attitude belongs to anyone who feels it, whether he has Hawaiian blood or not. It belongs to the Japanese—if they feel it. It belongs to the Chinese—if they feel it. It belongs to the Portuguese or to the Filipinos—if they feel it. In other words, the things on which the Hawaiians pride themselves most are things which do not really belong to any race but to the place. Therefore, it is really impossible for true Hawaiians to draw apart and be a separate group because there are many other people who are just as Hawaiian in this matter of attitude and point of view, as those of Hawaiian blood.

There is a phrase which the people of Hawaii may well remember. The more mixed the racial make-up of an individual, the more meaning this phrase has, because every racial type which is here in Hawaii has come from first-class stock. People who are of mixed Oriental, Hawaiian, and haole descent can apply this phrase with three times the force of anyone who represents one racial type only. The phrase is,

"Remember the dignity of your race."

Every single advanced human race today—Oriental, Hawaiian, or haole—each one represents millions of years of evolution, of selection of traits by climate, of struggles of ancestors to adapt themselves to better living on the earth. Every one represents extremely valuable and precious elements. If we remember the "dignity" of our race, we have an appreciation of all these years of evolution, and of these valuable and precious elements represented in every racial type.

REFERENCES

Handy, E. S. C., The Problems of Polynesian Origins, B. P. Bishop Museum Occasional Papers, Vol. 9, No. 8.

Dixon, Roland B., Racial History of Man, Introduction and pages 343-390.

Shapiro, Harry Lionel, The Physical Characters of the Society Islanders, B. P. Bishop Museum Memoirs, Vol. III, No. 4.

Sullivan, Louis Robert, A Contribution to Tongan Somatology, B. P. Bishop Museum Memoirs, Vol. 8, pt. 4.

Sullivan, Louis Robert, Marquesan Somatology with Comparative Notes on Samoa and Tonga, B. P. Bishop Museum Memoirs, Vol. 9 pt. 2.

Sullivan, Louis Robert, Observations in Hawaiian Somatology, B. P. Bishop Museum Memoirs, Vol. 9, No. 4.

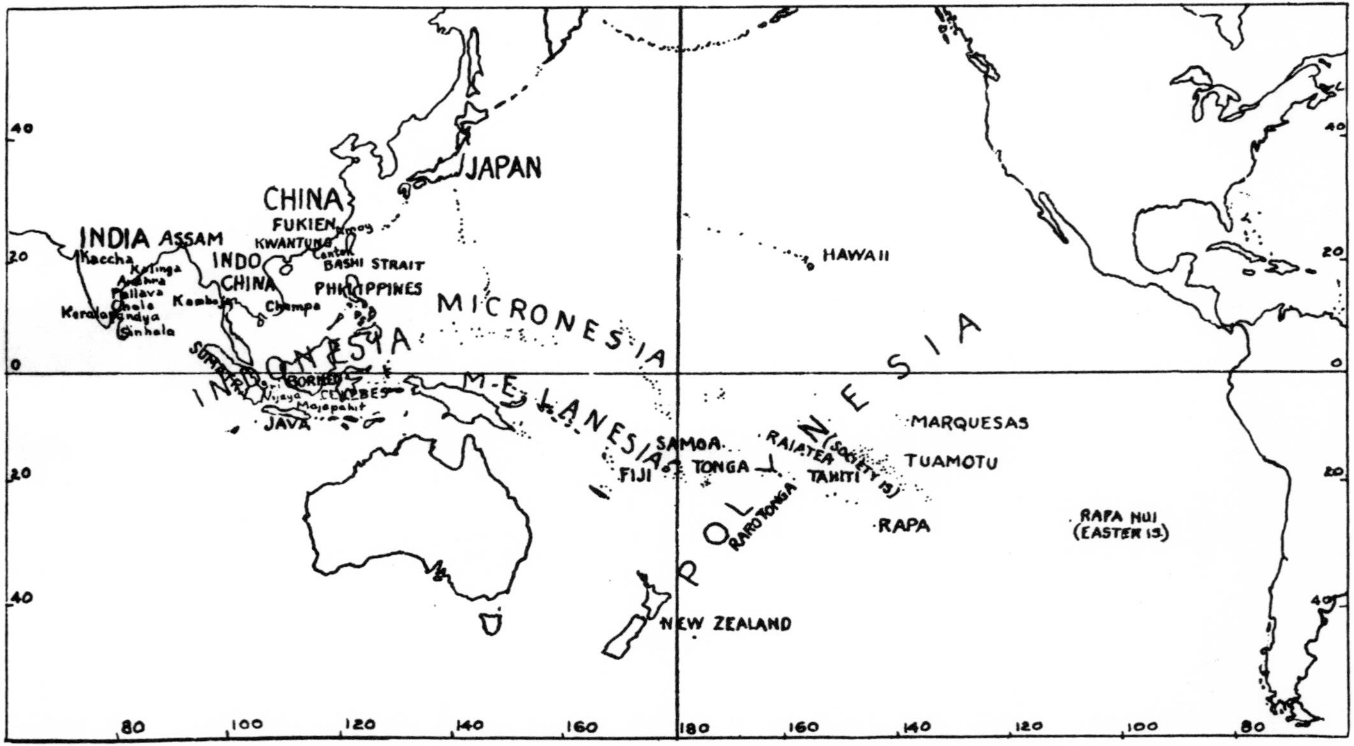

Chief Pacific Island Groups

CHAPTER 2

POLYNESIAN MIGRATIONS

PETER H. BUCK

The ancestors of the Polynesian people are held by most scientists to have been a Caucasian offshoot which worked east from south of the Himalayas and reached the islands of the Malay archipelago known collectively as Indonesia. There they came in contact with the Mongoloid ancestors of the Malays who had pushed south into the same region. A certain amount of intermixture took place, followed by conflict which resulted in the push east into the Pacific of the mixed Caucasian-Mongoloid people. This mixed people, largely Caucasian and to lesser degree Mongoloid, formed what are now termed the Polynesians.

The Polynesians developed the knowledge of seacraft provided with a single outrigger, and became a seafaring people. They made voyages between the large islands of Indonesia and so acquired the foundations of the knowledge that was ultimately to lead them to the farthest lands in the Pacific Ocean. Many writers have held that the Polynesians worked out into the Pacific at the beginning of the Christian era. This date has been arrived at largely from the studies of Abraham Fornander of Hawaii and Percy Smith of New Zealand. Both these scholars relied on the genealogies preserved by various branches of the Polynesian people. Later comparative studies, however, indicate that long genealogies are unreliable after they pass beyond the settlement of the islands in which the genealogies have been recorded. Even so, traditional stories with accompanying genealogies give some idea of the order in time in which historical events took place.

Migrations refer to the movements of peoples who leave one area of settlement and journey to another. It does not follow that the Polynesians moved in large numbers at the same time. It is more likely that small groups, owing to pressure from behind, moved out and effected landings on islands farther to the east. In islands already occupied, the immigrants exercised diplomacy or force to maintain their occupation. The first pioneers were followed up by other groups, and later again, those who had held on longest to the earlier home were forced to leave in order to avoid slavery or death. Thus there were movements of small groups or expeditions seeking new homes and such movements probably extended over a fair period of time. When the opposition encountered in the various islands was strong, the Polynesian group was forced to move on after periods of armed rest. So the movements to the east continued until unoccupied islands were discovered that could be converted into permanent homes. Two routes were open for the Polynesian migrations into the heart of the Pacific which they ultimately occupied. The evidence indicates that both routes were used.

The northern or Micronesian route extends from the Philippines through the Carolines with an eastern branching to the Marshall and Gilbert islands. While the Philippines form the western end of the route, it is possible that movements extended to the Carolines from Indonesia. To the north of the Carolines lie the Marianas, which Polynesian groups may have reached. From a somewhat uncertain Hawaiian legend recorded by Fornander, it has been assumed that an ancestor named Hawaii-loa may have reached Hawaii from the Marshall Islands. The divergence of a Polynesian ancestor from a general easterly route to a northeast course that would lead to Hawaii is also recorded in Maori tradition. The date of this voyage has been placed by Percy Smith as the year 450 A.D. Such traditions require support from other sources before they can be accepted. If the Micronesian route was followed it is probable that the Polynesians were the first people to occupy that region. Later, however, waves of Mongoloid people entered the area and the resulting Micronesian people became predominantly Mongoloid. The presence of pure Polynesian words in Micronesia, certain forms of stonework, and the use of the sling as a projectile weapon, are indications of affinity with Polynesia. Thus Polynesian movements through Micronesia to Polynesia may be assumed, but a more detailed field study of Micronesia is required to provide adequate material for scientific analysis.

The southern or Melanesian route passes from Indonesia along the north coast of New Guinea, the sea fringe of Melanesia to Fiji, and thence on to the Polynesian groups of Samoa and Tonga. New Guinea and Melanesia were too strongly occupied by people of Negroid stock for the Polynesians to obtain permanent footing. Various early Polynesian traditions record conflicts with dark-skinned people and students refer these allusions to the period when the Polynesians were fighting their way along to western Polynesia. In such contacts, conflicts did not always occur and some Polynesian groups may have dropped out on the way. The superiority of the culture of Melanesia to that of New Guinea has been held by some scholars to be due to the interaction between immigrant Polynesian groups and the aboriginal people. Such small groups were absorbed into the local masses. They ceased to be Polynesians and leavened the culture of the Melanesians. Other Polynesian groups again settled on a few outlying islands in Melanesia, such as Ticopia, Rennell, and Ontong Java. They seem to have retained the basis of Polynesian social organization but it remains for the publication of recent field work in these islands to reveal how far they were affected both physically and culturally by their Melanesian neighbors.

In Polynesia itself, the study of skeletal and living material has led some physical anthropologists to see traces of Melanesian characteristics. If they are correct, such traces indicate that intermixture took place back in Melanesia or in Polynesia itself. If it took place in Polynesia, the fact that the Melanesians were better navigators than they are usually thought to have been, would have to be admitted. Percy Smith held that such traces might be due to slave crews that their Polynesian masters brought with them. Another possibility is that drift canoes of Melanesians reached some Polynesian islands. In Easter Island, the strong preponderance of Melanesian physical characteristics in the collected skeletal material together with the long ear lobes of the stone images, creates a problem as to whether or not Melanesians actually reached that most eastern island of Polynesia. On the other hand we may express the doubt as to whether the so-called Melanesian characteristics in Polynesia are really due to Melanesians. Our physical survey of Polynesia has been practically concluded but an analysis of the data has yet to be made. The physical survey of Melanesia as an organized effort has yet to be commenced. At present, therefore, a comparison of Polynesian and Melanesian physical characteristics, rests on such insufficient data that the question of Melanesian voyages into Polynesia may be regarded as doubtful.

Let us now consider the Polynesian pioneer group who had arrived at the eastern bounds of Micronesia and Melanesia by various stages through a number of generations. By this time they were seamen of marked ability and courage.

They used the single canoe for ordinary purposes but for voyages of any extent they used a second canoe in place of the ama or outrigger float. If they were acquainted with metals when they left Asia, their metal tools had long ago worn out and could not be replaced with iron. They fell back upon stone to hew down trees and shape the wood into the seacraft required. In coral atolls where there was no stone they shaped the shells of the Tridacna into adzes. To supplement the paddles, they used triangular sails plaited from the leaves of the Pandanus. They had studied the signs of the skies and the vagaries of the ocean. They had named the stars that gave them direction and they were acquainted with the winds which blew from various points. They had a calendar based on the stages of the monthly moons, and an annual cycle that counted from certain positions of the Pleiades. They knew the seasons of the westerly winds and the run of the constant trades. They knew the hurricane season and so could divide the year into a period when it was unsafe to brave the sea, and when good fortune might sit in the belly of their sails. Above all they had leaders who had a supreme confidence in themselves and an intelligent priesthood who could not only placate the gods, but, more important still, read the signs of the heavens from the stars, the moon, the Milky Way, and even the Magellan clouds as guiding signs across the trackless ocean. They gazed east at the "hanging skies" where heaven and earth met, and there grew up the urge to pierce through to the lands which they were convinced lay on the trail of a guiding star. Perhaps some push from behind sent an early wave in small and detached groups voyaging east into the unknown. That the push or the urge was great we may assume from the fact that they took their women folk with them. Thus by stages the islands of western Polynesia were discovered and settled. Perhaps quarrels as to chieftainship and prestige led small groups, perhaps even in single canoes, to make further expeditions to the east. So intervening islands and the central region of the Society Islands became occupied.

From traditional narratives and the distribution of certain cultural elements, we may divide the movements of the Polynesians into an earlier and a later period. The earlier people were the pioneers who reached various islands and settled down without thought of returning whence they came. Such were the original settlers of Hawaii known as the Menehune, and also the earliest settlers of Tahiti named Manahune. The first settlers of New Zealand and the Chatham Islands may have belonged to the same early wave. The Maori traditions that the earliest settlers had marked Melanesian characteristics were recorded by the later people and cannot be accepted without reservation. The Chatham Islanders were a Polynesian people and it is probable that the earliest settlers in New Zealand were Polynesians also. The early wave thus settled in central Polynesia (Society Islands) and reached Hawaii in the north and New Zealand in the south. It is also probable that they extended east as far as Easter Island. From such evidence as we have, it seems that the early people had a simpler form of social organization in which the blood kinship of all members of the tribe was stressed. They had an open religious meeting place in which spaced upright stones formed the main feature. They thatched their houses with grass and with leaves tied to horizontal battens. They probably had no cultivable foods and relied upon the Pandanus largely for their vegetable food. They deserve admiration for their achievements in peopling Polynesia. Unfortunately, the records of their voyages have been submerged by the traditional narratives of those who came later on the scene.

The later period is characterized by the rich traditional narratives of the "long voyages." These voyages were made from central Polynesia in organized expeditions under the leadership of alii or chiefs, with learned priests as navigators. They discovered unoccupied islands and also rediscovered islands already occupied by the earlier people of the same stock. The main voyages extended from the end of the 11th to the 14th centuries, and then ceased. The voyages were actuated in the first instance by the spirit of pure adventure, the desire to break through the "hanging skies." In many instances, the voyagers returned to central Polynesia and not only related their discoveries but gave the directions by which the new lands might be reached. The crews consisted of picked men whose shoulders could bear the strain of the deep sea paddle. They were trained to endurance and to self-control with regard to food and water. They were brave men who feared neither adverse elements nor hostile forces. If they weathered the storm and emerged to a fair haven, all was well. If they were engulfed in the waters of the great ocean, they went down as men. Such are the terms applied to the early voyagers in the native narratives and today they give a thrill of pride to those of us who come of such stock.

The earlier voyagers of this period took no women or food plants with them. The later voyagers took cultivable food plants, and so the coconut, taro, yam, and sweet potato were spread through Polynesia. Where people of the early period were in occupation, conflict sooner or later occurred but in the end the alii chiefs of the later wave acquired dominance and rule. Though traditional narratives state that the earlier wave was conquered and practically exterminated, it is certain that such accounts have been exaggerated. The two peoples intermarried and fused. The earlier people formed the mass of the common people while the later alii families became the leaders and rulers. New elements were introduced into the culture by the later comers but where the earlier wave persisted in large numbers, elements of their culture survived and were adapted in the blended culture that resulted.

Raiatea and Tahiti in the Society Islands form the center of diffusion of the later period. The ancient name of Raiatea was Hawaii, and this name in various dialectical forms figures as the starting point of most of the "long voyages." Kupe sailed for Hawaiki to the south seas and discovered the "Land of the High Mists," subsequently named Aotearoa (the long white cloud) and later again, New Zealand, by the belated voyagers of another race. Kupe returned and gave the sailing directions as a little left of the setting sun in the Maori month which corresponds to the lunar month of November-December. From a number of genealogies, Kupe's discovery of New Zealand has been placed at about the period 950 A. D. Kupe reported that he saw no human beings but one tradition states that he saw smoke inland from the coast of the North Island. It is quite possible that the early wave of people had reached New Zealand at this period, but had not spread to the parts visited by Kupe.

Two centuries later a celebrated Maori ancestor named Toi sailed down to the Land of the High Mists in search of his grandson Whatonga, who had been blown out to sea during a regatta in Hawaiki. Toi found the country fairly thickly populated in parts by a people who had been blown away while journeying from one island to another. These people had no cultivable food plants. Toi was later joined by his grandson, who had returned to Hawaiki after Toi's departure, and in his turn set out to seek his grandfather. The two vessels brought no women. The two crews married wives from the earlier people and the mixed Toi tribes resulted.

An interesting Maori tradition relates the arrival of two chiefs who brought dried cooked sweet potatoes as part of their sea stores. The new food created a desire for the plant and an expedition sailed back into central Polynesia to secure sweet potato tubers for cultivation. Between the years 1150 A. D. and 1350 A. D. various voyaging canoes came to New Zealand from Hawaiki. It is also probable that during that period return voyages were made. Information regarding the new land in the south had been carried back to Hawaiki for traditions handed down by the East Coast tribes of New Zealand show that when their ancestor Paikea arrived, he went very definitely to places where the inhabitants were related to him. A number of famous canoes such as the Tainui, Arawa, Tokomaru, Mataatua, Kurahaupo, and Takitimu have been grouped together in narrative and song and this has led to the erroneous idea that they came in one fleet. The evidence shows that they were spaced in time. The Aotea and Te Ririno came together and after encountering a severe storm the Aotea called in at the Kermadec Islands, refitted, and made New Zealand. The Horouta and Mamaru are other well known canoes. The later canoes came definitely to settle and brought their women folk and the cultivable food plants such as taro, yam, and sweet potato. The year 1350 A. D. is usually regarded as the date when immigration ceased and the "sacred tide to Hawaiki was cut off." The shorter genealogies from the Mamaru canoe, however, may indicate that it came later.

The crews of the various voyaging canoes selected areas for settlement that would avoid clashing with one another. When they became established, they fought and fused with the earlier wave who were called the "people of the land," (tangata whenua). Family groups expanded into subtribes (hapu) and tribes (iwi) until the whole North Island was divided up into canoe areas occupied by tribes which acknowledged a common ancestral origin. In the greater area of land available for development, they became landsmen and the urge for the long sea voyages ceased. The glories of their achievements on the great ocean of Kiwa were perpetuated in narrative, speech, and song. The common welcome to visiting tribes harks back to the time when the canoe was the chief means of transport.

Toia mai, te waka!	Draw hither, the canoe!
Kumea mai, te waka!	Haul hither, the canoe!
Ki te urunga, te waka!	To its pillow, the canoe!
Ki te moenga, te waka!	To its bed, the canoe!
Ki te takotoranga i takoto ai te waka.	To the resting place where shall rest, the canoe.
Haere mai, haere mai.	Welcome, twice welcome.

The northern discovery and settlement of the Hawaiian islands had been made by the Menehune, at some early period. Later came the alii invaders from Tahiti (Kahiki). Those voyages appear to have extended from the 11th to the 13th centuries and thus ceased earlier than those to New Zealand. From Tahiti to Hawaii is 2400 miles but some of the intervening small islands may have been used for resting places. Bruce Cartwright advances the interesting suggestion that the annual migration of the golden plover (kolea) to the south from Alaska through the Hawaiian islands may have given the people in Tahiti the idea of land to the north. The Hawaiian myth of Papa, who after marriage to Wakea gave birth to the islands, contains what might be regarded as confirmatory evidence. Papa left the Hawaiian region on a visit to Tahiti and in her absence Wakea married Hoohoku-lani. The news of Wakea's infidelity was told to Papa in Tahiti by the kolea, or golden plover.

The dates of the alii voyages to Hawaii are like all others, approximate. The Hawaiian genealogies though long, are somewhat confused. An analysis by Stokes shows that a number of names personifying natural phenomena have been introduced among the names of human ancestors. This has occurred also in other parts of Polynesia. The dates of the outstanding alii immigrants are tabulated below from the recent analysis of Hawaiian genealogies by Bruce Cartwright. The number of generations is taken back from 1900 A. D. and I have allowed 25 years to a generation.

Ancestral line	Visitor to Hawaii	Generations from 1900	Approximate date of arrival
(1) Puna	Newa-lani	34	1050 A. D.
(2) Hema	Hua, or son Pau	31	1125 A. D.
(3) Nana-mua	Mawake	28	1200 A. D.
	Moikeha	26	1250 A. D.
(4)	Pili-kaaiea	25	1275 A. D.

The Puna line is well known in the Society and Cook Islands. The Hema line is also widely known even as far as New Zealand. The voyage of Moikeha from Tahiti brought up in Hilo Bay, when the bard Kama-hua-lele stood up on the platform of the double canoe and recited his chant to the land commencing with the words:

Eia Hawaii	Behold Hawaii
E moku	An island
E Kanaka	A people

The last voyage was brought about by the priest Paao who came from Tahiti and seeing that the chiefly stock had degenerated in the person of Kapawa, he returned to Tahiti to get fresh alii blood. He returned with Pili-kaaiea whom he established in high chieftainship on the island of Hawaii. Traditional narrative relates that he was responsible for a changed form in the heiau religious structures, and that he also introduced human sacrifice and the red feather girdle (malo ula) of the alii nui. From these introductions, Paao must be associated with Tahiti and not Samoa. The voyages of Lono-mai-kahiki, Kalana, and others are recorded in Hawaiian tradition. The channel between the islet of Kahoolawe and the huge island of Maui, named Ke-ala-i-kahiki (the way to Tahiti) remains as a record of the fact that the voyagers took their departure from this point when they ran south to Tahiti. They sailed south by keeping the North Star (Hokupaa) directly eastern and when they lost it in the sea behind on crossing the Equator (Te Piko o Wakea), they picked up the southern guiding star Newe and the constellation of Humu stood overhead. In the period of the "long voyages" the 2400 miles of sea were crossed and recrossed by the Hawaiian ancestors who have handed down a record of daring achievement of which their descendants may be justly proud.

In the central area, the Manahune original settlers were overcome by the Arii families who spread out from Raiatea. The later waves spread out from the central distributing center to the neighboring islands. Each island or island group has its own historical narrative, and most have evidence of an earlier wave of people followed by later adventurers who secured the chieftainship and rule. The Tahitian narratives and genealogies while quite clear about the conquest of the Manahune of Tahiti by the Arii families from Raiatea are stragely lacking in detail as to whence the Arii families came from to Raiatea. Lacking a separate origin, it is possible that they belonged to the same people as the earlier wave but developed a higher form of culture in Raiatea. The growth of the population and increase of knowledge in organization and seacraft may have led to the adventurous voyages that extended from the 10th or 11th centuries.

The farthest eastern outpost colonized by the Polynesians is Easter Island. The stretch of sea between Easter Island and the coast of South America is less than that crossed between Tahiti and Hawaii or New Zealand. That some Polynesian voyagers reached South America has usually been regarded as doubtful. Yet the problem of the distribution of the sweet potato in space and time cannot be lightly disposed of. Some botanists maintain that Central or South America is the original home of the sweet potato. We know from traditional narrative that the sweet potato had been carried to both Hawaii and New Zealand before Columbus discovered America. Professor Roland Dixon of Harvard supports the fact that if America is the original home, the sweet potato must have been brought into Polynesia by some Indian tribe or by Polynesians who reached South America and returned. The Indian tribes were not seamen and they had ample land to meet their requirements. It is thus a fitting climax to our sketch of the Polynesian migrations to say that the Polynesians by various waves and in various stages traversed the whole width of the great Pacific Ocean from Asia to America and returned with the sweet potato as evidence of their having reached the "Ultima Thule."

CHAPTER 3

GOVERNMENT AND SOCIETY *

E. S. C. HANDY

In the old days in Hawaii there was no organized system of government such as we have today. The organization of the community was very different from anything we have now. People lived differently, they felt differently toward each other. In those days the government was the king. All the power was in the hands of one man towards whom all the rest of the people felt the greatest respect and whose actions were not questioned. Under the king there was the great mass of the Hawaiian people, who may be thought of as falling roughly into three main classes.

THE CLASSES OF THE PEOPLE

In the old days, the mass of the people were called makaainana. The word is interesting because it refers to the relationship of the people to the land. The makaainana were the people who lived on the land. Aina means land, but it has a deeper meaning because it is derived from the word meaning "to eat." The word actually means the land on which a person is born and from which he gets his living. The makaainana were the common people, the laboring masses, the cultivators of the soil, the fishermen, hunters, and craftsmen. In wartime they fought for the chief or king. Amongst themselves, their goods and their labor were shared or exchanged, but it was the right of the chief or king to require of them what he pleased, in goods or in services. Compensation for labor was, for the most part, in the form of gifts—food, cloth, mats, utensils, etc. There was no medium of exchange or money. Those who worked for the chief had their livelihood from him as compensation.

There was a distinct division of labor on the basis of

* This chapter is arranged from stenographic notes of an extemporaneous lecture delivered by Dr. Handy. The notes were read and corrected by Dr. Handy.

sex. Fighting, fishing, canoe and house building, making implements and utensils, feather work, farming, and priest-craft, were men's work. Men did the cooking, making separate imus for themselves and their women-folk. Women made kapa, wove mats and baskets, and raised their children. There was no routine labor in the old days. This probably explains why most Hawaiians today do not like routine work.

Besides the makaainana, there were two other classes, one above them and one below them. There was the lower class called kauwa. They were without land and without rights in the community. They were outcasts. We do not know just why they were despised by everyone. Perhaps they had broken the laws of kapu, perhaps they were an ancient people who were here before the Hawaiians came. The people at the top, above the makaainana, were the alii. At the head of all the alii was the Alii Nui, or, as he is called in the books written about Hawaii, the mo'i (pronounced moee). In all the South Seas, in Tahiti, in Samoa, in New Zealand, in Hawaii, we find that there was a great alii who was the highest ranking man among all the alii. He was what would have been called in Europe a king. But the Alii Nui was different from the king in that his right to rule did not depend entirely upon straight succession in a family. Rank determined by genealogy was one factor determining his right to rule, and his power to establish himself as a ruler over all the other chiefs was the other. In other words, the Alii Nui was Alii Nui both by reason of his birth and by the fact that he outranked all other chiefs, and because he had the personal qualifications to make him a leader or ruler over the rest. The three classes in ancient Hawaiian society were then the makaainana, the kauwa, and the alii.

THE KING AND HIS OFFICERS

When we try to imagine a country in which all the power is held by one man, we realize that the system in such a state is different from anything we think of as government. The Alii Nui owned all the land. Every time an Alii Nui died or was overthrown, the new chief had the right to re-divide all the land among his faithful followers, the alii who were younger members of his family, and others who were dependents. A new king acted as a conquerer of the land, dividing the country among his chiefs and followers. This custom made a great deal of trouble. Nearly every time a new Alii Nui came in, there was war, because the people who had the land wanted to keep it, while followers of other alii wanted to set their chief on the highest place so that they could get the land. The situation may be compared to what happens when jobs are given out to members of a political party after our present-day elections. But in the old days, it was not a matter of voting, but of fighting, and land rights were the reward of the victor.

Before the time of Kamehameha the Great there were single Alii Nui on single islands. Each king had one faithful and loyal advisor called the Kalaimoku, the "man who carved the island," the "island carver" or the "kingdom carver." This Kalaimoku was an older man who had been with the family a long time and had much experience in government, strategy, and war, in everything that the king had to be sagacious about. The division of the land fell to the Kalaimoku and that is why he was called the "island cutter." It was as though he sliced up a pie to pass around among followers of the chief. It was really like slicing a pie because the islands are more or less round and the lines dividing districts were cut from sea coast to mountain top. These large districts were called ahupuaas, and were given to high chiefs. The ahupuaas were parcelled out by these chiefs among their followers in small strips or sections called ili. A simple ili was a strip running from sea to mountains. Then there were also ili lele, consisting of parcels of land in different places: one ili lele would have a piece on the seashore, a piece of taro land, and a piece of forest. An ili kupono was a single piece with perpetual title free from taxes levied by the chief of the ahupuaa, but still subject to taxation by the Alii Nui. (See figure in Chapter 7.)

The divisions on the Big Island—Hilo, Puna, Kau, etc.,—

were so big that they were called mokus, and they were sub-divided into ahupuaas or districts. On Oahu there were no divisions larger than a district or ahupuaa. Moanalua is an example of one district or ahupuaa on this island.

LAW AND ORDER

Next to the Kalaimoku, probably the most important personage was the Konohiki. The Konohiki saw that the land was cultivated. He was the tax collector. He was the general executive upon whom the Kalaimoku depended to see that what he ordered was done. These Konohikis, of whom there must have been a great many, were in charge of the separate pieces of land, or work going on under the Kalaimoku. Tenants were called on for contributions in goods or in labor on the occasion of any ceremony requiring offerings, or feast of the alii, or war, or other public activity. But the great annual tax levy came during the Makahiki when taxes were paid in foods, kapa, mats, and feathers, since there was no money or medium of exchange. Tenants were required by the Konohiki to labor when work was to be done in building and cleaning irrigation ditches, making roads, etc. In the days before the missionaries came there was probably no regular time requirement, but after the missionaries came and the seven day week was established, one day a week of labor for the king was required of the people.

In addition to the Konohiki there were constables called Ilamuku who were in charge of law and order in the country. They may be compared to the present-day sheriff and police. Law and order in old Hawaii was not a joke. Nobody ever made fun of the Alii in the old days. The law of the country was the kapu. Both Alii and Priests had absolute right of death over any subject. The discipline of the kapu in old Hawaii was very rigid and extremely severe, but it was also effective. Some descriptions by the people who came here in the early days prove this. Captain Cook, who discovered these islands, and Captain Vancouver, who visited them soon after their discovery, observed the extreme discipline which existed. The following paragraphs are taken from their records.

"A numerous train of natives followed us; and one of them, whom I distinguished for his activity in keeping the rest in order, I made a choice of as our guide. This man, from time to time, proclaimed our approach; and every one, whom we met, fell prostrate upon the ground and remained in that position till we had passed. This, I afterwards understood, is the mode of paying their respects to their own great chiefs."

"We returned towards the boats, accompanied by the chief and his ladies, and attended by the natives who conducted themselves in the most orderly and respectful manner."

"The unremitted attention of the superior chiefs, to preserve good order, and insure the faithful discharge of every service undertaken by the subordinate description of the people, produced a uniform degree of respect in their deportment, a cheerful obedience to the commands they received, and a strict observance and conformity to fair and honest dealing in all their commercial intercourse."

"The inhabitants were excessively orderly and docile, although there was not a chief or any person of distinction amongst them to enforce their good behavior; neither man nor woman attempted to come on board, without first obtaining permission; and when this was refused, they remained perfectly quiet in their canoes alongside."

This discipline was due in part to the kapu, which was a system of rules supposed to govern people not only by external force but even more by spiritual or inner dangers which they ran if they broke the kapu. A man was believed to die if he broke the kapu even if he was not knocked on the head by the Ilamuku or Konohiki. But the kapu actually depended for its power largely on the personality of the Alii and Kahunas. The kapu was fundamentally a system of rules designed to prevent spiritual debasement or defilement. The word itself can best be translated "forbidden." The king and all his family, his clothes and possessions, were kapu because of the alii's sacredness. Common persons were forbidden any contact with the alii. His sacredness gave the king the power to declare kapu anything that he pleased. All the rules and prohibitions (kapu) established by the alii controlled the people and made the government. Consequently they are defined as the "kapu system." Everything connected with the worship of the gods or akua, with the worship of the aumakua or guardian spirits, was sacred and kapu to protect it from profaning contacts. Such work as canoe building was kapu because it was consecrated to the gods. Heiaus were kapu, priests were kapu, prayers were kapu. Another class of religious kapus forbade contact with women during their monthly period or after childbirth. Contact with anything connected with sickness and death was considered spiritually defiling and was kapu. The kapu was the ancient social and religious law of Hawaii. It governed everything in the life of the people.

CHARACTERISTICS OF THE ALII

The people believed in the power of that kapu because of the magnetic personality of the alii. These alii were the first born of the people and they were men bred to rule, men of selected stock who were set apart from the people. From earliest childhood they were raised with the sense of being sacred, of being superior and were actually called akuas or gods. There are many descriptions from all parts of Polynesia which show that these old time alii were men of powerful personality. This magnetism was a thing that old voyagers who came to Hawaii and Polynesia noticed especially.

The alii had a sense of sacredness or divinity. This is something that goes with the idea of kingship everywhere in the world but it was nowhere more highly developed than it was in old Hawaii. The same idea exists in Japan in the feeling of the sacredness of the Emperor. When the English talked about the "divine right of kings" they were expressing this same idea. Feather capes are discussed in another chapter but there is one little thing about the feather capes which will make clear this old Polynesian sense of the sacredness of the king, and which is the fundamental significance of the feather cape. The feather cape is called ahuula, which actually means crimson or red cloak. The cloaks always had the shape of an inverted crescent, and they always had various colors on them. In the old folk stories of Hawaii, great alii whether men or women are described as being seen with the rainbow as their sign. If the alii was coming, or was present, the rainbow was a symbol over his person. In New Zealand this word ahuula is spelled kahukura and is the name of the god who was seen in the rainbow. Whenever the alii, who were supposed to be accompanied by the rainbow as a sign, moved about in ceremonies or went to battle, they clothed themselves in these gorgeously colored feather capes which were the shape of the inverted rainbow. The ahuula therefore perhaps symbolized the rainbow, the sign of the Alii's magnetism, power, and sacredness.

As has been said, the Alii were men of magnetism and personality. We shall look at some descriptions of the greatest alii of all, the great Kamehameha. Kamehameha was the first alii to control all the islands, and everything shows that Kamehameha rose to power mainly through his own strength, personality, and intelligence. He did have the help of white men who advised him, and he had the help of some guns which gave him an advantage over the other alii, but in the main his power came through his own gifts. Kamehameha's personality was such that men like Cook and Vancouver who came in contact with him, and others of their ships, have left records of their impressions of him. One of the descriptions of Kamehameha comments on his appearance as follows:

> "He walks erect, firm and graceful, with a dignity of deportment well becoming his quality and high station. His countenance, though not mild, is by no means displeasing. Its lineaments are strong and expressive and form a more perfect index of the emo-

tions of the mind than we find among the generality of his countrymen. In our broken conversation with him, he possessed a quickness of comprehension that surprised us, and in his behavior, he was open, affable, and free, which much attached us to him in this first visit."

Later, when he came on board the ship Vancouver was on, the "Discovery," he was described as follows:

"On his first coming on board, he first presented a variety of feathered capes and helmets to Captain Vancouver. Then taking him by the hand to the gangway, he told him there were ten canoes loaded with hogs for him, and desired that he would order his people to take them on board. This was done with such a princely air of dignity, that it instantaneously riveted our admiration, as the manner of presenting and the magnitude of the present far exceeded any thing of the kind we had seen before or experienced in the voyage."

Kamehameha was not a man who just strutted around in a feather cape and looked handsome, but he was a real king, fearless in action. Those old alii did not just imagine they had power but they had to prove it because they were the actual leaders in battle. We go out and do a little surf riding, and perhaps get scratched up; or we ride on a horse and run a little chance of getting thrown and breaking a bone; or we play football and get bruised up, but these alii played more dangerous games than these. Their sport was war and the weak alii did not stand much chance of survival.

One of the sports in the old days was a sham battle with spears. A description of one of these battles in which Kamehameha took part when Vancouver was here, follows:

"The warriors who were armed with pallaloos (pololus) now advanced with a considerable degree of order . . . presenting . . . a wonderful degree of improved knowledge in military evolutions. This body of men, composing several ranks, formed in close and regular order, constituted a firm and compact phalanx, which in actual service, I was informed, was not easily to be broken. Having reached the spot in contest, they sat down on the ground about thirty yards asunder, and pointed their pallaloos at each other. After a short interval of silence, a conversation was commenced, and Taio was supposed to state his opinion respecting peace and war . . . The arguments . . . not terminating amicably, their respective claims remained to be decided by the fate of battle. Nearly at the same instant of time they all arose, and in close columns, met each other by slow advances. This movement they conducted with much order and regularity, frequently shifting their ground, and guarding with great circumspection against the various advantages of their opponents . . . .

"In the afternoon of the next day, the king entertained us on shore with a sham battle, by drawing up his warriors on a fine sandy beach at the village of Kiloa in two parties of about thirty or forty on each side one of which was supposed to be Kahekili's warriors from Maui just landed from their canoes to invade Kamehameha's territories. They first fought with blunt spears which they darted from their hands at one another with amazing force and dexterity, making them pass through the air with a whirring noise and quivering motion, yet the party aimed at on either side would often catch hold of them in their rapid course and instantly turn their points with equal force and velocity on those who hove them. After the action commenced no regular rank was preserved on either side, each warrior ran back to pick up the spear that passed him, and advanced as near to the opposite party to take his aim as he could with safety, but during the conflict they lost and gained ground on both sides . . .

"The king was averse to our seeing this sham fight till the parties were a little heated, as he said they would then fight with more spirit and animation. After he stood along side of us for some time, looking on and giving directions, . . . he darted in to the middle of them without any weapon whatever, and placing

Kamehameha I

himself at their head, a shower of spears was instantly aimed at him from the opposite side. He caught hold of the first that came near him in its course and putting himself in a position of defense, with his eyes fixed on the spears coming towards him, and by the spear in his hand he parried every one of them off with the greatest coolness and intrepidity, and watching at the same time with a vigilant eye every favorable opportunity of getting a good aim, when he would instantly dart back the spear in his hand and get hold of the next that was hove at him. In this manner they continued the contest on both sides even with such apparent virulence that many of them received considerable hurts and bruises. At last they had resort to the polulus, which are spears of fifteen or eighteen feet long, pointed like daggers. These we were told were always their last resource in battle. They do not heave them like the other spears but charge with them in a close bodied phalanx to close action, and notwithstanding their unwieldy appearance, they manage them with great dexterity, by resting them on the forearms of one hand to guide their direction, while the other hand pushes them on or gathers them in with great ease and alertness."

King Kamehameha was not an alii who only imagined he had a right to rule but a man who could get into a fight with the best spearsmen and hold his own unarmed. He was a man great in head and heart and hand.

OUR RESPONSIBILITY TODAY

The days of the kings whose word was law over the people are absolutely ended. We are living in a time of democracy when the Demos, as the Greeks called it, that is to say, the mass of the people, is king. We are all part of the Demos. The old kings ruled by the power of magnetic personality. If we are going to have a decent country, the same thing must rule but it has to rule in every person of the community and not in just one person at the top. In Kamehameha we find a symbol of the type of personality which every member of a democratic community ought to achieve and set up as an ideal and as a goal. This is the meaning of the verse of "Hawaii Ponoi" in which Kamehameha is mentioned. It is the meaning of the lines:

Hawaii ponoi	Hawaii in the right,
Nana i kou moi	Look to your King
Kalani Alii	The sacred King
Ke Alii	The heavenly King,
Makua lani e	Father above us all,
Kamehameha e	Kamehameha,
Nakaua e pale	Who defends himself
Me ka ihe	With his spear.

That last line refers to the description which has just been quoted, in which King Kamehameha showed himself capable of defending himself with his own hand. In this community, in this society and government we have now, most of the pilikia arises out of the fact that very few people are strong enough to stand on their own feet as Kamehameha did. Instead of defending themselves with their own spear they expect to hide behind somebody else's skirts or slide through easily without taking trouble themselves. Well, if you want to do that, no one can prevent you but if you want to be a real power in this Demos, which is King among us now, I think you will be happier if you are like Kamehameha, standing on your own feet in the battle of life, using your integrity as your spear and fighting clean and strong and without fear.

References

Malo, David, Hawaiian Antiquities.

Handy, E. S. C., Cultural Revolution in Hawaii, American Council, Institute of Pacific Relations.

Alexander, W. D., Brief History of the Hawaiian People.

Ellis, William, A Narrative of a Tour through Hawaii.

(See also bibliography, chapter entitled The History of Land Ownership in Hawaii.)

CHAPTER 4

RELIGION AND EDUCATION *

E. S. C. HANDY

RELIGION

The chapter which follows this contains a description of some of the religious ceremonies and observances of the home in old Hawaii. In ceremonies such as those which marked the weaning of the boy and his entry into the eating house of the men, prayers were offered to the family gods or aumakua. Every home had its kuahu, or altar, erected to the aumakua. But these domestic religious observances were only a part of religion in old Hawaii. In addition to the family gods or aumakua there were the greater gods or akua, the gods of Nature and of Creation. These gods had their public temples, or heiaus. They had their priests and appropriate ceremonials.

The Polynesians had a conception of a Supreme Being, a god who was chief over all the others. We do not know much about the ideas of the ancient Hawaiians concerning this Supreme Being, because the priests were under oath, just as members of any secret order such as the Masons are today, not to tell what they knew of the most sacred things. The penalty for breaking this oath was death. Consequently, very little is known of the kapu secrets of the old Hawaiian religion. We do know that they had the idea of a Supreme God. Fornander states that the Hawaiians worshipped the Supreme Being under the name of Hika po loa, or Oi-e, which means "most excellent, supreme." We know that other Polynesian peoples had this idea of a Supreme Being. The following is a translation of a Maori sacred chant describing the creation of the world by the Supreme Being. This will give you an idea of the grandeur

* This chapter is arranged from stenographic notes of an extemporaneous lecture delivered by Dr. Handy. The notes were read and corrected by Dr. Handy.

At left is the hale pahu, the house for the priests and their sacred paraphernalia. In the back-ground is the oracle tower. Along the back of the stone altar and in front of it, rise carved slabs of wood, decorated with streamers of kapa. The court is enclosed by a high stone wall.

Heiau at Waimea, Kauai, sketched by Webber (Capt. Cook's artist.)

of the conceptions of those old Polynesian priest-philosophers. You will find it interesting to compare this with those verses in Genesis which describe the Creation.

"Io dwelt within the breathing space of immensity.
The universe was in darkness, with water everywhere.
There was no glimmer of dawn, no clearness, no light.
And he began by saying these words,
That he might cease remaining inactive,
  Darkness, become a light-possessing darkness.'
And at once light appeared.
He then repeated these self-same words in this manner,
That he might cease remaining inactive,
  Darkness, become a light-possessing darkness.'
And again intense darkness supervened.
Then a third time he spake, saying,
  Let there be a darkness above,
  Let there be a darkness below.
  Let there be a darkness unto Tupua,
  Let there be a darkness unto Tawhito
  It is a darkness overcome and dispelled.
  Let there be one light above,
  Let there be one light below.
  Let there be a light unto Tupua,
  Let there be a light unto Tawhito,
  A dominion of light,
  A bright light.'
And now a great light prevailed.
Io then looked to the waters which compassed him about
    and spake a fourth time, saying,
  'Ye waters of Tai-kama, be ye separate.
  Heaven be formed.'
Then the sky became suspended.
  'Bring forth thou Tupu-horo-nuku.
And at once the moving earth lay stretched abroad."

Next to the Supreme Being everywhere in Polynesia was a god who, in a sense, was the representative of that Supreme Being. In Hawaii this god was called Kane. In the other islands he was known as Tane. In New Zealand the story is that Rangi (who corresponds to the Hawaiian Lani), the sky-father, married Papa, the Flat Earth. The children of this union were Tane, (Kane), Rongo, (Lono), Tu, (Ku), and other akua. The word Tane or Kane alone means "man." As a creative force, Tane was the parent of all nature, as a man is the parent of children. Kane was the heavenly father of all men, the creator of men. As he was the father of all living things, he was a symbol of life in nature. One of the old Hawaiian prayers to Kane illustrates this:

"Green are the leaves of God's harvest fields.
The net fills the heavens—Shake it!
Shake down the god's food!
Scatter it, oh heaven!

* * *

"Life to the land!
Life from Kane,
Kane the god of life.

* * *

"Life to the people!
Hail Kane of the water of life! Hail!"

This prayer brings out one of the most interesting ideas that the old Hawaiians had about this god, for it shows that they identified the god with sunlight and fresh water, without which nothing can live. In the prayers to Kane the phrase, "Kane, the water of life," is often found. There is a mele about this "water of life." It came from Kauai. Two verses of this long mele, published in Mr. Emerson's study of the Hula, follow:

"A query, a question,
I put you:
Where is the water of Kane?
At the Eastern Gate
Where the Sun comes in at Haehae;
There is the water of Kane.

"One question I ask of you:
Where flows the water of Kane?
Deep in the ground, in the gushing spring,
In the ducts of Kane and Loa,
A well-spring of water, to quaff,
A water of magic power —
The water of life!
Life! O give us this life!"

You will notice that in the first verse there is the idea of the "water of Kane" in the east where the sun comes. There you find Kane representing the sun and light. In the second verse it is the water in the earth that is the "water of Kane." In other words, it is sunlight and fresh water which are life-giving for growing things.

In New Zealand the nature god Tane was the god of the forests. The forests were sacred to Tane, as was the work of the woodsmen and woodworkers. That the same idea was held in Hawaii is proved by a prayer which appealed to Kane as the god who had to do with woodsmen's work:

"These are the offerings for you, oh Kane,
For the benefit of the carpenter's adze,
The woodsman's adze,
The little adze,
The reversible adze,
An adze to finish off the image,
The image of you, oh Kane, the god of life."

Besides Kane, two other great gods were worshipped. These were Lono and Ku, called in New Zealand Rongo and Tu. In New Zealand Rongo was the god of cultivated foods, and Tu the god of war. In Hawaii, Lono was the god of rain and of agriculture, and Ku was the god of chiefs and of war. In New Zealand a boy was dedicated either as a farmer to Rongo, or as a warrior to Tu.

Lono was the god of peace. In his honor, the great annual festival of the Makahiki was held. This is described in the next chapter, but we may note here that during the whole period of the Makahiki, October through February, war was kapu. This was because Lono was the god of peace. Two prayers offered to Lono during the Makahiki illustrate his position as the god of rain and cultivated food.

"Send gracious showers of rain, oh Lono,
Life-giving rain, a grateful gift,
Symbols of Lono's blessing . . .
O Lono of the broad leaf,
Let the low-hanging cloud pour out its rain,
To make the crops flourish,
Rain to make the tapa-plants flourish,
Wring out the dark rain-clouds
Of Lono in the heavens."

You can imagine people living in the old days at Hahaione in dry seasons, when day after day would go by without rain and the only food they had was sweet potato and fish. Rain was so essential to their life that they had to pray for it, and they prayed to Lono whom they saw in the clouds. The other prayer to Lono follows:

"Oh Lono in heaven; you of many shapes.
The long cloud, the short cloud, the cloud just peeping (over the horizon), the widespreading cloud, the contracted cloud . . .
The body of Lono has changed into glory.
The Kanawao grows in the moist earth;
The body of that tree stands in high heaven,
Established is the holy assembly of Lono in the distant sacred place."

Ku, or Tu, was the god of the warriors. Vigorous prayers were offered to him when a child was dedicated as a warrior. A Maori prayer dedicating a boy to Tu illustrates this:

"Rely on the powers below, the powers above,
(For) thy strife shall be all above, all below.

* * *

"Call on the first Heaven,
Call on the second Heaven,
When thou dost exercise thy warlike spirit

Be brave indeed.
To uplift thy weapons,
To carry thy arms,
To parry fierce blows,
To catch the bravest
Be thou strong and able,
To grimace in the war dance,
To be lithe and quick
And acquire the power of Tu
Possess it! Hold it!
Come forth to the world of being
To the world of light.

* * *

"Invoke (the powers) inland (the powers) at sea,
Invoke the ancestors,
Invoke the female priests,
Invoke the (spirit of the) ancestral homes,
Invoke the wind (or spirit) that is present,
Be strenuous, be brave, be courageous,
Stare fiercely, stride with high action, showing the
white of the eyes,
Stare wildly, that those of old may see thee.
So be it; possessed! So be it; holden!"

Each of the great gods had temples in which they were given appropriate offerings. In the Bishop Museum may be seen an excellent model of a war temple. Ku was offered human sacrifices. These might be people who had broken a kapu, or low class people who were killed and placed on the altar to please the god of war. Human sacrifices were offered in New Zealand also, where the priest tore out the heart of the victim and offered it, or perhaps ate it himself. But to Lono, the god of peace, no such sacrifices were offered. He was always offered pigs, taro, potato, cloth, and other things from growing nature. Each of the great gods had not only his own temples and his own appropriate sacrifices, but also his own order of priests. The priesthoods of Ku and of Lono were distinct groups with genealogies of their own. In each of the temples where the gods were served, were wooden images representing the different gods. These may be seen in the Museum. They are described in this book in the chapter on carving.

EDUCATION

The story of religion is closely related to the story of education in old Hawaii. When a child was dedicated to a god, it was necessary that he understand the kapu belonging to that god, and the prayers he should use. But in old Hawaii there was also provision for education in the sense in which we refer to it today in connection with schools and colleges.

Among all peoples of the world, education begins in babyhood. We get our fundamental education before we ever begin to go to school. The very small child is educated through play, and through imitation of, discipline from, and association with, the other members of the family. The child plays with toys which imitate the equipment of his home and the occupations of his elders. As he gets a little older he joins in the things which are going on. In Tahiti today children make the ti leaf mats to cover the imu. They help to gather stones for the imu. No one gives them lessons in building an imu; they learn by taking part in the experience. This is the only kind of learning which makes much difference in our lives, this kind of learning which comes from sharing in worthwhile experiences interesting to us. Children learn to talk in just this way. No one teaches a child to talk, but he learns. Children learn about the relationships of the family in this way. No one teaches them about the members of the family and their duties, but they learn what these are. Children learn customs, manners, ways of doing things in the home, not so much by direct teaching, as by direct learning through living and taking part in the life of the home. Children in old Hawaii learned a great deal in this way. In the old days, family life and customs were governed by strict kapus which were learned in the family in the manner described. Every child grew up under a very strict discipline in those days and learned in the home much of what he had to know.

In the home in those old days, he got much of what we call "vocational education." He still gets it there, in certain situations. In Kona, Hawaiian women are still making lauhala mats. Younger girls are sometimes there, preparing material and assisting. Some of them will go ahead with the weaving with which they have become familiar, without being "taught." Two years ago, in Kaupo on Maui, I talked with a Hawaiian woman who had some twenty varieties of sweet potatoes in her garden. When a question was asked, the older woman directed her daughter who was with her, "You get mohihi," or "You get auahi o pele," and the daughter brought in the different varieties. She had acquired her knowledge by working with her mother in the garden. Margaret Mead went to Samoa and studied the life of the young people there today. The children practice dancing together in imitation of the dances of the older people. By and by they know the dances. How many Hawaiians today have been taught to dance or sing or play the guitar? Most of them learn these things by joining in with those who do know, and taking part until they are able to go ahead by themselves. Doubtless in the old days, the boys learned to build an imu, to prepare food for an imu, to pound taro, to make poi, to prepare fishing gear—not by direct instruction, but again, by joining the men and helping and assisting until they acquired skill. The girls, in the same way, learned to make kapa, to weave mats, and to perform the household duties which fell to their lot.

But vocational education in the old days did not end with the training received in the home. There was, in addition, instruction by experts. It was sound and excellent instruction, for it was really apprenticeship. Apprenticeship means that the young person takes part in the work, learns under an expert, and works on the job until he has mastered the skills and crafts involved. This is much more effective training than school instruction in an unreal situation unlike the practical situation of the worker. Education in old Hawaii was very practical and effective. Young people were placed under the expert at a very early age, and they remained with him for years. They might be placed under an expert in genealogies, or meles, or herb medicine, or canoe building, or land boundaries, or any one of the various fields in which specialized knowledge and skill were necessary. Each expert was called a kahuna, and each young man became a kahuna when he had finished his training. The kahuna kalaiwaa, for instance, was the expert canoe builder. His sons, or his friends' sons, worked under him for years. When they were capable of doing all the work themselves, they received the title of kahuna and undertook not only to make canoes, but also to train other young people in this work. In this way the skills and arts and craftsmanship of old Hawaii were passed on from one generation to another.

One of the most interesting schools in which specific training was given was the Hula Halau. The Halau was the house in which the Hula was taught to young women who danced and to the men who chanted and played. Each alii had at least one kumu hula, who was the teacher or master of the hula. When the time came for preparing the hula and the meles in honor of the king's child or in honor of Lono during the Makahiki, the king ordered the Hula Halau built. The kumu hula got together in it his musicians, people expert in the hula, and young fine looking girls who were good dancers. All of these people stayed in the Halau and practiced for a long time. The Halau was kapu. The people in the Halau were not allowed to go out of the house. They had no contact with anyone else. During all the time they were practicing the hula, they were consecrated. The whole performance and the training period were considered sacred. In the Halau there was a kuahu decorated with green things from the mountains. At the end of the training period there was a regular ceremony of "graduation." At this ceremony the altar was consecrated and a young pig was killed and eaten as a sacrament. After this, the group went and danced before the king and the people.

The ancient Polynesians also had higher education which may be compared with our university training. Not much is known about this in Hawaii for knowledge of it died out long ago with the priests. More is kown about it as it existed in New Zealand, and without doubt the Hawaiian system was similar to the Maori practice about which we do know something. These advanced schools in New Zealand were called Whare Wananga. In Hawaiian this would be Hale Wanana, which means a house of learning or house of sacred knowledge. The Whare Wananga was built in the style of a regular Maori house, except that it had a sacred post at one end and in the middle a fireplace with stones set around it. The pupils sat around the fireplace on these stones. All the pupils were the sons of chiefs. No common people were allowed, because the knowledge given was considered sacred. The teachers were priests or Tohungas, and the chief teacher was called Whatu. The Hawaiian equivalents of these are kahuna and haku. There were two great divisions of knowledge. One of these was the Kauwae-runga (Upper Jaw). This was considered the higher division. In this the pupils learned about astronomy, about the gods, about the heavens and heavenly things in general. The other division was known as Kauwae-raro (Lower Jaw) and in this lower division the pupils were taught history, genealogy, and the religious things that had to do with war, self-protection, and health. The school met from April to October, which is the winter in New Zealand. The teaching was always from sunrise to noon, because it was thought proper to teach only when the sun was rising, and never when it was going down. Teaching was always oral, by word of mouth, because the people had no writing. In the old days, both in Hawaii and in New Zealand, knowledge of the higher sort was regarded as very sacred, a thing to be kept secret and not to be used except for sacred purposes. When they entered the school the young chiefs were dedicated by very interesting prayers to the Supreme Being whose name was never mentioned in a common place but only in the sacred school or in the deep forest. This is part of one prayer:

"Enter deeply, enter to the very origins,
Into the very foundations of all knowledge,
Thou of the hidden face!

Gather as in a great and lengthy net, in the inner recesses of the ears,
As also in the desire, the perseverance, of these thy offspring, thy sons.
Descend on them thy memory, thy knowledge,
Thou the learned! Thou the determined!
Thou the self created."

At the end of the course there was a very peculiar ceremony. You will find, if you read Hawaiian lore or Hawaiian stories, how stones were often very sacred. You know how today many old Hawaiians use stones in planting or fishing. In this Maori university each student had a small stone which he swallowed and later recovered and kept all his life as a symbol of his learning. The final consecration is described as follows by Elsdon Best:

"An interesting form of the final ceremony performed over a scholar was conducted in the flowing waters of a stream, where, in native belief, man is less liable to be affected by evil influences than at any other place. This was assuredly a singular performance. A small piece of stone, the whatu whakahoro aforementioned, was placed upon the tongue of the scholar as he stood in the flowing waters on the left side of the priestly expert. The latter then placed his left hand on the head of the scholar, as they both faced the rising sun that is the very lord and genius of knowledge, the personified form of which brought knowledge of occult lore into this world. With his right hand the priest pointed at the ascending sun as he intoned an invocation to the Supreme Being, to Tane, to Ruatau, Rangi, and Pawa. Tane is the personified form of the sun, Rangi the Sky Parent, while Ruatau and Pawa are two important celestial beings. One of the principal objects of this function was to 'bind' the acquired learing of the scholar, to render it permanent. At the recital of the words 'O Io the Parent! O Ruatau! O Tane-te-waiora!' the scholar swallowed the small stone."

Oftentimes people who do not know about life in old Hawaii speak of it as if it were on a very low and ignorant plane. This is not true, in any way whatsoever. Life was so organized that people learned to do well the work which was expected of them. They learned specific things under competent instruction. Either through participation in the life of the home, or through definite apprenticeship, they learned all the complicated skills of the craftsman. The life situation, the way of teaching, were such as to bring about real learning. Modern schools cannot approach the effectiveness of the old instruction which involved life in the home, and practice, under skilled leadership, right on the job. Modern schools try to bring back into the school some of the effectiveness of the old situation. They must do it, because the home is no longer the constructive source of instruction that it once was, and, in the development of modern industry, the apprentice system has gone. Nevertheless, the fact remains that the most successful of modern schools scarcely bring about the quality of learning which was achieved in the old days in Hawaii, when the whole situation was real and every man, woman, and child had his definite part to play in the life work for which he must be educated.

References: Religion

Malo, David, Hawaiian Antiquities.

Handy, E. S. C., Cultural Revolution in Hawaii, American Council, Institute of Pacific Relations.

Beckwith, Martha Warren, Kepelino's Moolelo Hawaii, B. P. Bishop Museum Bulletin No. 95.

References: Education

Buck, Peter, Polynesian Education, The Friend, Oct. 1928 and March 1931.

Mead, Margaret, Coming of Age in Samoa.

Mead, Margaret, Growing Up in New Guinea.

CHAPTER 5

FEASTS AND HOLIDAYS *

E. S. C. HANDY

The feasts and good times of the old Hawaiians were not just social good times when people got together and ate and talked and sang and enjoyed themselves. Every feast in the old times followed some religious celebration. There was always a sacred part which came first. The old Hawaiians had feasts at the birth of a child and at the time the child was weaned. There were feasts to celebrate marriage and feasts when death occurred. Other feasts had to do with work. Work in old Hawaii had its solemn and sacred side. Every finished piece of work had to be consecrated, and a part of the consecration was the sacred feast at which the akua, the god who helped in that work, was supposed to be present and to share the feast with the workers who had completed the canoe or the house or whatever was being dedicated.

The first thing we should understand about these old Hawaiian feasts and holidays is that the aumakuas or akuas were spirits which belonged to the particular family, or to the particular kind of work. Aumakuas were guardian spirits. For every kind of work and for everything one did, there were certain aumakuas. At every feast, the aumakuas were supposed to be present. Some of whatever food there was—fish or pig or chicken or taro—was presented on the kuahu, a sort of little altar set up like a table for the aumakuas. It was believed that this food was eaten and enjoyed by them. The idea behind the offering to the aumakuas may be compared to the idea behind the Christian celebration of the Lord's Supper or the sacrament of communion. At this sacrament the Lord is supposed to be present in the food shared by the people. Similarly, in

* This chapter is arranged from stenographic notes of an extemporaneous lecture delivered by Dr. Handy, who read and corrected the lecture notes.

old Hawaii the offering of food was supposed to be shared by the gods and by the people.

This idea is particularly noticeable in the old hula ceremony. The hula, in the old days, was a sacred dance in honor of the aumakuas and the akuas. Many weeks before they performed before the king, the dancers were kept apart in the Hula Halau. They ate special food and were under struct kapu until they had learned all the songs and dances. Then came the time when they were consecrated and ready to perform. The teacher in charge of all the work killed a young pig, and a little bit of that pig had to be eaten by every member of the group. That pig had been consecrated to the akua of the hula. When it was killed and eaten as a part of the consecration ceremony, this was again an instance of sharing consecrated food among worshippers.

David Malo, who lived long ago and knew much about the ceremonies and customs of old Hawaii, wrote descriptions of many of these ceremonies. Among his descriptions is that of the family feast held when the small boy was weaned, taken from his mother, and allowed for the first time to enter the eating house of the men. In the old days men and women did not eat together, because men were supposed to be sacred in certain ways in which women were not. Food was thought to be sacred and the men would lose kapu if they ate with women. So when a boy was old enough to be weaned, it was necessary to have a special consecration ceremony to make him sacred, and to put him under kapu so he could come into the eating house of the men and share their food.

Lono, one of the great gods of the early Hawaiians, was the god worshipped particularly in the ceremony of weaning. First, the father consecrated a pig to Lono. This pig was baked in the presence of all the people who had come together for the ceremony. The head of the pig was cut off and placed on the altar which was at the end of the mua, or men's eating house. On this altar stood also an image of Lono. Around the neck of the image hung an ipu or gourd.

In this ipu an ear of the pig was placed. Bananas, coconut, awa root, and a bowl of awa were then put before the image as a feast for Lono. Holding the awa bowl, the father called to the akua, "Here are the pig, the coconuts, the awa, oh ye gods, Ku, Lono, Kanaloa, Kane, and ye Aumakua." The father then said the prayer quoted below. It was called the Pule Ipu. In this prayer there are lines about the gourd vine which is a vigorous growing vine. These lines probably mean that the father prayed for the vigorous growth of his boy and asked that he be big and strong like the gourd vine. The prayer also mentions sweet potato, taro, and other things, because Lono was the god who was believed to make these grow. This was the prayer:

"Arise, O Lono, eat of the sacrificial feast of awa set for you, an abundant feast for you, O Lono!

"Provide, O Kea, swine and dogs in abundance! and of land a large territory—for you, O Lono!

"Make propitious the cloud-omens! Make proclamation for the building of a prayer-shrine! Peaceful, transparent is the night, night sacred to the gods.

"My gourd vine this; and this the fruit on my gourd-vine. Thick set with fruit are the shooting branches, a plantation of gourds.

"Be fruitful in the heaped up rows! fruit bitter as fishgall.

"How many seeds from this gourd, pray, have been planted in this land cleared-by-fire? have been planted and flowered out in Hawaii?

"Planted is this seed. It grows; it leafs; it flowers; lo! it fruits—this gourd-vine.

"The gourd is this great world; it covers the heavens of Kuakini.

"Thrust it into the netting! Attach to it the rainbow for a handle!

"Imprison within it the jealousies, the sins, the monsters of iniquity!

"Within this gourd from the cavern of Mu-a-Iku, calabash of explosive wind-squalls,—till the serene star shines down."

This prayer requests that all evil which might come to the child during his life be shut up in the gourd which the god had taken to himself. This idea of protecting the child is very similar to the idea behind Christian baptism which is also thought to be a protection to the child. In these old Hawaiian consecration rites there are two of the ideas which exist in the Christian religion today. These are the idea of sharing the sacred feast and the idea of protection through life.

This particular ceremony which took place when the child was weaned may be compared to similar ceremonies described in the Bible, which were evidently a part of the Hebrew religious practice in the earliest days. The story of Abraham and Isaac, in Genesis 21:8 contains this statement: "The child grew and was weaned and Abraham made a great feast the same day the child was weaned." In Samuel I, 1:24-27, we find, "And when she had weaned him, she took him up with her, with three bullocks, and one ephah of flour, and a bottle of wine, and brought him unto the house of the Lord in Shiloh; and the child was young. And they slew a bullock and brought the child to Eli. For this child I prayed . . ." Practically all over the world, among the people of India, of China, of Japan, among the American Indians, among the old Hawaiians and the ancient Hebrews, there were family ceremonies marking birth, weaning, marriage, and death.

When we think of holidays today we do not think very frequently of family celebrations of the type just described. We think of Christmas, Thanksgiving, and those times when everyone stops working and when everyone is feasting. The old Hawaiians had this sort of holiday too. The great celebration of the ancients was the Makahiki which was the Hawaiian Thanksgiving. This Makahiki was a holiday covering four consecutive months. During this period there were religious ceremonies. The people stopped work, made offering to the king, and then gave their time to sports and feasting and dancing and having a good time. During those four months which began in October or November and ended in February or March, there was no war. War was kapu and the whole nation was given over to this great festival in honor of Lono. The king always played the part of Lono in this celebration.

The first period of the Makahiki in Hawaii was the kapu time when the whole country was sacred and the people, although they had stopped working, were not yet allowed to play. Before they could play, the taxes for the king—the pig, the taro, the sweet potatoes, the feathers, the kapa, the mats, all things that were made—had to be brought together and offered on the altars of Lono. The gifts from the people were divided up by the king and his followers and by the priests. These gifts were called hookupu. Everybody brought gifts which were regarded as taxes but were originally thank offerings, and laid them on the ahu-puaa, or stone altars set up at the boundary line of every district. The first part of this holiday was this period of kapu when the land was sacred to Lono and the offerings were brought and laid on the altar. Then an image of Lono was carried right around the island by the priests. At each one of the ahu-puaas the chief of that district presented the gifts to the image, or in other words to the god who caused things to grow and who gave plenty and prosperity to the country. The priests accepted the offering to the god and said a prayer which ended with these words, "The land is free, gird yourselves for play." In other words, "We have accepted the offering to the god, the rest of the food is free, the rest of the mats, feathers, and kapa is free to the people. Now go ahead and enjoy yourselves." The image was carried from district to district until the whole country was free from kapu. Then came the time of celebration, of hula dancing, of sports, of singing and of feasting.

There was a very interesting incident at the end of the Makahiki festival. The king went off shore in a canoe.

When he came in he stepped on shore and a group of men with spears rushed at him. Most of the kings had guardsmen with them to ward off the spears, but Kamehameha the Great stood the test alone. It was believed that unless the king was sacred enough to be superior to death, he no longer was worthy of representing Lono, the god of plenty. The interesting thing is that just this sort of ceremony existed in many other ancient religions in the world. For instance, in ancient Rome Jupiter was the god of rain and fertility. The king represented Jupiter, and each year, according to ancient Roman tradition, the king had to submit to tests to prove his sacredness and his right to embody the fertility of Jupiter. The test was either a foot race or a fight in which the man who won became king. This ceremony was celebrated in Rome in February, exactly the time of the ending of the Makahiki.

Some sort of thanksgiving ceremony is found almost everywhere in the world, and in all periods of history. Our own Thanksgiving Day is a holiday that was originally dedicated to the giving of thanks to God, but meaning to most people nowadays just the time of a big dinner. However, to the New Englanders who originated the day, it was a sacred festival in which thanks were given for the corn and the other good things of the harvest. As in the case of the old Hawaiian festival, the New England feast followed the religious worship. There are similar festivals in China. They were a part of the life of the people of ancient Rome and Greece and Egypt. There is evidence in the Bible that the Hebrews made thanksgiving offerings. In India at the present time there is a tremendous festival of thanksgiving when offerings are made to the gods who are believed to have caused the growth of rice and other things. During this great festival everything which is going to be used during the coming year is brought out and consecrated, and thanks are offered. The Hindus, who are a religious people, feel that everything should be used for some good purpose as well as for the enjoyment of life. So they bring out all these things which they are going to use so that they may be consecrated. The old

Hawaiian had the same idea when he consecrated the little boy, praying that he might be kept safe and sound for the coming year.

In all of our present day feasts and holidays, we are too apt to forget the real meaning of the celebration and to think only of the social enjoyment of the occasion. The meaning goes from these holidays when we have no other purpose than having a good time, desirable though that is. It would not be a bad idea if we should think more about the real meaning of our religious and national holidays—Thanksgiving, Christmas, the Fourth of July. We cannot state that all the old-time Hawaiians remembered the solemn and sacred character of the celebrations in which they took part. Perhaps they did not, but instead merely repeated the words, with their thoughts on the good times which were soon to come. Nevertheless, the fact remains that these feasts had their religious side, which, if it were truly remembered, was very solemn and had great significance. Consider the prayer to Lono, for instance. It was filled with religious feeling, with desire for the welfare of the child, and with belief that through this ceremony Lono would guard the child. The words meant all this. Whether the heart did, we cannot know, any more than we can know about such things today, except in our own individual case. We can all know about our own personal understanding, feeling, and sincerity. No one else can tell, but after all, in such matters we are responsible only for ourselves.

The mind is like a tree which should have its roots deep in the ground, if it is to stand firm and unshaken. Here in Hawaii, the roots of our minds should go down into Hawaiian learning, as well as into the learning of the Occident and the Orient. The greater our understanding and appreciation of the real meaning of these past or distant cultures, the deeper our roots, as it were, and the stronger the growing tree.

REFERENCES

Malo, David, Hawaiian Antiquities.

Handy. E. S. C., Polynesian Religion, B. P. Bishop Museum Bulletin No. 34.

CHAPTER 6

HOUSES AND VILLAGES

E. S. C. HANDY

In very ancient times, people depended on their environment to shelter them from peril, cold, storm, and all the hardships from which they needed protection. They got along as best they could with the natural shelter of caves, as we do sometimes when we are hunting or fishing. As time went on, people learned to do something for themselves in the way of making shelter, and they ceased to depend wholly on nature to protect them from the cold of winter or the intense heat and rain of summer. Different forms of houses were developed in different countries. The type of house developed depended partly on the material the environment provided. For example, the Eskimo builds his house out of stones, or blocks of ice, or makes a shelter of the skins of animals, because these are the things he can find about him. But the Polynesian, as we should expect, used other materials to make his shelter.

FACTORS CONTROLING THE HAWAIIAN HOUSE TYPE

There are three things to be remembered in discussing the old Hawaiian house. The first is, that when the Hawaiians first came to these islands, they had to build their homes out of the materials they found here. They had no lumber as we have today, but they did have stone, timber, lauhala, and pili grass. They made the best use of the things they could find, but the materials at hand necessarily had their effect on the style of the house. In the second place, the tools the Hawaiians used had to be made out of what they found here. In the old days there was no metal in Hawaii; every bit of metal we find today is imported. These old-time Hawaiians who had no metals had to learn to make and to use stone tools. Probably they first used shells and later learned to make stone tools which could cut better and straighter than shells. Their favorite tool was the stone adze with the blade crosswise.

These stone adzes, along with some bone tools, were the only implements they had, and with them they did some very fine work. The old canoe in the Bishop Museum shows the quality of their workmanship. The Maoris, cousins of the Hawaiians who live in New Zealand, do poorer work nowadays with metal tools than the old-timers did with their crude stone tools. They have become careless because the tools do all the work. The workmen in ancient Hawaii took great pride in their work, such pride that with their rough tools they were able to do fine exact work. The third thing we should remember is that the old-time Hawaiians were sailor men and they therefore built their houses as sailors would. Sailors do not nail or peg things, but instead they tie and lash them together because at sea lashings hold better than nails or pegs. When they first landed on these shores, the old Hawaiian colonists set up houses and lashed them together as a sailor would. All Polynesian houses were made this way, and lashed together in the same way as a canoe.

HOUSE BUILDERS

In Hawaii, canoe building was a profession. Expert canoe builders were called Kahuna-kalai-waa, or Master-canoe-cutters. Some of these experts were attached to the different alii, while others worked for anyone who would employ them. But there seems to have been no distinct class of house-builders, although there were some who were termed kuene hale who were known to be skilled in putting up houses and who might be called in to help. Every man built his hale for himself. His relatives and friends assisted him. In the South Seas, however, house building was a distinct profession, practiced by expert carpenters who were organized in guilds or trade associations comparable to the trade guilds in China or medieval Europe. These associations of expert carpenters (Tufunga-fai-fale) still exist in Samoa, where they control the building trade. Any man who wants to build a good house employs carpenters from the local builders' association. Handsome lashings made with colored coconut fibre cord are to be seen in the interior of fine Samoan houses. These show what builders' association worked on the house, for each guild of tufungas has its own designs.

BELIEFS CONCERNING THE NEW HOUSE

When a man was to build a house in old Hawaii, it was important for him to get the advice of a diviner, or kilokilo, as to the location and as to the house itself. It was considered a sign of death for the owner to build a dwelling in a temple enclosure or on a burial ground, or fronting on a cliff, or on a mound, or facing a stone wall. It was thought that if the house opened on a highway, the members of the household would be afflicted with constant illness. If one house in line with several others stood above the rest, it was thought that its owner would become rich. If houses were built in the rear of others, there would be constant quarreling.

It was believed that the owner's death would result if, in the erection of the house, it had been necessary after the completion of the main frame, to remove the rafters, or a plate beam supporting the rafters; or to pull up a post; or to remove thatch framing, or thatching. It was thought that the owner's death would result if faulty construction or cutting of parts was discovered after the house had been completed and occupied. Death of the owner was expected if anyone climbed up to inspect the ridge-pole while the ridge was being thatched, or if a priest stuck his head inside to examine the unfinished house.

Crooked side posts gave interesting indications. Two side by side with their crooks toward each other meant that the owner would be stingy. A crook bulging inward meant that some member of the household would be afflicted with dropsy. One bulging outward indicated that some member of the family would be a hunchback. There was a great variety of good and bad luck signs of this type.

BUILDING THE HOUSE

After the site had been chosen timber had to be cut and trimmed in the forest. The pili grass or lauhala had to be collected for thatching. Hau bark, ieie vine, or morning-glory runners were gathered and rolled into great balls (like balls of twine) ready for use. And all these materials must be brought together at the site that had been selected. Here the ground was cleared and leveled up by building low walls with stone, and filling in with earth; or sometimes the whole platform (paepae) was built of stone. Then, at the corners and along the sides and ends of the leveled floor (kahua) the men dug postholes by means of digging sticks (oo). The side posts (pou) were set up and the holes filled in with stones and earth which was firmly tramped down. At either end, midway between the corners, were set up the two main posts (pou hana) that supported the ridge pole (kauhuhu). On top of the posts along the sides were placed the plates (lohelau), which were heavy hewn pieces of timber to support the lower ends of the rafters (o'a). These rafters, resting on the ridge pole and plates, were small poles. Light horizontal rods (aho) were then lashed across the rafters and on the posts all around the four sides of the house, binding the whole frame together. Where upper ends of the rafters crossed over the ridge pole, was lashed a light pole (kaupaku). Small rods to hold the thatching materials were lashed to the aho. Now the frame was complete, ready for the thatching (ako). Standing alone, it looked like a very large birdcage. On a frame to be thatched with pili grass the rods to hold the thatch were spaced four fingers apart. When lauhala was used for the covering, the rods were only two or three fingers apart. The thatching was a long tedious job, for every bundle of grass and every leaf had to be laid on carefully and bound with bark or vine. The thatching of the ridge required especial care; here and at the corners of the roof the grass had to be plaited tightly to prevent leaking.

Sometimes, after the trimming of the thatching on the ridge and on the corners, a central pillar of ohia wood, termed pou manu or halakea, was erected inside the house. For good luck an aholehole fish or a red weke or kumu was planted beneath this pillar. The family slept with their heads towards this post. "Always sleep in the middle of the house," admonishes an old Hawaiian, "lest a murderer stab with a stick from outside, and tie your hogs outside so that they will grunt if a marauder comes. The dog should sleep within to bite the marauder who might enter."

In cold regions, as Waimea, Hawaii, a dwelling was equipped with a fireplace (kapuahi) in the middle of the floor, a shallow depression walled with flat stones set on edge. There was no chimney. The smoke simply seeped through the thatching. This fire was never used for cooking, because under the old kapu, food could not be cooked in the sleeping house. Kane-moe-lehu (Kane-sleeping-in-the-ashes) was the akua of the fireplace.

CONSECRATING THE HOUSE

The old Hawaiians regarded the home as a living thing. The new house had to have its consecration ceremony exactly like that for a newborn child when its navel-string was cut. This ceremony was performed after the thatching was completed. The builders left the thatch over the doorway hanging rough. No one was allowed to enter the house. A kahuna was sent for to consecrate the dwelling. He put the finishing touch to the work by trimming this thatch over the doorway. Holding a chopping block in one hand and an adze in the other, and timing his strokes to the rhythm of the pule kuwa, the kahuna consecrated and freed from kapu the new dwelling by "cutting its navel string." A pule kuwa follows:

"Ku lalani ka pule a Keoloalu i ke akua,
O Kuwa wahi'a i ke piko o ka hale o Mea.
A ku! A wa! A moku ka piko,
A moku, a moku iho la!"

"Orderly and harmonious is the prayer of the multitude to God.
Kuwa cuts now the piko of the house of Mea.
He stands! He cuts! The navel string is cut!
It is cut! Lo it is cut!"

The following is a Molokai pule used at this time:

"A moku ka piko i ele-ua, i ele-ao,
I ka wai i Haakula-manu la.
E moku!
A moku ka piko o kou hale la,
E Mauli-ola!
I ola i ka noho-hale,
I ola i ke kanaka kipa mai,
I ola i ka haku-aina,
I ola i na 'lii,
Oia ke ola o kau hale, e Mauli-ola;
Ola a kolo-pupu, a haumaka-iole,
A pala-lau-hala, a ka i koko.
Amama, ua noa."

"Severed is the piko of the house, the thatch that sheds the rain, that wards off the evil influences of the heavens,
The water-spout of Haakula-manu, oh!
Cut now!
Cut the piko of your house, o Mauli-ola!
That the house-dweller may prosper,
That the guest who enters it may have health,
That the lord of the land may have health,
That the chiefs may have long life.
Grant these blessings to your house, o Mauli-ola.
To live till one crawls hunched up, till one becomes blear-eyed,
Till one lies on the mat, till one has to be carried about in a net.
Amen. It is free."

A Hawaiian, writing in the days when there were no kahuna pule, advises that the following be done at the final trimming of the thatching, "It is well to bring an aholehole (fish) and some sugar cane and also cut them; at the same time say, 'Here I am a house builder; I am cutting the piko of the house; therefore ward off evil influences from the house. Amama'."

While the thatch over the doorway was being trimmed, a feast of pig, chicken, and fish was cooking. Before eating it, and after the trimming ceremony, the family ancestors were invoked in the following prayer:

"Na aumakua i ka po,
Na aumakua i ke ao,
Mai ka hikina ke komohana.
Eia ka ai, eia ka ia, eia ka puaa
Ke komo nei ka hale hou.
Ka ai nei,
Ke ike mai la oukou i na pulapula,
E hoola mai ia makou apau, a e hoola aku i na haku aina.
E na akua wahine,
Mai hikina a ke komohana, mai ke komohana a i ka hikina,
E ola ia'u mau pulapula, kaika-mahine, moopuna.
E ola, e ke akua.
Amama. Ua noa."

"O ancestors of the night,
Ancestors of the day,
From the east to the west,
Here is the food, the fish, the pig—
We are entering a new house.

Eat thereof,
Observe us, thy offspring,
Preserve us all, and the landlords.

O female gods,
From east to west, from west to east,
Preserve my offspring, daughters, grandchildren.
Long life, O akua.
It is ended, it is free."

Then all enjoyed the feast of house entering (ahaaina komo hale). These prayers and the feast removed the kapu on the new dwelling, so that the owner and his family might safely enter and set up housekeeping. The akua of the threshold, which was sacred and must not be sat upon or stood on, was Kane-hohoio, while the interior was sacred to Kane-i-loko-o-kahale.

TYPES OF HOUSES AND THEIR FURNISHINGS

The floor of a good house on a stone foundation would be covered with small pebbles, but in poorer houses with earth floors the ground was simply covered with dried potato vines and grass, and old mats. A fine house had beautiful heavy lauhala mats for floor covering.

The sleeping house was very simply furnished. On the floor were the lauhala mats (moena) and the kapa moe which formed the bed coverings. Here also were the small rectangular pillows (uluna) made of lauhala. The interior was lighted at night by kukui nuts stuck on a coconut leaf midrib or a small stick, standing in a hollowed-out stone lamp (poho kukui).

Men and boys ate and cooked in a house separate from the eating house of the women. Nearby were the ground ovens. In the eating houses were kept the various utensils for eating and serving. These included wooden bowls (umeke); gourd containers and water bottles (huewai); smaller containers (ipu); and dishes (pa, kanoa, etc.) Here also were the poi board (papa ku'i ai) and the stone poi pounders (pohaku ku'i).

The residence of a well-to-do Hawaiian consisted of six separate houses, as follows:

Heiau, a chapel in which images of the family aumakua were kept, and private worship was held. Sometimes an altar in the mua served this purpose.

Mua, the eating house of the men, kapu to women.

Noa, where the wife lived, not kapu to the husband.

Hale aina, the eating house of the women.

Kua, also kuku, where kapa was beaten in bad weather.

Pea, where the wife lived during the period of uncleanness.

Besides these the householder who lived by the sea had

a canoe shed (halau waa). Some farmers had food sheds (hale papaa or hale hoahu), which were floors elevated on posts and roofed.

FAMILY CUSTOMS AND RELATIONSHIPS

Today we have rooms under a single roof for various needs—sleeping, cooking, eating, working, and so on. But in ancient times the Hawaiians built a separate house for each purpose, because the kapu forbad eating and sleeping under the same roof; it forbad men eating with women, and it forbad men and women working together.

"The division of the household into two halves, male and female, and their segregation by kapu, did not, however, affect the solidarity of the family as a social unit. For the Hawaiian, the social and emotional tie of relationship was exceedingly strong, including in the visible world blood relatives of any degree of relationship and members of the family by adoption, some of whom would be members of the domicile, while others were attached only through bonds of sentiment. In the unseen but tangible 'other world' the bond of affection and sense of interdependence embraced the ancestors (kupuna, grandfathers,) and the aumakua or spirit guardians incarnate in animal forms.

. . . "Leadership in the family lay with the male and female parents or with elders substituting in their roles. The fundamentals of a child's education were acquired through companionship with elders, and participation in their activities, as in performing minor functions in connection with cooking or plaiting mats, or carrying the father's hooks, accompanying him in his canoe, . . . and so on."

VILLAGES (KAUHALE)

In old Hawaii and elsewhere in Polynesia there were no cities or towns because the civilization was not industrial or commercial as it is nowadays. In early Hawaii, concentration of population for governmental and business purposes was not necessary. The people gathered together in small villages near good fishing grounds, or in the vicinity

Hawaiian village at the mouth of Waimea valley, Kauai, in the time of Capt. Cook. Sketched by his artist, Webber.

of the lands which were planted with taro and sweet potato. The houses of the chief were generally built near the best fishing places. The houses of his relatives and retainers were built nearby, as were the homes of the men working for him. In this way, little villages grew up, mostly along the coast. When Captain Cook came to these islands, he found such a village at Waimea, Kauai, for instance, and wrote a description of it. Drawings made at the time show the appearance of this village. Captain Cook's description follows:

> "Though they seem to have adopted the mode of living in villages, there is no appearance of defense, or fortification, near any of them; and the houses are scattered about, without any order, either with respect to their distances from each other, or their position in any particular direction. Neither is there any proportion as to their size; some being large and commodious, from forty to fifty feet long, and twenty or thirty broad, while others of them are mere hovels. Their figure is not unlike oblong corn, or hay-stacks; or, perhaps, a better idea may be conceived of them, if we suppose the roof of a barn placed on the ground, in such a manner, as to form a high, acute ridge, with two very low sides, hardly discernible at a distance. The gable at each end, corresponding to the sides, makes these habitations perfectly close all around; and they are well thatched with long grass, which is laid on slender poles, disposed with some regularity. The entrance is made indifferently in the end or side, and is an oblong hole, so low, that one must rather creep than walk in; and is often shut up by a board or planks, fastened together, which serves as a door; but having no hinges, must be removed occasionally. No light enters the house, but by this opening; and though such close habitations may afford a comfortable retreat in bad weather, they seem but ill-adapted to the warmth of the climate. They are, however, kept remarkably clean; and their floors are covered with a large quantity of dried grass, over which

they spread mats to sit and sleep upon. At one end stands a kind of bench, about three feet high, on which their household utensils are placed. The catalogue is not long. It consists of gourd-shells, which they convert into vessels that serve as bottles to hold water, and as baskets to contain their victuals, and other things, with covers of the same; and of a few wooden bowls and trenchers of different sizes."

The normal way to live in the climate of these islands is this old Hawaiian way with houses scattered, rather than in the modern style of packing dwellings close together on streets. You see the old way of living in Kona today where the houses are scattered all along the shore and along the road. You see it today also in the vicinity of Honolulu back in the valleys of Kalihi and Nuuanu for instance, where the houses are scattered along in the valley bottom and on the hillsides. This is the healthy and natural way to locate homes in Hawaii.

REFERENCES

Malo, David, Hawaiian Antiquities, B. P. Bishop Museum, Honolulu, 1903.

Brigham, William T., The Ancient Hawaiian House, Memoirs of the Bishop Museum, Vol. 11, No. 3, Honolulu, 1908.

Handy, E. S. C., Cultural Revolution in Hawaii, American Council, Institute of Pacific Relations.

CHAPTER 7

THE HISTORY OF LAND OWNERSHIP IN HAWAII

JOHN H. WISE

The story of land ownership in Hawaii is a very fascinating one. Many present-day problems arise directly out of ancient rights and therefore a clear understanding of the ancient system and the ways in which it was changed, is essential. In ancient Hawaii, all the land belonged to the Alii Nui of the island. Control over the various districts was allotted to his chiefs and followers. All lands were redistributed when a new chief came into power. Right down through the time of Kamehameha I, all land was redistributed on conquest or on the coming of a new chief into power. Kamehameha I established peace throughout the islands and from his time on it was generally understood that the tenant could reasonably expect to be allowed to remain on the land which he cultivated. Liholiho, the son of Kamehameha I, wished to follow the old custom of redividing the land, but he was strongly opposed by Kaahumanu who possessed considerable influence. Consequently, Liholiho managed to dispose of only a few lands to his personal friends and supporters. When Liholiho died, the regent reported to the chiefs that Kamehameha I had intended to abolish the custom of redividing the land and to substitute instead the principle of hereditary ownership by the royal family. The chiefs said, "All the laws of the Great Kamehameha were good. Let us have the same!" In this simple manner, the principle of hereditary royal ownership of the land was accepted in Hawaii. In 1840, in what was known as the Bill of Rights, Kamehameha III definitely gave to the people the right to remain on their lands, stating, "Protection is hereby secured to the persons of all the people, together with their lands, building lots, and all their property, while they conform to the laws of the kingdom, and nothing whatsoever shall be taken from any individual except by express permission of the laws."

However, the land still belonged to the king and no transfer of any kind could be made without his consent. Considerable pressure was brought to bear upon Kamehameha III to make it possible for people to acquire land and hold it in fee simple ownership. Growing industry, expanding trade, immigration,—all these exerted their influence to show that changing conditions demanded a changed system of landholding. Moreover, Kamehameha III honestly desired to secure the Hawaiian people more firmly in their possession of the land. The Great Mahele, or division of the lands was planned, arranged, and carried through. It was decided that three groups of people had just claims to the land. These were the king, the chiefs, and the common people. The basis of this was the idea that whoever had had a share in making the land valuable had an interest in the land. Then it was necessary to provide for the expenses of government. Kamehameha III waived his title to Hawaii providing a satisfactory arrangement could be made for the chiefs, for the people, and for the government. To provide for the government and for the people, it was necessary that the chiefs give up much of what they considered theirs. However, the complicated and difficult adjustments were made and the Great Mahele was completed.

Roughly, one-third of the lands was reserved for the king one-third for the chiefs, and one-third for the people. Out of the share of the king and chiefs, came the government lands. The part remaining to the king was known as Crown Lands. At the time of the Great Mahele, it was considered that the Crown Lands belonged to the king, to sell, lease, or mortgage. The succeeding history of the Crown Lands is interesting. Kamehameha III left a will leaving the crown and the Crown Lands to his heir, Kamehameha IV. Kamehameha IV died without a will. Kamehameha V was chosen king but Kamehameha IV's widow, Queen Emma, put in a claim to half the Crown Lands and to her dower right in these lands. The question to be settled by the court was, did the Crown Lands belong to the king as a person or to the office? It had been thought earlier that they were the personal possession of the king, but it was apparent that if these lands could be sold, leased, or mortgaged, if they could be left at the personal disposal of the king, very soon there would be nothing remaining to the Crown. As it was, the lands were seriously burdened with debt, and decreased in extent. Consequently, the decision was made that these lands belonged to the Crown, not to the person. It was decided that these lands could not be sold or mortgaged; that the king could use and enjoy their revenues, but must pass the land on to his successor intact. In other words, these lands were no longer considered a personal possession, but were held in trust for the heir. Later, when Liliuokalani was deposed, she put in a claim for the revenues of the Crown Lands. This claim was refused, on the ground that if some member of the royal house had been placed on the throne when the queen was deposed, the revenues would have gone to the new ruler, and that this was still the case though the form of government had been changed. Throughout Hawaiian history except for the brief intervals of time just described, land ownership or revenues after the Great Mahele, have gone with the office, not with the person. In the old days, we say that the land belonged to the Alii Nui. It did—just as long as he held the power. When he lost the office, he lost the land.

THE WAY THE LAND WAS DIVIDED IN OLD HAWAII

In the old days, each island was ruled by an Alii Nui. The whole island, or mokupuni, was divided into districts called moku. The division lines ran from the top of the mountains to the sea. The ruler of the moku was the alii ai moku, appointed by the Alii Nui. Each large district was again cut into smaller sections known as ahupuaas. The name was derived from the ahu or altar which was erected at the district boundary line and on which the yearly payments were made at the time of the Makahiki. On this altar was also placed a small image of a pig or puaa, hence the name name ahupuaa. The ahupuaa was in charge of a konohiki. Ahupuaas varied greatly in size and shape. A typical ahupuaa was a long narrow strip running from the sea to the mountain. On the windward side of an island, a single valley often formed one ahupuaa. On East Maui, the principal lands radiated from a large rock on the edge of the crater Haleakala. In several districts, the ahupuaas widened as they went inland and the larger ones cut off the smaller ones from the mountains. Waikapu and Wailuku on Maui took in almost the whole isthmus and cut off half the lands of Kula from the sea. Some districts were divided into ahupuaas rather uniform in size, perhaps one-quarter of a mile wide and several miles deep. In other districts, ahupuaas such as Honouliuli on Oahu, contained over 40,000 acres. Hawaii contained the great mountain lands of Kahuku, Keauhou, Humuula, and Kaohe. The first of these included over 184,000 acres.

People living in one ahupuaa had a right to use what grew there. They could go to the mountains for timber. They could gather pili grass and olona. They could fish in the waters off their district. Their rights extended to the boundaries of the ahupuaa and no further. If there were breakers, it was considered that the ahupuaa extended to them. If there were no breakers, it was considered that the ahupuaa extended a mile and a half out to sea. It the ahupuaa did not extend to the sea, the inhabitants of that district were barred from all in-shore fishing, and must go out to the deep waters for their fish. It was customary for the konokiki to select one kind of fish, generally the most plentiful variety of the district, for his exclusive use. With this restriction, fishing was free to the people within the boundaries of the ahupuaa. No person could cross the boundaries of his ahupuaa to take anything. This being the case, it was important that the boundaries be well known.

Boundary lines followed natural lines to some extent and in some cases. Frequently the boundary was a ridge or a depression or a stream. But it might be the line of growth of a certain tree or herb or grass, or the home of a certain bird. The boundary might be even more intangible than this, as is shown by the following: "The ancient

Hawaiian method of determining the dividing lines between hillside and valley property is illustrated in testimony before the Land Commission in 1848 to affix the boundary between Kewalo and Kaimuohena. 'The dividing line between them is where a stone would stop when rolled down the ridge. Kewalo is any place where a stone running down would stop and below where a stone would stop is Kaimuohena.' " Certain people were trained in knowledge of the different boundaries. This knowledge was passed on from generation to generation. In every community were experts in the subject of the boundaries. When disputes arose, or when a man was accused of trespass, these experts were called in to settle the question.

The ahupuaas were generally, though not always, subdivided into ilis. The ili sometimes reached the sea. A moo was a small division of an ahupuaa which generally did not reach the sea. The very small subdivisions of the land, and the large number of native names for tiny pieces of land, give some idea of the dense population which must have lived in the islands in the old days.

An individual might move from one ahupuaa to another. If the konohiki was unusually severe in his treatment of the people, it is probable that the people would move. Since the Alii Nui and the konohiki were interested in having a large number of fighting men to be called out at any time, it is reasonable to suppose that the konohiki did not, as a general rule, treat the people with extreme severity so that they would move out of the district. When there was war, the Alii Nui called the konohiki and stated the number of men he wished from each ahupuaa. If the konohiki could not furnish them, the Alii Nui would demand an explanation. If the men had left the ahupuaa, the Alii Nui would make an investigation. If he found that the konohiki had ill-treated the people, he would remove him and place another man over the district, because he wished always to be able to secure all the fighting men he needed. When we speak of ill-treatment and severity, we must not imagine that modern ideas of kindness and consideration prevailed. The people expected a certain amount of severe treatment. It was customary in those days. Human life was not thought to be of particular value anywhere in the world, in the times of which we are thinking. The idea that human life is of any value in itself is very new in the world and is still not accepted in large parts of the world even at present.

Streams ran down through some of the ahupuaas and the water from these streams was often carried through the villages in ditches. Wet-land taro is raised, not in still water, but in very slowly moving water, and in many cases the water from the streams was run through the taro fields in ditches from which the plants could be properly irrigated. The stream water was used for bathing, washing, and drinking, but it is interesting to note that it was kapu to bathe or wash except at the mouth of the stream. This kapu, and others of a similar nature, kept the streams clean.

LAND TENURE

In the old days, though the common people were not land owners, and though they might be dispossessed at any time, as a matter of fact it was not customary to remove the people from their homes and fields when the island was redivided by a new chief. Though they had no legal security, they had a certain general security, particularly after Kamehameha I established peace throughout the islands. Though they were more secure after the time of Kamehameha I, in some ways they were better off in the earlier days. When the konohiki depended on the ahupuaa to furnish his fighting men, when his own power depended on the number and ability and strength of his fighting men, he was interested to some extent in the welfare of the men of his district. He lived in the district and took an active part in the life of the people. When, however, there was general peace and when the interest of the chiefs was centered more in the court about the king than in the life of the people, the chiefs left their lands to the control of agents. Very frequently the agents were concerned only in the amount of revenue they could obtain from the people and the people were oppressed. Since they could not live in reasonable comfort in their ahupuaas, many people left their lands, attached themselves as hangers-on at the court, or wandered about the country. The system which had maintained them to some extent in the old days, did not work when the conditions changed.

Kamehameha III was aware of the fact that the welfare of the people was not assured under the changing conditions in the islands. He was concerned for his people. He was influenced by advisors who were used to private land ownership, and who urged that owning their own land would be a source of pride to the Hawaiian and give him an incentive to work. Moved by all these considerations, Kamehameha III instituted the Great Mahele. The Great Mahele was an unusual affair. It has been described as a "phenomenon in national history not often repeated . . . in one sense a revolution."

We have spoken of some of the problems which arose concerning the Crown Lands and the way in which the royal holdings were protected. More serious problems arose in the case of the kuleanas or small farms allotted to the people, and in their case, no means of protecting these holdings were provided. Though 1,000,000 acres of land were set aside for the Hawaiian people, very few Hawaiians now hold kuleanas. It is interesting to know how the people lost their land, and how the Great Mahele did not bring about the permanency of ownership and the security which Kamehameha III had desired.

Though 1,000,000 acres were set aside for the common people, only 8,000 to 11,000 kuleanas were claimed, and they extended only over some 28,000 acres. There were several reasons for this. For one thing, the ownership of land was not in any way a part of the tradition of the Hawaiian people. They never had owned land. They did not understand the privileges and responsibilities of land ownership. They had been cared for by the chiefs and they expected to be cared for by the chiefs. In some cases, they were intimidated by the local konohikis who discouraged them from putting in claims. In other cases, they were unwilling to seem to be taking land away from their alii. They were confused by the problems presented. Accustomed for generations to communal rights to forest and upland produce, to fishing and to land, they could not imagine life on another basis. The whole idea of fee simple ownership was so new to them that they could not comprehend it and take advantage of it.

The kuleanas allotted to claimants varied considerably in size. This was because in awarding lands no consistent policy was followed. For instance, one surveyor might include in the land allotted to the claimant, only the land actually under his cultivation at the time. In such a case, the individual kuleana would be two or three acres in extent and would not be sufficient to support the owner, for in raising taro, lands cannot be cultivated year after year but must be allowed to lie fallow for a time. Consequently, a kuleana consisting only of cultivated fields would be inadequate. Another surveyor, aware of the need of other lands besides those fields actually under cultivation, might include upland regions and award from fifteen to forty acres to an individual. Another surveyor, not knowing how to allot fallow lands fairly, might adopt an arbitrary measure and recommend six to twelve acres for a single kuleana.

The kuleanas not only varied very considerably in size, but they were often made up of two or three or four parcels of land separated from each other and located at the shore, farther inland, and in the mountains. We can easily understand this when we remember how the ancient ahupuaas usually gave the tenants access to the different things they needed from the mountains to the sea. The people were used to this privilege and expected to retain the type of rights to which they were accustomed. But this type of ownership complicated enormously the task of defining the boundaries of the kuleanas. The task of surveying and describing the 11,000 or more kuleanas was an extremely difficult one, particularly since the islands had never been surveyed, and since there were few men available qualified to undertake this enterprise. The surveyors should have been men of exceptional honesty and integrity, men who were technically trained, and men who thoroughly understood the Hawaiian language and customs and who had the confidence of the people. And, to accomplish this task, a small army of such men would have been necessary. Of course, there was no such army of specialists to be found. Also, the surveying instruments of this date were crude and inadequate to the task. As a result, the enterprise of defining the kuleanas was only partly accomplished. There was no uniformity in the methods used. Every conceivable method of measurement was adopted. Everything was left to the man who was hired for $2 or $3 a kuleana to do the measurement. Kuleanas in one district might be surveyed by a dozen men, no one of whom guided himself by the notes of another. In some cases titles were awarded below high water mark, and sometimes to the reef. In other cases this was not done. There was consequently much confusion and overlapping. Within a single ahupuaa there might be a perfect patchwork of kuleanas and other lands which were not claimed. There should have been a master map into which the pieces surveyed could have been fitted, but instead, only the claimed kuleanas were defined. And they were not always defined very exactly. Sometimes the land was not surveyed at all and the boundaries were defined in terms of the old Hawaiian landmarks. It is easy to see why the mere difficulty, the impossibility, of surveying and defining the kuleanas introduced insecurity into the land tenure. If a question arose, how could it be settled? What redress had the kuleana holder, particularly when he did not understand the whole affair at all?

Another factor operated to make the kuleana holder insecure. For the first time in his life and for the first time in generations of Hawaiian life, people unused to land ownership found themselves in possession of something which could be leased or mortgaged or sold. Very frequently the kuleana owner disposed of his land entirely. Often he leased it to a corporation interested in the plantations which were being developed throughout the islands. The Hawaiian had been accustomed for generations to boundaries and district lines which were rigidly maintained. He could not possibly imagine the erasing of landmarks, the obliteration of distinguishing characteristics. He could not imagine that it could ever be made impossible for him to identify his land. After he had leased his land to a corporation, he might return after a number of years, hoping to live again on his kuleana. But where was the kuleana? Mr. Lydgate has described the kuleana holder's perplexity. He saw before him an expanse of land covered with rice or sugar cane. Ditches had been filled in, dikes had been levelled off, hedges had been cut down. He might go to the plantation office to see what could be done. Here he might find his name and the record of a lease on a "kuleana in the ili of Wai-Momona, Hanalei." That was all. Where was the ili of Wai Momona? No one knew. In the early days, every man, woman, and child for a dozen miles about could have told just where it was but now no one knew. It was somewhere in this rice field, or in this cane field. The owner might have gone to law to recover his holding. It would have been a long expensive process to prove ownership of a kuleana originally so poorly defined and now lost in the great fields of the plantation. And if the owner could have afforded this, if he had gone to law and won his case, he would have found himself in possession of separate pieces of land surrounded by cane or rice, cut off from the life of his people. Faced with this, many of the kuleana holders lost their property.

Few kuleanas remain today. For the sake of the Hawaiian people it is too bad that their lands were not made inalienable, as were the Crown Lands when it was seen that they were in danger of being lost. The Hawaiians could have been protected if it had been made impossible for them to sell or mortgage or lease their lands for a long period of time, during which they could have become used to the new privileges and responsibilities of land ownership, and adjusted to the new social and economic order. When an old custom is being overturned for something quite different, it is a good plan to protect the people involved from the otherwise inevitable misunderstanding and loss. It is too bad that the generosity of Kamehameha III and his willingness to surrender his land for the good of the people, could not alone accomplish the ends he desired. With the gradual disappearance of the kuleana, small farms held in fee simple vanished from Hawaii. They are appearing again in some degree in lands which are homesteaded, but whether the small farm will ever again be an important factor in the landholding system of the islands, is open to question.

RENT AND TAXATION

In the old days, the common people were required to work for the konohiki every fifth day. This constituted a part of the rent paid for the land. In addition, there were services which might be required by the Alii Nui at any time, and there were the regular payments made during the Makahiki. These payments were made in produce. After the time of Kamehameha I, the labor tax was first regulated by law. Every tenant was required to work every Tuesday for the king and every Friday for the konohiki. Later laws reduced the number of days of annual service for the king and the konohiki to thirty-six each. This law was passed in 1840. The whole system of paying taxes in money, not in labor or produce, has evolved in Hawaii since 1840.

PROBLEMS REGARDING FISHING RIGHTS

In the old days, fishing rights were carefully defined and rigidly observed. After the Great Mahele, kuleana owners who did not hold to their fishing rights lost them. Generally speaking, only the great estates retained their fishing rights. At the present time, for instance, the John Ii Estate, the Bishop Estate and the Damon Estate claim fishing rights in Pearl Harbor. Since Pearl Harbor is a great naval base, it is easy to see why it is difficult even for influential groups to maintain these rights and also, why it is impossible to preserve the fish in these waters. Many difficult cases involving fishing rights originate in the customs of old Hawaii and represent an attempt to hold to ancient rights.

The circle represents the island, known as the mokupuni,

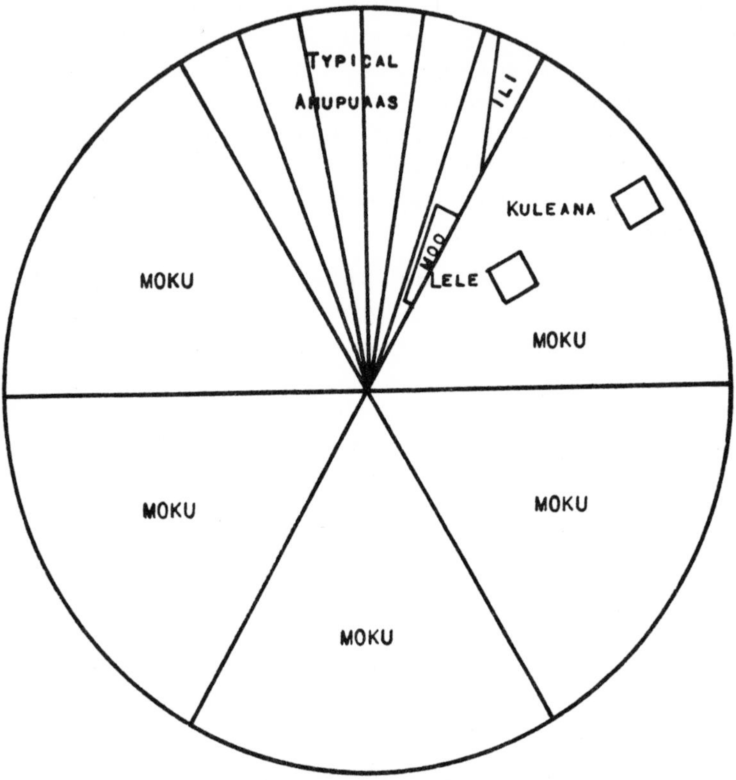

A MOKUPUNI

ruled by the Alii Nui. The large wedge-shaped divisions represent the moku ruled by the Alii Ai Moku. The subdivided moku shows typical ahupuaas. An ili was a small division of an ahupuaa which sometimes extended to the sea. A moo was a small division of an ahupuaa which generally did not reach the sea. The little squares on the third moku show a single typical kuleana. The kuleana proper is nearest the sea. The other parcel of land belonging to the same holding (kuleana) but separated from it was known as the lele.

REFERENCES

Spaulding, Thomas Marshall, The Crown Lands of Hawaii, University of Hawaii Occasional Papers No. 1.

Thrum's Annual, 1890:65

Alexander, W. D., A Brief History of Land Titles in the Hawaiian Kingdom. Thrum's Annual, 1891:105

Dole, S. B., Evolution of Hawaiian Land Tenures. Hawaiian Historical Society Papers, No. 3, 1892.

Lydgate, J. M., The Vanishing Kuleana. Thrum's Annual, 1915: 103.

Lyons, C. J., Land Matters in Hawaii. The Islander, 1875, July 16, July 30, Aug. 6, Aug. 13.

CHAPTER 8

FOOD AND ITS PREPARATION

JOHN H. WISE

There were certain facts about life in old Hawaii which affected very considerably the diet and eating habits of the people. (1) The people were of course entirely dependent on what the islands and the ocean produced in the line of food. Today we import much of what we eat, and do not begin to produce enough food for a population smaller than the population in the old days. (2) We know that the Hawaiian people were splendid physical specimens and that their diet must have contained the elements necessary for health. The stature and physique of the old-time Hawaiian was proof of the values his diet must have contained, just as the smaller stature of such people as the Japanese is suggestive of defects in their native diet. (3) We know that the old Hawaiians had no fire-proof cooking utensils, so that they had to manage without much of what we think of as "cooking." (4) Certain foods were kapu to women. It was kapu for men and women to eat together. Consequently, the preparation and serving of food must have been complicated by these facts in the social organization and customs of the times.

THE CHIEF FOODS OF OLD HAWAII AND THEIR FOOD VALUE

The staple foods of old Hawaii were taro and poi, breadfruit, sweet potato, bananas, taro tops and some other leafy vegetables, limu, fish and other sea-foods, chicken, pig, and dog. The food values of fish, sea-foods, and meats are generally understood, but perhaps the food value of poi, taro, and limu is not so well known. Taro is essentially a starchy food with a high water content. Both taro and poi are good sources of Vitamins A and B. As taro and poi are digested, they produce an alkaline reaction in the body. This is highly important, because most starches, noticeably polished rice, have an acid reaction. Dr. Buck often wondered why the Polynesians were physically so much better developed and larger than the various stocks from which they probably originated. It may be that the Polynesian became larger because he changed an acid starch, low in Vitamin B, for an alkaline residue starch with plenty of fish and sea weed. It has been found that when he replaces poi and fish with polished rice, his children have rampant decay of the teeth. Because of their alkaline reaction, poi and taro have the desirable effects of fruit in the diet. Fruits were lacking in old Hawaii, as only coconuts, bananas, and mountain apples were here originally. Another fact to be noted about poi is that the acid in the fermenting poi preserves it, and it becomes a food which will keep several weeks without refrigeration. This is interesting, because of course in old Hawaii there was no such thing as refrigeration.

There are many varieties of limu or edible sea weed. Some of these have been analyzed for their food values. It has been found that they perhaps furnished a small amount of calcium, and doubtless certain vitamins. Their chief value probably lay in the fact that they provided variety in an otherwise monotonous diet. They probably also served a useful purpose in preventing constipation. Opihi, the little limpets to be found on the rocks along the shore, are a very high source of Vitamin A.

Certain vitamins lacking in the diet were supplied by the direct rays of the sun to which the people were continually exposed. The combination of sunlight, sea-foods, and the meats and vegetables mentioned, provided the Hawaiians with everything needed for healthy bodily growth and for splendid physical development.

FOODS AND COOKING

Though they did not have fire-proof cooking utensils, the Hawaiians managed to boil liquids by dropping hot stones into a calabash containing the liquid. In this manner, they prepared certain foods by steaming. Most of the cooking, however, was done in the imu or underground oven, and without the aid of containers of any kind.

The imu used today in the preparation of a luau is much the same as the imu used in the early days. The first step in making an imu was to dig a hole in the ground. This hole was used over and over. Today it is customary to build a shelter over an imu, just as people sometimes build shelters over their out-door picnic fireplaces at their beach or mountain homes. Wood was placed in the hole. If plenty of wood was to be used, kindling was placed in first, then larger pieces, and then still larger ones. The laying of the fire was similar to the laying of any open fire today. Stones were placed over the wood and the fire was lighted. Sometimes arches were built with long stones and the smaller stones were placed over the arches. After the stones were heated the arches were knocked down and the imu was then used in the same way as the other type. The stones used were of a certain kind which the Hawaiians knew would hold the heat and which would not burst when hot. After the stones were hot, grass (honohono) was laid in. On this were placed the taro, the breadfruit, the sweet potato, and the bananas, to be cooked. Over the food a layer of leaves, preferably ti leaves, was placed, and then the imu was closed with old mats and kapas. It took taro from three to four hours to cook in an imu. Taro and taro leaves must be thoroughly cooked before they can be eaten. The reason for this is that the root, the stem, and the leaves all contain needle-like crystals which are extremely irritating and which must be broken down by thorough cooking. Sweet potato, breadfruit and bananas required a shorter time to cook than taro. Three or four days were required to cook the ti root, which was a confection.

Besides chickens, there were only two land animals which could be used for food in old Hawaii. These were pig and dog. Meats, as well as vegetables, were roasted in the imu. After the pig was killed it was dressed and heated stones were placed inside it. It was salted and placed in the imu for one-half to two and a half hours. Then it was taken from the imu, the stones were removed, and the meat cut up. Except in the case of some particular celebration, small pigs were not killed. However, for family use, the large hogs were used but were never put in the imu. After the hog was dressed, hot stones were put in after the inside had been salted. It was then wrapped in old kapas and mats, placed on a poi board, and left for forty-eight hours. Then it was unwrapped, the stones were removed, and the meat was cut from the inside, not the outside. This was because these inner portions which had been next to the stones were more thoroughly cooked than the other portions. A large pig lasted some time and did not spoil because of the salting of the meat.

Meat which remained and which had been imperfectly cooked, was sometimes cut up and placed in laulaus for re-cooking. Sometimes it was cut up and placed in calabashes with hot stones. The Hawaiians ate only thoroughly cooked meat, and re-cooked any portions which had come partly cooked from the imu. If several animals were to be cooked in one imu, the imu was built flat, so the heat would be even. The cone-shaped imu was hotter in the middle than at the sides.

Chickens were wrapped in ti leaves and cooked in the imu. Chicken prepared with luau and coconut is a modern adaption of the old Hawaiian use of luau and coconut. If the old method of steaming through the use of hot stones dropped into the calabash is followed, rather than more recent cooking methods, this dish is particularly delicious.

Fish was one of the chief foods of the Hawaiian people. The fish resources of Hawaii were extensive. Bryan, in his "Natural History of Hawaii," says, "Some idea of the fish resources of Hawaii can be gained from the fact that of the 600 or more species which scientists have found in Hawaiian waters, more than 350 are sold in the markets of Honolulu for food, each species having an Hawaiian name by which it is designated." The Hawaiians not only fished in the open ocean, but they raised fish in carefully made and protected fish ponds. The favorite pond fish was the mullet. On one side of the mullet pond was a smaller pond in which the little fish were kept until their variety could be recognized. Most of those which were not mullet were destroyed and the mullet were then placed in the big pond. This protected the mullet against game fish which would destroy them. Awa and aholehole were also run into the fish pond, as they did not destroy each other or the mullet.

Fish was cooked in several ways. One way was to wrap it in ti leaves, in packages called lawalu, and put it on the coals. Another way was to broil it over hot coals. A third was to place it in a calabash, put a little water on it, and drop in hot stones. Fish cooked in this way is very delicious.

The Hawaiians had different ways of preserving uncooked fish. Their uncooked fish was always preserved by salting or drying or both. The Hawaiians never ate fish raw just as it came from the ocean. They always dried it or preserved it in some way before eating it. Small fish which were to be eaten uncooked were split open, salted, and hung in the sun. Dried fish and poi are a very good combination, a favorite today as well as in the old days.

The leaves of several plants were cooked and eaten as greens. Among these were popolo, pakai, aweo weo, naunau, haio, nena, palula, and of course taro tops or luau. Pia was another vegetable food. David Malo describes its preparation in these words, "When ripe the tubers are grated while yet raw by means of rough stones, mixed with water and then allowed to stand until it has turned sweet, after which it is roasted in bundles and eaten." David Malo has an interesting comment on the sweet potato. He says, "The body of one who makes his food of the sweet potato is plump and his flesh is clean and fair whereas the flesh of him who feeds on taro poi is not so clear and wholesome." Whether this is accurate or not, at least it gives an idea that the sweet potato was well thought of by the early Hawaiians. Sugar cane was grown throughout the islands in little patches in every little community. Every group of houses had its patch of cane. The people developed no artificial methods of extracting the juice; they chewed the stalks of cane and enjoyed them just as people do today, whenever they manage to get a stalk of cane. We find today that the Hawaiians very frequently raise a little sugar cane in their yards, just as they did in the old days.

Nearly all food was eaten cold. This practice is followed today in such places as Samoa where native customs still prevail.

POI-MAKING

Cooked taro was peeled through the use of shells, sticks, or stone knives. Fresh cooked taro, called ai paa, was much liked. Sometimes it was sliced and dried in the sun. So prepared, it furnished a convenient and portable food called ao, suitable for long voyages.

Most of the cooked taro was pounded. The poi board used was a single board five or six inches thick, twenty-four to thirty inches wide, and three to six feet long. Any hard close-grained wood, to be obtained in pieces sufficiently large, was used. Koa and ohia were most used for this purpose. The poi pounder was fashioned from hard lava or coral rock. It had to be just the right weight, neither too heavy nor too light. It might be porous. It was generally made in pestle form, though ring and stirrup pounders were used in certain localities. Poi pounding was heavy work and was always done by the men. The workman seated himself on the ground, with his legs extended on either side of the board. He wore nothing but the malo, for it was necesary that he have perfect freedom of motion. On one side was placed a pile of cooked taro, and on the other, a calabash of water. The board was well moistened with water and some cooked taro was placed on the moistened board and was mashed with short quick strokes. At every blow, the pounder was lifted high in the air. The intensity was increased as more taro was added and the quantity on the board became greater. Between strokes, the face of the stone poi pounder was moistened with the hand dipped in water. This was done to keep the pounder from sticking. A firm doughlike mass called paiai was produced. When it was needed for storage or transportation it was made with the minimum amount of water, and was tied up in ti leaves, in bundles. Poi was made by pounding this substance and adding water until it reached a smooth somewhat fluid consistency. Poi was also made from sweet potato and from breadfruit. Both of these were much easier to make than poi made from taro since they required so much less pounding.

Down to very recent days, each Hawaiian family still cooked its own taro and prepared its own poi. Taro was generally cooked once a week, pounded, and kept rather hard so that it would not turn sour. The poi was prepared from this as it was needed throughout the week. Nowadays, all the work is done in the poi factory. Here the taro is cleaned, cooked, peeled, run through a machine, mixed with a little water, and placed in bags for delivery. This is a lot easier than it was in the old days but something has been lost from the life of the people.

THE WATER SUPPLY

The chief drink of the Hawaiians was water. Spring water was most desired. There are many springs in the islands. Some are in the mountains, some are in the lowlands, and some are along the shore covered by the ocean. The water in these springs along the shore is perfectly good, though not as fresh as the water from the other springs. To secure the water from the springs along the shore, the Hawaiian took a covered gourd, located the mouth of the spring, uncovered the gourd just at the mouth of the spring, filled it, and covered it. Cattle grazing along the shore today may be seen going into the water and drinking. They are drinking from one of these fresh springs along the shore under the sea.

Streams of fresh water were another source of the water supply. The Hawaiians never dug wells. They found and utilized the water of streams and springs, and if it was necessary, carried the drinking water in gourds from the source of supply to their homes.

ANCIENT CUSTOMS REGARDING PREPARATION AND USE OF FOODS

David Malo, the Hawaiian who reported so many of the customs of the old days, has some very hard words to say about the kapus governing eating. He says, "The task of food providing and eating under the kapu system in Hawaii was very burdensome, a grievous tax on the husband and wife, an iniquitous imposition, at war with domestic peace. The husband was burdened and wearied with the preparation of two ovens of food, one for the husband and a separate one for his wife." This was necessary, since men and women were not allowed to eat together. The women might not even enter the eating house of the men, though a man might enter the eating house of the women. As soon as boys were weaned they were not allowed to eat with women.

David Malo goes on to describe just what the man had to do, because of this necessity of preparing food for men and women separately. "The man first started an oven of food for his wife and when that was done he went to the house (mua) and started an oven of food for himself. Then he would return to the house, open his wife's oven, peel the taro, pound it into poi, knead it, and put it in the calabash. This ended the food cooking for his wife. Then he must return to mua, open his own oven, peel the taro, pound and knead it into poi, put the mass into a separate calabash for himself, and remove the lumps."

The fact that certain foods were kapu to women complicated the daily routine still further. Among the articles of food that were set apart for the exclusive use of men and which women were forbidden to eat, were pork, bananas, coconuts, ulua, kumu and some other fish, and some sea-foods. These kapus and customs touched the every-day life of the people to a great extent, and all the time. When Liholiho sat down with the women and ate with them; when, at the same time, the women ate pork and bananas, the whole daily routine of the people was overturned. Restrictions which had governed them for generations were set aside. We speak of the "breaking of the kapus." The fact that the king ate with the women seems to us to be a rathe simple happening. In reality, this was the beginning of the great change which has taken place in Hawaii in the last hundred years or so, and which has involved the overturning of the ancient culture.

References

Malo, David, Hawaiian Antiquities.

Miller, Carey D., Food Values of Taro, Poi, and Limu., B. P. Bishop Museum Bulletin 37.

MacCaughey, Vaughan, and Emerson, Joseph S., The Kalo in Hawaii. Hawaiian Forester and Agriculturist, April, 1914.

Larsen, Nils P., Nutrition as Affected by Race and Climate. Proceedings of the Pacific Regional Conference of the W. F. E. A., Honolulu, 1932.

Jones, Larsen, and Pritchard, Dental Disease in Hawaii. Dental Cosmos, May, June, July and August, 1930.

CHAPTER 9

AKU AND AHI FISHING

THOMAS MAUNUPAU

Fishing was one of the most skilled occupations of the early Hawaiians. It demanded knowledge of the stars, of the winds, of the currents, and of the clouds. The night fisherman needs the stars to guide his course. Wind and current affect the run of the fish, and knowledge of the clouds is helpful in enabling the fisherman to decide whether he should go fishing the next day. These things are just as true today as they were in the days of ancient Hawaii. However, there was in the old days a great deal more to fishing than this understanding of the sky and the waters. A man did not become a fisherman in those days just by going out and fishing; he had to go through many stages in his preparation, before he was accepted as a fisherman. The fisherman was an honored person in those days, and not everyone could become one.

There were a great many religious ceremonies connected with fishing. There was a particular ceremony when a new canoe was christened and when a new net or a new hook was taken out for the first time. Certain customs of a religious origin were observed when the first fish was caught. Kapus were observed when the fisherman prepared his fishing gear, and when he went out to see to the launching of his canoe. Some of these old-time customs still remain as habits of the Hawaiian fisherman today, but most of them have been given up. In the olden days, every heiau or temple had in it a fish god or kuula. Each fisherman had his own kuula. Perhaps it might be a stone or image he had pulled up in the ocean, and which he regarded from then on as his kuula, or it might be the family god or aumakua. The kuula was supposed to bring luck and success in fishing. The fishermen of old Hawaii believed that they needed some supernatural power to aid them in their undertaking, and hence religion and fishing were closely connected by ceremonies and customs.

There were many methods of fishing. They demanded different equipment and different training. There was night fishing, inshore fishing, offshore fishing, and deep sea fishing. We shall consider only aku and ahi fishing, because these were considered by the early Hawaiians as first in importance. If we wish to understand the way fishing was regarded by these old-time Hawaiians, we can get that understanding best by considering aku and ahi fishing of which they thought so highly. Only the man who handled the pole and line and trolling hook used in aku fishing, was called the fisherman or lawaia. The man who steered the canoe was called the kaohi. All the rest were merely paddlers, and were not called fishermen though they went out and fished.

The fisherman had to make careful preparation before going out to fish. Strict kapus governed the making and the lashing of the hooks. When hooks were to be lashed, the fisherman informed the family the day before, so that they could be ready to observe the kapus. While the fisherman was busy lashing the hooks, no one was allowed to make any kind of a noise, or to run in and out, or to peek through the door or window. Everything had to be kept quiet, and no one was allowed to interrupt the fisherman; no one could look at his work, or ask him questions, or talk to him, or visit him. Lashing had to be done at a particular time of day. It had to be done in the afternoon and could never be continued after sunset. If the fisherman did not finish before sunset, he put his work away very carefully and did not touch it again until the next afternoon. When the hooks were all lashed, they were put in an ipu or container and this was placed near the ceiling of the house, and never left lying around carelessly. Before he left for the fishing ground, the fisherman went to a little corner and said a prayer to the aumakua. He asked for luck for the day. When he left the house, he reminded his wife to obey the kapus. A wife was not supposed to gossip, or to sleep, or to quarrel with anyone while her husband was fishing. On the way to the canoe landing, the fisherman was not supposed to stop and talk to anyone, and if he met a blind man he turned back, because this was thought to bring him bad luck. When he arrived at the canoe landing and started out for the fishing ground, no one was allowed to call to him or to anyone else in the boat and tell them to come back. In the canoe, no one was permitted to speak to the fisherman. All eyes were forward; the men paddled and watched in silence until they arrived at the fishing ground.

Much of the success of the fishing depended, of course, upon what the fisherman did after he had arrived at the fishing ground or koa. Probably one of the first things he had to do was to wait for the sunrise, for he started very early before the sun came up. As soon as daybreak came, the fisherman studied the course of the current, because aku swim with the current, not against it. Aku have to be caught at the surface, so the fisherman waited for the noio bird which hunted the small fish which the aku were after. For this reason, aku were found where the noio bird could be seen. The fisherman told the man who steered, "When you see the noio birds, paddle toward them." Sometimes when the canoe had come to the place where the birds were, still the aku could not be seen because they had not yet come to the surface. As soon as they began to come to the surface, the fisherman threw his hook and line and tried for a catch. Very often he might not catch anything right off, and at the beginning of the season, which is January, February, or March, his whole catch would be small. Each hook the fisherman carried was named according to its color—muhee, lehua, etc., and if the fish did not bite, the fisherman thought there was something wrong with the color, and changed the hook. If the aku bit after the hook was changed, the fisherman took the fish, cut it, and looked inside to find out surely just what kind of a hook the aku wanted that day. The hooks these fishermen used sparkled as they were skimmed on the surface of the water; they resembled the belly of the small fish the aku ate, and therefore the aku bit. In the early part of the season the fisherman often wished to offer the first fish to the aumākua. In this case, he took the first fish caught and marked it by cutting off its tail. This fish was then placed in the bow of the canoe and was kapu. As soon as the fisherman returned to shore, he took this fish and went to the little shrine of the aumakua and offered the fish as a sacrifice. This was done to bring him luck and success.

A new fisherman was initiated in a particular way and with certain ceremonies. When the regular fishing had been finished and the canoe was returning home, the pole and line were given to the new fisherman so he could try his luck. As soon as he caught his first fish, he was not allowed to continue. When he got on shore, he took this fish and gave it to the old fisherman or to a kahuna. The man who received the fish cut it into small pieces, wrapped them all in ti leaves, and cooked them. When the fish was cooked all the leading fishermen were invited to come to the celebration. The pieces of cooked fish were spread on the table and the regular fishermen said a prayer to all the aumakuas of the East, of the North, of the West, and of the South; to the aumakuas of the sky and of the deep sea, asking all to get the aku to bite for the new fisherman. When the prayer was finished all the fishermen sat down and ate. This was one occasion when everyone watching around was not asked to sit down and eat. However, though the watchers could not be invited to join the feast, they might sit down and help themselves without any invitation. Every fish bone was kept and placed on the table. The new fisherman gathered them up, wrapped them together and took them to some point where he said a prayer and threw them into the sea. Only after this had been finished was he a full-fledged fisherman. Not everyone was given a chance to become a fisherman; only those men who lived up to certain standards and requirements were allowed to be admitted to the fraternity.

The koa or fishing ground has been mentioned. This was an area in which fish were always found. It was a depression in the bottom of the ocean and was particularly deep. The Hawaiians knew just where to go to find fish. They did not fish just anywhere over the ocean, but only in those places where fish were always found. They found good fishing grounds, located them by certain marks, and never missed the place. The koa is not so important in aku fishing because aku swim with the current, but it is very important in deep sea fishing. However, the fisherman who knows where the koa is can always go there and get his fish. Today a person can watch from shore and see schools of aku going in a certain direction and disappearing at a certain spot. This is a koa. The fish either go to that hole and sleep or they simply remain there. At any rate, they may be found there the next day. The experienced Hawaiian fisherman of the present does not fish outside the koa. The Japanese fisherman today uses iron hooks and kerosene, but the Hawaiian fishermen do not use these because they spoil the fishing grounds.

Ahi fishing is deep sea fishing and also requires great skill. The old time fisherman went out to the fishing ground and dropped his line which was probably 1200 feet long and marked every fifty feet. He used this measured line because he knew the depth of the koa and he did not wish to let his line out to the bottom because then the bait would not spread. The skilled fisherman let his line out 90 fathoms, and then jerked the line. The palu, which was just mashed meat, spread in all directions when the line was jerked and the fish came for it. The man who fished at 90 fathoms got all the fish if the other men in the canoe were fishing on the bottom. As soon as sharks came in, the fisherman left that koa for a time, so that the fish may go to the bottom to escape the sharks. When the fishermen returned the koa was still full of fish, and lasted for ages as a good fishing ground. Present-day fishermen who go out and fish all day and all night spoil a koa in a few months and when a koa has been spoiled, it is spoiled forever.

Every Hawaiian who went out to fish had to know not only all the arts of fishing, but he had to know how to manage his canoe. He must be able to float it if it overturned, for instance. If the canoe was simply swamped, it was easily managed because in rough weather the waves helped the men to float the canoe. But it was harder to right a canoe which overturned. This demanded a great deal of skill and hard work. The sails and mast were taken off and wrapped up. Then the men worked to right the canoe; the task might keep them in the water all day. The Hawaiian was not afraid of sharks, and he is not afraid of them today. If a favorite hook was bitten off by a shark, the fisherman thought nothing of jumping after the hook and trying to get it back.

The ancient Hawaiian did everything he could to preserve the fishing ground. No fishing ground can be preserved unless precautions such as the Hawaiians observed are taken. This is true not only of aku and ahi fishing but of every other kind of fishing. The Hawaiians had a kapu on alongshore fishing in certain places when deep sea fishing was open. The kapu places were marked with coconut leaves. In the case of inshore fishing, one place was kapu for a month; then this area was opened and the next was kapu. At certain times of the year, certain seaweeds were kapu, because when fish food was preserved by this means, the shore fishing was saved for the people. There used to be plenty of fish in Hawaiian waters, but these have to a great extent disappeared because constant fishing has wiped them out. The fish are gone for good unless we have closed and open seasons for different kinds of fishing. The government is trying to place certain restrictions on fishing. If the ancient form of kapu used by the old-time Hawaiians could be revived in these new governmental restrictions, we should again have plenty of fish, provided the restrictions were observed as were the kapus in the old days.

The old Hawaiian fisherman was a skilled and selected person. He had knowledge of, and respect for, the traditions and customs of fishing. He was careful to observe these customs, because through them, fishing was preserved for the coming generations, and his children were trained in the skill they would need as they became fishermen. Fishing in those days was not a matter of getting all the fish and moving on to another fishing ground. The Hawaiian fisherman was much too clever to do this, and he respected the traditions of his people too much to do it. Laws today cannot help to preserve the fish in Hawaiian waters, unless in addition to the laws, we have a feeling of respect for them and observe them because we see that they are beneficial.

CHAPTER 10

AGRICULTURE

JULIET RICE WICHMAN

The Hawaiians were skilled agriculturists. Possessing only the crudest of tools, the oo, which was nothing more or less than a crooked stick, they tilled the soil and raised great and successful crops of taro, sweet potatoes, and yams. They developed systems of irrigating their wet-land taro. They understood how to enrich the soil and how to treat it so that its value was not destroyed They were industrious. They performed, with regularity and dependability, the heavy labor demanded by the crops they raised with the tools at their command. But the Hawaiians were something more than skillful farmers. Their agriculture was tied up with a body of religious beliefs and observances which are, by the unthinking, sometimes labelled as "superstitions." They suggest to the thoughtful that the Hawaiians who lived close to the world of nature may have glimpsed truths to which our eyes are blind. Certainly anything which works is not superstition, and the Hawaiian agricultural practices were most effective. At the present time, survivals of these old beliefs exist, but their deepest significance has been lost even for the people who observe certain practices which have come down from the old days.

The Hawaiians observed the phases of the moon in determining the right time to plant. The peasants of Asia and Europe have similar practices, and scientists in Germany and England and the United States have thought these ways of doing things worth investigating, to find out just how the planting date influences the growth of plants. It seems reasonable to suppose that there must be some scientific principle underlying these beliefs which are so widespread and which have such uniformly successful results. It is interesting to note that the days selected by the Hawaiians as the best for planting are the same days selected by the peasant farmers of Europe and Asia. The Hawaiian year was divided into twelve months. Each day of the month had a separate name, and the month began with Hilo. The night of Hilo was the night of the new moon. Counting from the night of Hilo, the two days named Mohalu and Hua were selected as very favorable for certain types of planting. If you wish to follow Hawaiian planting tradition, plant on Mohalu and Hua, which are the twelfth and thirteenth days, counting Hilo, the day of the new moon, as the first. Certain things were most successfully planted on the first two days of the moon, Hilo and Hoaka. The custom was to plant on the new moon days those things used for their leaves, as luau, and to plant on Mohalu and Hua those things used for their roots, as taro, sweet potatoes, and yams. Practices differed in different districts and on separate islands as to just the favorable time to be chosen.

The successful times for planting sweet potatoes were from about the 20th of December to about the 20th of January and from the 20th of August to the 20th of September. These months belonged to Kane-puaa, the special god of the sweet potato. Special varieties were planted on particular days. In Vol. VI of the Fornander collection, is given a list of favorable days for planting sweet potatoes, together with a description of the kind of growth yielded, as, for instance, "Kulu—this is a good day to plant potatoes; they are long, but full of ridges," or "Hunu—a favorable day. The potato sprigs planted this day would yield fine large potatoes." Bananas were planted at midnight, just when the full moon shone directly into the holes prepared. Undoubtedly many practices of this type are still followed, and perhaps some day a study of them will be made. These traditions deserve respect, for they worked.

Not only was the planting date carefully selected, but the planting itself was always attended with religious ceremony and prayer. Successful gardeners everywhere have a reverence for plant life and for nature. If they lack this, they are not successful. One cannot go through the experiences of planting little brown seeds in the brown dry earth, and of seeing them come out and grow and flourish and bear fruit, without feeling that here is something which is wonderful. The people of ancient Hawaii felt this; they interpreted nature as a godlike force, and they—as did all other early peoples—always invoked the help of the gods of nature before planting. This seemed to them to be natural and right.

There is a legend about one of the farmers, an old planter of Hawaii, called Makua-kaumana. He lived over the Pali on the windward side of Oahu. He had a very famous garden. He always prayed to the gods asking them for help in his garden, but he was not satisfied with his prayers. One day two strangers came to visit his garden. He did not know it, but they were two of the gods of the planting. He told them about his work, and his prayers to the gods, and they taught him this prayer:

"O Kane, O Kanaloa,
Here is the taro, the banana,
Here is the sugar cane, the awa,
See, we are eating it now."

The strangers told the farmer, "You must worship your gods not only by prayer but also by sacrifice. When you offer them food, ask Hina-puku-ai to carry the food to the gods for you." Following the advice given in this legend, the Hawaiians made offering to the gods of the produce of their land, when they asked help for growing things.

In planting traditions, the great god Kane was identified with the sun, and the great god Lono was identified with the rain. The goddess Laka was the goddess of the wild wood and of wild growth. She was respected by the planters and had particular rites. There was a special demigod for sweet potato planting. He was called Kane-puaa, for he was half man and half pig. When the sweet potato was planted, a special prayer was offered to Kane-puaa.

"O Kane-puaa, root toward the mountain;
O Kane-puaa, root toward the sea;
Root to the windward, to the lee;
Root in the middle of our potato field!
O Kane-puaa, root from that corner to this corner,
From the far border to the near!
O Kane-puaa, root from that corner,
That fruit may appear at the end of the stalk,
  along the stalk,
And roots creep between the hills!"

Hina, the moon goddess, had a great deal to do with the planting date and therefore with the growth of plants. Ku was the patron of hardwood trees, from which, among other things, agricultural tools were made. When trees for tools for planting were cut in the forests, and when the tools were shaped, prayers were offered to Ku that the implements might be strong and worth using. The tool-maker first of all selected the day according to the moon, and a day favorable for implement making. He went up into the woods and selected alii, maki, lehua, hala, flower-bearing hau (not seed-bearing), and when he had made his selections, he offered this prayer to Ku:

"Ku of the far-stretched hillside,
Ku of the mountain,
Ku the watcher,
Ku, giver of strong and twisted branches!
Behold the hewing of our implements!
Sharp cut the oo for the fields of sweet potato,
  yams, and dry-land taro, these vegetables for
  dry-land planting!"

The god was told everything for which the tool was to be shaped, so that it might prove successful in the cultivation of these things.

The Hawaiian respected his tools. The oo was thought to have certain powers. An oo that had been used in producing successful crops was considered to possess a certain ability in itself. It was treasured and preserved.

If the oo was particularly successful it was often kept in the family and used in the breaking of the soil of the first crop and in the planting of the first row of the field. It was not commonly used because it was too valuable. The untried tools were used for rough work. They might later become potent and be passed on to bring good fortune with them.

The Hawaiian planters were clever in selecting their land. They always looked for land growing well with wild growth. They said that if the wild growth was plentiful, Laka liked the land and it would be fertile. They always turned the wild growth under or burned it after it was cut down. They never took it away, but left it to enrich the soil. The Hawaiians thought of the wild growth as containing some of the vital essence of the land which must not be wasted.

The most important food crop of the Hawaiians was taro. Dry-land taro was grown on elevated lands. It was most successfully grown on Kauai and Maui. Wet-land taro was grown in fields in valleys, and in river valleys where patches were built up and diked and the water brought in. Sometimes the wet-land planting was done high above the river bank, and one wonders how the water was brought in to irrigate the plants. The people brought the water down in bamboo pipes. They evidently had a remarkable knowledge of water engineering because the fields were well laid out and the water was brought in in such a way that it never took the land out.

The first important step in taro planting and growing was the cutting of the seed tops. These were always bundled together so that, as was said, none of the vital essence might be lost. As a matter of fact, if you have one little plant and put it aside for planting, it will quickly dry out, but if you fasten a bundle of them together, they all keep much better. Planting was attended by ceremonies. In the case of dry-land taro, prayers and offerings were made to Lono, the god of rain, whose help would be needed, but in the case of wet-land taro, the prayers and offerings were made to Kane, the god of the sun.

When the wet-land patches got sour and the crops were poor, the farmer said, "My field is no longer pleasing to Laka; she has destroyed the field." He set about it to restore his patches to Laka's favor. He wore a lei, which was Laka's symbol, and he and his family and perhaps some helpers went out to the wild growth along the river and cut young hau branches. They brought great bundles of these hau branches and threw them on the field. They covered the branches with mud and invoked Laka. The field was left to lie until the hau had rotted in the patch. Then taro was planted again and the crop flourished. The farmer said, "Laka smiled on the field and restored it to favor." As a matter of fact, hau has a peculiar ability to restore sour acid land. Hau leaves, mixed with sour soil, turn it back again to natural soil and make it good. In gardening, one of the best things you can use to make soil fertile is rotted hau leaves. Soil under hau trees is one of the best types of soil you can get. It is splendid for potting plants. Fields on which hau trees have grown are good lands for gardening when the trees are cut down and the roots are removed from the soil. So we see that the Hawaiian farmer knew what he was doing when he got the wild growth, the hau of Laka, and spread it on the sour taro lands.

When the Hawaiian farmer weeded his plants, he did not take the weeds away, for this would, he thought, be removing some of the vital essence of the soil. He banked the weeds around the plant and mulched them. Moisture around the plant was thus conserved.

When the first fruits were ready in the dry-land fields, rites were celebrated and offerings made in honor of Lono and Kane. A pig was cooked with taro, and a certain amount set aside for the gods as a thank offering. The farmer invoked the gods, "The food is cooked—our fresh taro; here is the taro; here is the pig. Come, partake of this our food, O god of farming!" After the new leaves had sprouted and spread out in the wet-land fields, the farmer gathered a bundle of the strongest and best from the field, and prepared and cooked the leaves. A portion of this luau was set aside and the god Kane was thus invoked:

"Kane, great giver of life,
Here is the luau,
The first fruit of our field.
Come thou—eat of it;
Preserve me, thy child, thy cultivator,
All life is from thee, O Kane,
The word is spoken—the prayer is freed!"

A similar offering was made of cooked taro after the field was ripe.

In the old days, the island of Niihau and the district of West Kauai were famous for their yams. When Captain Cook and other early voyagers visited here, they soon discovered that these yams had certain splendid keeping qualities not characteristic of the yams of other islands. They stocked at Niihau and Kauai and recorded observations of Hawaiian agriculture, in their journals. They stated that the fields were splendidly cultivated and that the farmers seemed to know their business. Ellis, in one of his volumes, recorded that the Hawaiian farmer was very intelligent, cultivating his crops with care and industry.

Agriculture in the old days was an integral part of the life of the people. It was tied up, not with earning a living, but with religion, traditions, and customs. Of all industries, agriculture, which has to do with growing things and is to a great extent dependent on the powers of nature, is the one which is most successful when it is infused with a vital belief. In old Hawaii, every step in the process of preparing the land, planting, caring for the growing plants, and harvesting, was marked with appropriate ceremonial which invested the work with significance and dignity. This solemn and sacred aspect of life and work in old Hawaii was lost. Only a few remnants of the ancient belief remain in the form of half-understood practices. Vital belief disappeared and with it went the vitality of the agricultural labors of the Hawaiian people. This was a tremendous loss, never to be replaced with anything of equal value to all the people. However, anyone with a real interest in growing things may build in his own life an integration of philosophy, garden lore, skills, customs, and traditions, which will be absorbing and vital to him. The person who does this, will regard with respect and interest the customs of the great agriculturalists of any nation and any time, and will perceive their significance. Moreover, his own gardening work will become transformed and it will, in turn, transform his life.

The disappearance of small farming in Hawaii has brought about our dependence on other countries for nearly all our food. Dr. Adams of the University thinks that Hawaii is the most dependent community of its size in all the world. In the old days it was entirely self-dependent and self-supporting. Of course, I am not saying that the reason for our dependence today is the fact that Hawaiian planting traditions have largely disappeared. It is plain that conditions of living have been revolutionized here in the islands, and that our dependence has grown out of all the changes of the last century. However, following peasant agricultural customs has proved valuable in Germany and in England, and it seems that those of us who live in Hawaii might well learn and follow some of the Hawaiian agricultural tradition. It is probably based on an understanding we do not possess, and which was successful in enabling the Hawaiian people to raise great food crops. And a study of that tradition opens up a new world of interests. Gardening and farming in Hawaii offer opportunity not only for these new interests, but for work in the open in a consistently beautiful setting. In all the islands, there is scarcely a spot whose natural beauty is not marked. The gardener with any imagination and powers of observation—and a good gardener must have both—

cannot fail to derive pleasure and satisfaction from his surroundings. The possibilities of gardening in Hawaii are endless and fascinating.

REFERENCES

Wichman, Juliet Rice, Hawaiian Planting Traditions. The Star-Bulletin, 1931.

CHAPTER 11

WOODEN UTENSILS AND IMPLEMENTS

KENNETH P. EMORY

In all Polynesia, there were no metals and no workable clays. Consequently, the Polynesian people were much more dependent on wood than we are today. Indeed, today we tend to use wood less and less. Cement is frequently used for exterior construction. Celotex and Canec and similar materials have been perfected and take the place of wood in many interiors. Chromium and glass are finding an increasing number of uses in house building and furnishings It is not at all difficult for us to imagine getting along without wood. But in ancient Hawaii, where all these modern materials were of course quite unknown, and even metals and clay were lacking, the people turned to wood for nearly everything they used—their household utensils, their weapons, their canoes.

The Hawaiians became expert in selecting and working wood to meet their needs. They knew the hardness, the color, the grain, the smell, the durability, of the woods of each of the trees that grew about them. They chose the light wiliwili for the ama of their canoes. Hau was selected for the iako. Koa and breadfruit were used for the hull of the canoe. Certain other woods were found best for the strips along the sides and for the end pieces of the canoe. The milo was especially sought after for small bowls, because of the beautiful effect produced by the contrasting heart and sap wood. Koa was never used by the Hawaiians for bowls in which food was to be placed, for it imparted an unpleasant taste to food. Only in recent years, when poi bowls have been manufactured to be sold as curios and ornaments, has koa been used for bowls. Certain temple images were made of ohia lehua, and the houses on the heiau dedicated to Lono were constructed with lama posts.

SELECTING AND CUTTING A TREE

The Hawaiians were not only very particular in the choice

of wood for certain purposes, and scrupulous to follow the established practice in making their bowls, images, canoes, and other things, but they observed ceremonial custom in cutting the tree and bringing the wood down from the mountains. When a tree was chosen for a great heiau image or for an important canoe, the service of an expert was called upon. It was a great task to fell a large tree with stone adzes, and if the tree should after all prove unsuitable or defective, all this work would have gone for nothing. If the tree was destined to be carved into a temple image, it was all-important that the proper rituals and sacrifices be carried out and that no kapu be broken. When the kahuna was choosing the tree, he watched the elepaio bird. If it visited a tree, it was an indication that decay had set in somewhere, and another selection was made. On the day that the tree was to be cut, the kahuna, clad in a white malo, took his men with their consecrated adzes and reverently went about the task. When the tree had been reduced to a log suitable for hauling, ropes were tied around a knob at one end, and it was skidded and hauled down to the coast. There, under a comfortable shed, it received its final shaping. Fire was not used anywhere in the felling or shaping.

SHAPING AND POLISHING

Two principal kinds of adzes and a chisel were the tools used in shaping wood. One of these adzes was like a pick, in that it had a relatively narrow cutting edge and a thick body. The other adze was thin and broad. The pick-like adze was used for making deep gouges, while the ridges between were adzed down by the broader blade. The chisels were used for carving. Shark teeth hafted in wood were also used for carving. Curiously enough, the Polynesians did not develop the ax. When the ax was introduced by Europeans, the Polynesians took to it very easily, but up to a hundred years ago, they were distinctly an adze-using people. All adzes in Hawaii were made of hard close-grained basalt which was found everywhere in the islands. They were shaped by flaking with a hammer stone, and grinding on a stone slab with sand and water.

Great skill and patience were necessary for this work of making adzes. The stone adze is inferior to the steel adze or to the ax, in the speed with which it will cut and in its fragility, but it has some advantages over the steel adze. It gives the workman better control over the finishing processes, for a false stroke cannot do as serious damage and the chips are smaller. Another advantage is that the blade of course cannot rust and wounds caused by a stone adze, in the case of accidental injury, are less serious.

After the adzing had been completed, then came the rubbing with rough lava and coral, then with finer coral, then with shark skin or the skin of the sting-ray. Final polishing was done with sand or earth on a pad of kapa, or even with leaves. Last of all, the article was rubbed with kukui-nut oil.

WOODEN IMPLEMENTS

Hawaiian spears were not carved, beyond a few dull barbs and a grip on the butt end of the long pololu spears. In the Museum may be seen spears from the Cook Islands and others of the South Sea groups, which show very beautiful workmanship. Spears from the Cook Islands are made of ironwood. Their jet black color is produced by immersing them in a swamp during the seasoning of the wood after the spear is shaped. Hawaiian clubs were not carved as were the magnificent clubs of Tonga. The ancient Hawaiian paddle had a tiny knob or ridge on one side of the end of the blade, a survival of the knob on the tip of the paddles in southeastern Polynesia, used to protect the tip of the blade when pushing off or poling in shallow water. These paddles may be examined in the Museum, as well as all other objects of wood made by the Hawaiians, such as boards on which olona fibers were scraped, kapa anvils, kapa beaters, and a great variety of bowls and dishes.

UMEKE OR BOWLS

Nowhere else in Polynesia were there bowls equal in quality or in variety to the Hawaiian umeke. Nothing but shallow bowls were used in all the rest of Polynesia, and in Samoa and Tonga there were few bowls except the kawa bowl. Dr. Buck wondered why this was, and suddenly realized the reason. The western Polynesians had little use for food bowls for they ate their food in a more or less solid state and served it on platters of coconut leaves. In eastern Polynesia, vegetable foods were mashed and made into hard pudding-like substances. But the Hawaiians went a step farther and mixed water with the pounded food. The semi-liquid paste which resulted could not well be served on a coconut leaf platter; bowls were necessary containers and were therefore developed. Bowls were made out of wood which was first soaked, often for months, in some pool. The outside was then adzed down to final shape as nearly as was possible by this process. Next, the inside was excavated first to a depth of perhaps one or two inches. Then the diameter of the cavity was made an inch or two less, and the excavation carried deeper. This was continued to the bottom. Then the ledges were cut out and the inside was perfectly smoothed so that food would not stick to the sides. The woods commonly used for bowls were kou, kamani, and milo. Other woods, such as the heart wood of the coconut, were occasionally used. The most typical Hawaiian bowl is the umeke poi. It is perfectly round in cross-section and is tall and thin-lipped. The bottom, however, is heavy. This heavy bottom is what keeps it from upsetting. The bottom of the ancient bowl was rarely perfectly flat; it did not need to be because the bowl rested on soft mats, or a pad, or the sand. A few of the bowls of the chiefs were propped on little grotesque figures wonderfully carved, but the vast majority of the bowls were ornamented in no way whatever. They rank with vases as objects of art because of the beauty of their lines. The upper part of the ordinary bowls has a graceful recurve. Certain bowls, called umeke opaka, were finished off with a number of flat faces meeting at angles. Certain others were peculiar for their constriction in the middle and the two or three graceful points rising on the rim. These are very rare and old. Most of the bowls that have survived in collections have been varnished and all recently made bowls are usually varnished. The old dull finish is coming in again and collectors are sand-papering off this modern finish.

The Hawaiians made some tremendously large bowls. One of these in the Museum measures more than seven feet in diameter and twenty inches in height. Bowls that split or cracked were carefully mended and a mended bowl was not considered in any way inferior to a perfect bowl. The mending patches implied age and age implied that the bowl was a family heirloom. Good patching was an exhibition of good craftsmanship which was appreciated.

The Hawaiians had one low bowl with a thick rim. These can be distinguished from the typical Marquesan bowl, with which they are often confused, only by the fact that the upper edge is slightly recurved. The Hawaiians probably brought this low bowl with them when they came to these islands, for it is the only Hawaiian bowl closely resembling the bowls used elsewhere in Polynesia. Most of the Hawaiian bowls were probably developed locally.

Poi bowls were covered when not in use. The cover was usually any available wooden plate of suitable size. The finer bowls of the chiefs were fitted with a special cover which might be used as a plate. The common plate was round or oval, quite thick, and slightly dished. There were platters of all kinds, for fish, fowl, dog, and pig. Some of the platters were rounded or squared at one end only. Some platters are so deep that they cannot really be distinguished from bowls. None of the true Hawaiian bowls or platters had legs, but some of the ancient platters were propped on two runners, something like sleigh runners. In Hawaiian collections you will occasionally see oval pointed bowls with four legs. These are not Hawaiian, but are recent importations from Tahiti. With the development of the poi bowl to care for the poi, came the creation of finger bowls, ipu holoi lima. These are small vessels of varied forms. Most of them have projecting into the bowl, a ridge or spur on which the fingers could be scraped.

The high kapus surrounding the Hawaiian chiefs called

into existence another class of wooden bowls, namely the ipu aina or slop basins, and the ipu kuha, or spittoons. It was of extreme importance to the chief that no enemy secure anything which came from his body. The ipu aina were often studded with the teeth of enemies, as a sign of contempt. The ipu kuha were open bowls with a handle on the outside. As these were carried about with the chief, they were made to be admired. Therefore, among these ipu kuha are the finest examples of Polynesian woodwork.

Coconuts served as natural containers for water. Coconut shells served as cups. Varieties of the gourd were cultivated to supply water bottles, and to serve as containers for clothing and other light material in traveling. The gourds were sometimes ornamented with geometric patterns by a staining process. The Hawaiians alone, among the Polynesians, did this.

CHAPTER 12

FIBERWORK

E. H. BRYAN, JR.

If you were suddenly to find yourself alone on an uninhabited island, how would you attempt to provide yourself with baskets, mats, nets, rope, fishline, and other much needed articles made of fiber? Pioneers arriving in every new land have had to solve this same problem, for the few articles which they could bring with them would soon wear out. The Hawaiians who left their former home in the South Pacific, and settled these islands, were such pioneers. During the centuries their fiberwork became one of their principal fine arts.

Their first problem was to seek out the various raw materials which they could use in this work. They needed strong, pliable vines and rootlets; they had to have straight, smooth, tough leaves; they had to look for plants whose bark contained long, strong fibers.

FIBER PLANTS OF HAWAII

In their former home they had made mats and baskets of coconut leaves, and cord from the fibrous husk of the coconut. It is not unlikely that the early immigrant Hawaiians brought the coconut to these islands and planted it here. Another plant which they probably introduced was the paper mulberry or wauke, which they used in making kapa, sandals, and cord. The bark of the breadfruit, cuttings of which they doubtless brought for a future food supply, also yielded a coarse fiber material.

Certain other plants, with which these early immigrants were familiar in their former island home, were probably found already growing in Hawaii upon their arrival. These included the pandanus or hala, the hau, varieties of banana, ti, and various kinds of grass, sedge, and fern. Other plants were new to them, but similar to kinds they had known before; and of these they readily made use. These included the ieie vine, whose aerial roots were strong and pliable; the mamake (Pipturus), whose bark was filled with coarse but strong fibers, the loulu palm (Pritchardia), whose fan leaves were an excellent substitute for the coconut; and the olona, the inner bark of which furnished the finest fiber of them all.

THE NEEDS OF THE PEOPLE

The needs of these early Hawaiians were simple. The warm, equitable climate demanded little in the way of clothing. Their chief concerns were the gathering and preparation of food, warfare, adornment, amusement, and the propitiation of their gods. In each of these activities fiberwork played a part. They needed baskets and slings for carrying food; nets, lines, and snares for fishing; mats and thatch for the home; sails, lashings, and rope for canoes; kapa, sandals, and other articles of clothing; fans, cords for leis, and later the network backgrounds for their gorgeous featherwork; slings and lashing cords for weapons; and various materials used in their worship.

The loom was unknown in Hawaii. They did not weave cloth. Instead they beat kapa from the bark of the paper mulberry, or occasionally from the bark of the mamake, breadfruit, or other relatives of the nettles. It is curious that this usually repulsive group of plants should have so many species useful to man. The olona also belongs to the nettle family.

KAPA MAKING

The process of making kapa was briefly as follows. Straight stalks of wauke or paper mulberry were cut about six feet high, and their tops lopped off. This left a piece about four feet long and the size of a man's finger or thumb in diameter. When a straight cut was made down one side of the rod, the bark could be peeled off. After it was soaked in a stream for several days, the pulp became sufficiently soft so that it could be scraped from the tough fibers. The scraping was done on a smooth board with a shell. The thin strips of fiber were then spread out flat in two or three layers, so that they might dry and adhere somewhat together. They were then laid over an "anvil" and beaten out flat and thin by women with wooden mallets. The process was called "kuku." First the round "hohoa" beater was used to felt the fibers together, the strip being folded and doubled so that all the fibers would not run in the same direction. Other strips were added and beaten in at the edges, until a sheet of the desired width and thickness was obtained. The final beating was done with a square beater, on the flat faces of which were carved lines or geometric designs. These gave a pattern of distinctive impressions of "watermarks" to the finished prduct. The sheet was ornamented with designs or decorations which were painted or stamped on with native vegetable or mineral dyes. The stampers were made of pieces of bamboo, on which the designs were carved; the paint brush, from a piece of pandanus fruitlet.

LAUHALA

Much of the plaited work, such as baskets, mats, pillows, and fans, was made from lauhala, the leaf of the pandanus. Mat sails, sandals, balls, and various other objects were also made of this durable material. The pandanus leaf was first trimmed along the edges and midrib to remove the spines, and then dried quickly, either in the sun or by passing it through a fire. Then each individual leaf was flattened out by winding it around the hand, and several leaves were coiled into a roll for further drying and for storage until needed. Pillows were made with a square plait; mats, baskets, and sails, usually with a diagonal plait. Great variety was obtained by different widths of material and forms of weave. The regular checkerboard plait was varied by different combinations of twill. (More details regarding technique will be found in B. P. Bishop Museum Memoirs, vol. II, no. 1, 1906, and for Samoan fiberwork, in Bulletin 75 of B.P. Bishop Museum.)

Lauhala was more important in Hawaii than the leaf of the coconut, so widely used in other regions of the Pacific.

But coconut and even native loulu palm leaves were used to some extent in Hawaii.

MAKALOA MATS

The finest of the Hawaiian mats were made from the leaves of a sedge, called "ahuawa" (Cyperus laevigatus), found growing in and around brackish swamps, especially on the little island of Niihau. The sedge was best for use when it was young, so that the time of weaving was limited to a few weeks out of the year. Thus it might require several seasons to make a large mat. When dried over a fire the leaves were whiter and made a more attractive product. The mats were made with a plait or twill, the material being so fine that there might be a dozen to twenty strands to the inch. The largest "makaloa mat" in B. P. Bishop Museum, presented in 1923 by the late Princess Elizabeth Kalanianaole Woods, measures 19 x 26½ feet.

A favorite material for making baskets, fish traps, and framework for feather images and helmets, was the aerial root of the ieie vine, a close relative of the hala. This common forest liana is called by scientists Freycinetia, after the famous French explorer. The tough, pliable rootlets were coiled or twined into both open and close weave containers. Such a weave was sometimes used as a covering for a calabash or gourd for containing clothing and other articles for storage or on a voyage. This was called a "hinai."

OLONA FIBER

Chief among the cordage fibers in Hawaii was the bast of the olona, a plant of the nettle family, scientifically known as Touchardia latifolia. An interesting article on this plant by Vaughan MacCaughey (Science, vol. 48, pages 236-238, September 6, 1918) enthusiastically describes it as "Hawaii's unexcelled fiber plant." Now rather rare, this species of plant was formerly fairly abundant in the lower and middle forest zones of our mountains, principally in deep, cool, gloomy ravines. Here it received a kind of "cultivation" by the natives, good patches being searched out and cleared of weeds and obstructions.

Long, straight shoots were cut when they had reached a diameter of about an inch. The bark was carefully stripped from pieces about six feet long, rolled into coils and carried into the lowlands. Here it was unrolled and placed in running water for some time, until the pulp was partly macerated. It was then scraped on a long, narrow board with a scraper of pearl shell or turtle shell, until all the pulp had been removed from the long fibers. These were bleached in the sun until ready to be rolled or braided into cord of various size and kind.

It was extensively used for making fish line, fish nets, koko or slings for carrying calabashes, and the network to which feathers were tied in making the famous Hawaiian feather capes and cloaks. The fiber is so strong that it could be used for several generations without apparent deterioration. Several nets and capes of olona fiber, now in B. P. Bishop Museum, which have had over a hundred years of use, are still in a good state of preservation.

OTHER FIBERS

Coconut fiber was twisted or braided into sennit, and coarser rope was made from the bark of the hau and mamake tree and from the fibrous stalk of the banana. Some fish traps, baskets, and modern hats were made of fern fiber; hats of sugar cane tassel-stalk; sandals and rude "rain coats" of ti; and house thatch of pili grass. Various grasses and sedges were used for rough, temporary mats.

Thus, it will be seen that the Hawaiians made good use of the raw materials with which nature provided them, and made a great variety of objects both useful and ornamental.

CHAPTER 13

FEATHERWORK AND CLOTHING

LAHILAHI WEBB

Nearly everyone who knows anything about Hawaii has heard of the famous feather cloaks of the old days. They were so unusual, so beautifully made, so spectacular, that they always attracted attention and interest. Other countries have used the feathers of different birds for decorative purposes, but nowhere was the featherwork more beautifully and skillfully done than it was by the feather craftsmen of old Hawaii.

The ahuula or feather cloak was endowed with great significance and could be worn only by chiefs of high rank, and by them only on special occasions. Ahuulas were of all sizes. They ranged from short capes to long cloaks reaching nearly to the ground. These cloaks had simple but striking designs worked out in different colored feathers, or perhaps no design at all. The most famous cloak of all is the great cape of Kamehameha I, which is made entirely of mamo feathers and is undecorated. This cloak was last worn when King Kalakaua was crowned, February 12, 1883. It is now in the Bernice P. Bishop Museum.

The foundation of the feather cloak was a closely woven net of olona fiber. Fibers of olona were also used to fasten the feathers to the net. The feathers in one row covered the bases of the feathers in the next row, and were arranged much as shingles on a roof today. They were very securely fastened. Skilled men did this work. The feathers were light in weight, but the olona netting was so closely knit that a large cloak might weigh as much as six pounds. However, all Hawaiian chiefs were powerful men, easily able to wear these great cloaks into battle where the cloaks of the chiefs were one standard around which the warriors rallied.

Helmets and images were made of featherwork. In these cases, the foundation was made from ieie, a vine which grew in the forests. To this foundation the feathers were attached by means of olona fiber. Helmets were worn with the ahuulas on the battlefield and on other special occasions. Kaili, or Kukailimoku, known as Kamehameha's war god, is the most famous feather image in the Museum.

Kahilis were made with feathers, but the featherwork involved was quite different from that used in the fashioning of cloaks, images, and helmets. The large kahilis were a sacred emblem of Hawaiian royalty. They were standards and insignia of the highest rank, used only on state occasions. Kahilis were dismantled after they were used, and the feathers were put away by the caretakers, or kahu hulu. All of the large old kahilis were named after some ancestor or favored person. Small kahilis, while a sign of royalty, were used not only on solemn occasions, but were also used over royalty while they were eating, or sleeping, or conversing with their friends.

The choicest kahilis were made from o-o feathers and were black and yellow. All kinds of feathers were used in kahilis, however. The handles were made from the bones of defeated chiefs, or from kauila or some other hard wood. Men did the binding of the feathers on the poles of the large kahilis, for they were too large to be handled by the women. Women assisted in the making of the small kahilis.

Lei hulus or feather leis were made from early days up to the present as a decoration for women. In olden times, only women wore the feather leis. The lei was worn on the head or on the neck. Sometimes one lei was worn, sometimes two—one long and one short. Leis were made all one color, or of different colors. All kinds of feathers were used. The choicest leis were made of the mamo, o-o, iiwi, and o-u feathers. The feathers were bunched, then sorted, and the longer feathers placed in the center of the lei, while the shorter ones were used at the ends.

Both men and women made the feather leis.

There are two very unusual articles of featherwork in the Museum. One of these is King Liloa's kaei kapu, a cordon made of o-o and iiwi feathers on both sides. It has been thought to be a malo, but it is not a malo. It is the only article of its kind in existence and very probably it was sacredly used in religious ceremonial. The other unusual article is the only garment of featherwork ever worn by a woman, and it was worn only after the kapus had been broken. It is a pa'u of yellow o-o feathers with small triangles of black o-o and red iiwi feathers at the ends. It was made for Princess Nahienaena who wore it only once, when Lord Byron was here in 1825. At her death, it was cut in half and put together to be used as a pall in her funeral. It was used as a pall for succeeding monarchs. It was last used in 1891 when King Kalakaua died.

The featherwork required much time and patience. Not only must the feathers be sorted, tied, and attached to the foundation network, but they must be collected in the first place. There were in the islands few birds of brilliant plumage, and these lived in the depths of the forests. The feather hunters or Poe Kawili knew the haunts of the birds they sought. They were familiar with the habits, songs, and food of the different birds. They knew the season for gathering the feathers when they were at their best. Feathers were gathered in the moulting season just before the birds dropped their feathers, so that few feathers were shed by the birds in the forest and lost. The moulting season was the time when the forest trees were in full bloom and the wild berries were bearing. The birds came out of the deep forests to feed. The feather hunters had their own method of trapping the birds. They broke a branch of the flowering trees and put bird lime or gum on the broken branch. Sometimes they used a net. After setting their traps, they concealed themselves, and awaited the birds. The birds were rarely killed when the feathers were collected. If the feather gatherers needed more feathers from the bird than it could stand, then the bird was killed and eaten. The plucked feathers were tied in small parcels bound together with strong fiber. After the hunters returned home, the women sorted and rebunched the feathers and padded the main feathers with a few iiwi feathers called pa'u.

Among the birds whose feathers were most highly prized was the beautiful mamo. Its body was brownish black, its tail feathers a rich golden or orange yellow. The feathers on top and under the tail were known as koo mamo. There were short feathers on the lower part of the thighs, called ae mamo. The mamo was found only on the island of Hawaii. Its feathers were used for cloaks, leis and helmets.

The o-o had a body of brilliant black, and under each wing a tuft of beautiful yellow feathers called e-e. The feathers over the rump were called pu-e, and the tail feathers were called pu-apu-a. The o-o was fairly common on several islands in the old days. Its feathers were used for all articles of featherwork. Under the tail of the o-o were two black and white feathers called pilali o-o, used for very choice kahilis. One of these kahilis is in the Bishop Museum.

The iiwi is bright red in color. In olden times the iiwi was the most abundant bird found on all the islands. Its feathers were used in great abundance in all the featherwork and decorations of the Hawaiians. It was often used under other feathers, as well as on the outer surface of the articles. It is said that the iiwi may be found today in the National Park area around Kilauea, and it is thought that these birds are increasing in numbers.

The o-u was of a dull green color. For some reason, their green feathers were little used. The apapane was dark red or crimson. Its feathers were rarely used but at times they are found in cloaks, helmets, leis, and kahilis. These—the mamo, the o-o, the iiwi, the o-u, and the apapane, were the birds of the upland regions sought by the feather hunters of old Hawaii.

Feather hat bands and leis are popular in the islands

today, and are worn by both men and women. People who know nothing about the gathering of feathers, slaughter birds for their feathers, and destroy the beautiful birds which are being imported into Hawaii. As has been pointed out, ruthless destruction of this kind never happened in old Hawaii, and it is not at all necessary today, provided people are willing to spend time in perfecting the art of collecting feathers, as they did in the old days.

All featherwork may be considered as decoration, rather than clothing. Even the great ahuulas, though they might cover almost the entire person, were not clothing, but were instead, decorations, signs of rank, and insignia of the chiefs. The clothing worn by the old-time Hawaiians was made of kapa. The men wore a kapa malo or loin cloth. It was one foot wide and three or four yards long. It might be dyed red or yellow. The pa'us or skirts worn by the women were dyed and printed in many different designs and colors. They were prettier and had more elaborate designs than the malos. A pa'u was thirty inches wide and three or four yards long. It was worn about the waist and the end was tucked in to secure it. Hula dancers, both men and women, wore the pa'u. The grass skirt, so-called, was never known in old Hawaii. When the weather was a little cool, both men and women wore a sort of kapa shawl, called kihei, over the shoulders. All articles of clothing were straight strips of material. Complete covering of the body by fitted, sewed garments was not necessary in this climate, so anything resembling a needle was not developed by the people. The style of the clothing was such that the direct rays of the sun reached the people and contributed to their health. Today, we go to great lengths to secure the "sun baths" which were a natural part of the every day life in old Hawaii.

Kapa designs were intricate and interesting. While most women could make kapa, the really skilled work of decorating it was done by those of high rank. Most kapa was not dipped into the dye. Instead, pieces already

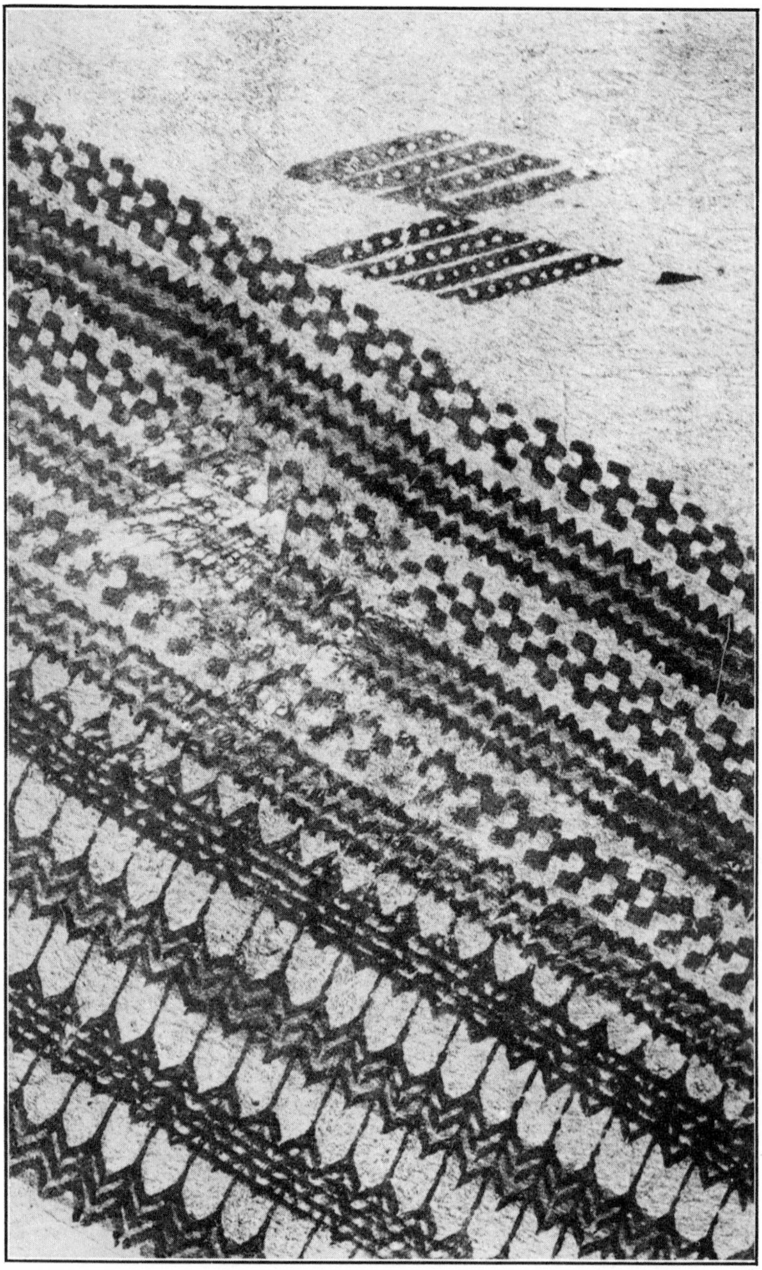

Kapa Designs

stained were pressed into it, or it might be marked or printed with the color. Fine and delicate tools of wood and bamboo were used in this work. Dyes were made from the native plants.

Brown and black were obtained from charcoal made from roasted kukui nut. The charcoal was mixed with water or kukui nut oil.

Orange was obtained from the turmeric root.

Yellow was obtained from the wood and root of the noni, from the fruit pulp of the nanu, and from the bark and root of the hoolei tree.

Red was obtained from the roots of the noni. They were pounded, mixed with fresh water, and strained. The article was first dipped in this solution, and then in sea water, whose salt brought out the red. Red was also obtained from the bark of the kolea tree and from the fruit of the ohia ai.

Blue was obtained from the berries of the uki.

Kapas of different colors and qualities had different names. Some of these were:

Ouiholowai—black and dark brown, scented.
Paipaikukui—dark yellow.
Akoa—reddish brown.
Aeokahaloa—grayish.
Holei—light yellow.
Mahuna—dark brown and black.
Kalukalu—very thin, transparent, creamish in color.
Uauahi—gray.
Paiula—pink.
Puakai—red malo.
Ninikea—pure white.
Halakea—whitish.
Ma'o—greenish, scented.
Pulou—black.
Pukohukohu—creamish, used for pa'u.

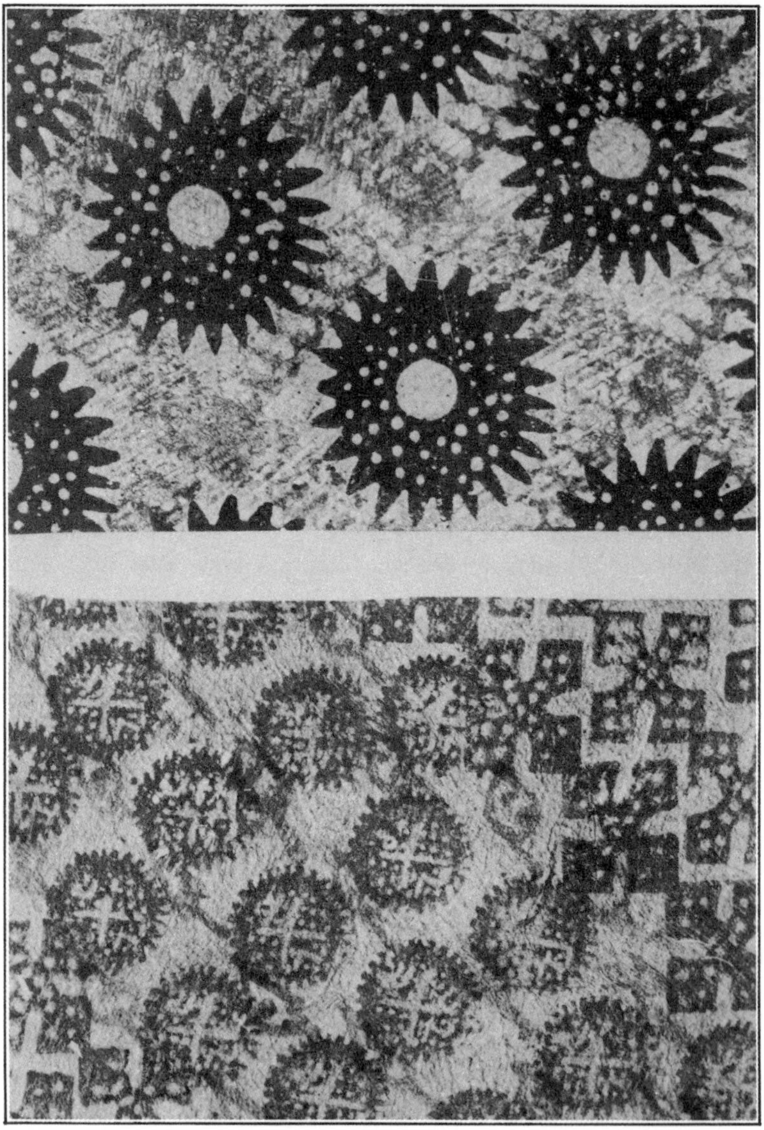

Kapa Designs

The priests at ceremonial times generally wore white kapa. Kapu sticks were covered with white, gray, or pink kapa, according to the occasion. Oloa fiber was prepared and reserved for ceremonial occasions, and for covering the temple tower in the heiau, as in the heiau model at the Museum. This kapa was pure white, undyed, and undecorated.

Bed coverings were made of kapa. They consisted of five separate sheets fastened together at one end with olona fiber or with strips of kapa rolled like string and knotted at each end. There might be four white sheets, and one colored or dyed or painted as the maker preferred. These blankets were from two and a half to three yards long.

Soiled blankets and clothing were washed. Since kapa is not cloth, but paper, the fabric could not be rubbed or scrubbed, but it could be carefully cleaned. The one soiled sheet was removed from the blanket; it was folded, and placed to soak in a stream. It was removed, and spread out in a prepared place to bleach in the sun. If it was not perfectly clean, the process was repeated. Soiled articles of clothing were washed in the same way.

Kapa coverings were light, but warm. Kapa clothing was suited to the climate of Hawaii. It is interesting to note how the Hawaiians used even the inner barks of trees, to secure for themselves what was necessary for their comfort. And, having secured the material, they then developed the crafts of dyeing and decorating it, until we find that the Hawaiians produced the finest and most beautiful kapas of all Polynesia.

CHAPTER 14

SPORTS, GAMES, AND AMUSEMENTS

KENNETH P. EMORY

When the Polynesians were living their own life, there was probably not a people anywhere devoting such a large share of its time to athletic sports, to games, and to amusements. These not only served to keep them physically in fine trim and mentally alert, but they afforded a welcome relief from a life which, contrary to popular conception, was for most of them toilsome. What was of even more importance, they served as a wholesome release from the oppressive weight of the kapus. Without these diversions the Hawaiians could not have been the cheerful sane people Captain Cook discovered. A complete list of Polynesian diversions would be a very long one and in it you could find the equivalent of practically every European sport, game, and amusement. For example, the Hawaiians had the following, or their equivalents—boxing, bowling, coasting, stilt-walking, kite flying, top spinning. In addition, the Hawaiians had many games and sports unknown to the European.

In spite of the fact that so many of the Hawaiian pastimes were in every way equal to those brought in by the European, and often better suited to the island environment and Hawaiian temperament, they have with the single exception of surf-riding been almost entirely replaced by their European equivalents or have been dropped. In the great shock to Hawaiian culture occasioned by the first contact with the Europeans, most of the Hawaiian athletic sports and games immediately went almost or completely out of existence. This was due to two main factors. The first was the absorption of the Hawaiians in their adaptations to the new life. They were busy learning to read and write. They were earning money to buy clothes and other foreign articles and to pay the greatly increased taxes of the chiefs. The second was the fact that because their pastimes were bound up with their ancient mode of life, religious belief and practices, all these ancient pastimes were discouraged by the missionaries. A stigma or feeling of inferiority and disgrace was attached to everything connected with their former life.

In their sports and games the Hawaiians differed from all other branches of the Polynesians in their passion for betting. While this added to the intensity of the excitement it led to the falling of many of their sports and games into the hands of professionals and caused much individual suffering on the part of the betters. In the intensity of the moment a man would sometimes rashly bet all his most precious possessions and lose all, then in desperation he might bet his bones, and so lose his life or his personal liberty. One of the officers with Captain Cook describes a typical sight, after a foot race.

> "I saw a man in a most violent rage, tearing his hair and beating his breast, after losing three hatchets at one of these races. These hatchets he had just before purchased from us with half his possessions."

In justice to the Hawaiians, let it be said that this betting probably became more common and exerted its worst influence in the first years of European contact, and that gambling may not have originated with them but may have been introduced by castaways from lands to the west of Hawaii, where gambling is commonplace.

In Hawaii, games, sports, and dances were indulged in throughout the year, and the occasions for them were many and various, but four months of the year were set aside especially for them. Even during this period there were some days when sports could not be engaged in, and throughout the other eight months there were many kapu days.

The Makahiki was the great festival period. It stretched over four lunar months, from October to and including January. It was a time when men, women, and chiefs were by law compelled to leave their ordinary work and religious observances. It might be called a national holiday, though a carefully regulated one. Boxing matches, sliding on sleds, the hula, all had their appointed times. The taxes for the government were levied and collected during this period, as were also the offerings to the god Lono who presided over their sports and games.

The Makahiki festival is described in another chapter. We need here only to note that the great boxing and wrestling tournaments, and other competitions of the year, were held during the several days immediately after the image of the god Lono had passed through a district and the offerings to him had been presented with due ceremonies. This was some time in the month of November.

The crowds that gathered at great public tournaments often numbered into the thousands. Their orderly conduct, the splendid display made of colored garments, feather cloaks and feather headdresses, neck, wrist, and ankle ornaments, and the decorations of greenery and fragrant flowers, the remarkable show of hospitality and spirit of gaiety prevailing afforded a spectacle that struck the early visitors to these shores with wonder and admiration.

The missionary Reverend William Ellis, in speaking of such a gathering at a wrestling match in Tahiti (vol. 1, p. 207), says:

> "It is not easy to imagine the scenes . . . presented at one of their . . . great wrestling matches, when not less than four or five thousand persons dressed in their best apparel and exhibiting every variety of costume and brilliancy of color, were under the influence of excitement. One party was drumming, dancing, and singing, in the pride of victory, and the menace of defiance; while . . . the other party was equally vociferous in reciting the achievements of the vanquished, or predicting the shortness of his rival's triumph.

> "However great the clamour might be, as soon as the wrestlers who remained in the ring engaged again, the drums ceased, the song was discontinued, and the dancers sat down. All was perfectly silent, and the interest of the second struggle was awaited with as great intensity as the first."

No important contest was engaged in without first consulting auguries, and without approaching the gods with prayers and offerings to win their favor. Over every sport some god presided. When a man felt he was in harmonious relations with the mysterious forces about him, he was quite likely to accomplish superhuman feats of strength and skill. He would have true mana.

Brief descriptions of the most characteristic sports, games, and amusements, follow.

SURF RIDING

Surfing was the most popular and delightful of Hawaiian pastimes. Crowds of men, women, and young people, both of the chiefly and common classes, might be seen surfing almost any day of good surf at the favored localities. The Hawaiians far excelled all other branches of the Polynesian race in this art. In the other islands, a short, pointed breast board, not more than two or three feet long, was all that was ever used, whereas the Hawaiians possessed magnificent boards, and canoes especially designed for surf riding.

The art nearly went out of existence between 1860 and 1900. One person writes in 1853 (Haole, p. 299):

> "Lahaina is the only place where surf riding is maintained with any degree of enthusiasm and even there it is rapidly passing out of existence."

About 1910, surf riding on boards was revived in Hawaii and now has not only come to stay as the sole survivor of true ancient Hawaiian sports, but is being introduced to other lands and has given rise to the world-wide sport of aquaplaning.

During the half century when the beautiful sport of surf riding nearly died, the surf boards which only the chiefs were allowed to ride went out of use. It is noteworthy that in the attempt since 1910 to perfect the surf boards then in use, employing all the modern science of speed designing, a long board has been re-invented that approaches closely the ancient model.

Surf boards (papa hee nalu) were of two sorts. The ordinary boards were called a-la-ia and were generally five to seven feet long, quite thin, and almost flat on both sides. The wood was koa or breadfruit. The long boards, called oro, were used by chiefs only. They were about sixteen feet long, very convex on both sides, and consequently very thick down the middle. The wood was wiliwili. Surf boards were often stained a glossy black. After use, those who cared for their boards dried them thoroughly, then oiled them, wrapped them in cloth, and suspended them in the house.

Upon choosing a tree from which to hew the board for a champion, an offering of a red kumu fish was made. After the board had been finally shaped in the halau, or canoe shed, it was dedicated with special prayer before being put to use.

The wave sought in surfing by board or canoe was one that welled up high and smooth, and did not break quickly or all at once. That sort of a wave was called an ohu, or opuu, whereas the long wave breaking all at once was called Kakala. In competitions, a buoy was anchored inshore. When two players were able to come in as far as the buoy, or both failed, it was a tie; but when only one succeeded in reaching the buoy, he scored. Famous surfs were all named, as, for instance, Kalehuaweha at Waikiki.

A number of chants were known which it was thought would cause the surf to come up when it was low or small. One of these is:

"Ku mai! Ku mai! Ka nalu nui mai Kahiki!

Alo poi pu. Ku mai ka pohuehue.
Hu. Kaikooloa!"

In addition to board surfing there was body surfing, kaha nalu, and canoe surfing. These are so familiar they need no description.

COASTING

Coasting down slopes was another sport in which the Hawaiian eclipsed their southern kin. Sliding on specially constructed sleds was practiced only in Hawaii and New Zealand. The Maori sled, however, was quite different from the Hawaiian and quite like a European toboggan. One of the Hawaiian sleds, to be seen in Bishop Museum, is the only complete ancient sled in existence. The narrowness and the convergence of the runners towards the front should be noticed. Coasting on these sleds was a pastime confined to the chiefs and chiefesses. Before use the runners were oiled with kukui nut oil to make them as slippery as possible. The sliding course was carefully prepared by being made even, by paving with stones, then by a covering of hard-packed soil overlaid by a layer of slippery grass. A track was about eighteen feet wide, and might be from 150 to several hundred yards long.

In sliding, a man took up a position several yards back of the take-off, and held the right rail in the right hand. He then ran forward, took hold of the left rail with the left hand, and on reaching the brow of the hill threw himself headlong on the sled. Of course, he tore down the slope with terrific speed and ran the risk of severe injury if he got off the track or became upset. Holua was practiced at mid-day or in the early afternoon. One person slid at a time, and the victory belonged to the one who slid the farthest.

Ti-leaf sliding on hill slopes is a survival of the children's hee holua of ancient times. They used not only ti-leaves, but the butt-ends of coconut leaves, and a little sled made of coconut mid-rib runners.

MAIKA

A game almost as distinctly Hawaiian as surf riding or sledding was the maika, or bowl. In this a round stone ball was sometimes used, but the usual bowl which was called an ulu or olohu, was a disk, 3 inches in diameter and an inch and a half thick at the center, and 1 inch thick at the rim. Some of these discs were of wood, but most were of stone. The game was played on a smooth, level, hard packed track of ground. On Molokai and Lanai some of these tracks, kahuna maika, may still be seen. In competitions, the ulumaika was rolled for distance, or rolled clear between two stakes set up in the ground several inches apart at a distance of 30 to 40 yards. Only men played at this sport.

Sometimes the half-grown breadfruit was used for the bowl. Evidently the game originated with the rolling of breadfruit, because in Samoa the only bowl used was a disc made by a central slice of breadfruit. The game was played also in the Cook Islands, but with a wooden disc as well as slices of breadfruit. In Samoa it was sometimes thrown with a strip of hau bark; in the Cook Islands it was generally so thrown.

PAHEE OR MOA

This game was played on the same course as the maika. A wooden dart, 2 to 5 feet long, thick and blunt at one end and tapering at the other, was glanced along the track. These darts were of heavy wood highly polished. They were thrown with great force and exactness. The player, balancing the pahee in his right hand, retreated a few yards from the mark, and then springing forward to a mark, threw. The darts remained wherever they stopped until all had been thrown. Then the whole party ran to the other end of the track to see whose darts were the most successful. The one who first scored ten was the winner. When skill rather than strength was on trial, two darts were laid down on the ground at a certain distance, and 3 to 4 inches apart, and the dart was thrown between them. He who in a given number of times threw his dart between these two without touching them, won. Another variation was to throw the dart between wickets. The dart could be thrown to 200 yards. The ihe pahee were long; the moa were short.

ARROW DARTING—KE'A PUA OR PA PUA

While pahee or moa was, like maika, a very arduous sport practiced by men only, there existed a much lighter form of dart throwing, engaged in by great numbers of men, women and children, when the Makahiki period came around, because that was the season when sugar cane put forth its tassels, the stalks of which were used for arrows. When the tassels were ripe the stalks were plucked and dried. The lower end of the stem was tightly bound with string, after which the point thus made was wetted in the mouth and thrust into the dirt to become coated with a clay.

The player, posting himself so as to take advantage of a knoll or any slight eminence, and holding the arrow well towards its tail end, ran forward a few steps in a stooping position, and as he reached the desired point, with a downward and forward swing of his arm, he threw the arrow at such an angle that it just grazed the surface of the ground, from which it occasionally glanced as it shot along. This arrow throwing was widely practiced in Polynesia. As an easy spear practice for children, these arrows were also thrown at each other and caught.

Matches were often arranged between two persons and bets were made in which the arrows themselves might be wagered. First one and then the other would throw. The first to score ten points won the bet.

BOW AND ARROW

As in Tahiti and the other islands of Polynesia, the bow and arrow was not used in warfare, but only in sport. The sling took the place of the bow in Polynesian warfare.

We know very little of how the bow and arrow were employed in Hawaii. They seem in their simplest form to have been playthings for children. Yet the sport of shooting rats (pana iore) was considered a noble pastime and permitted only to chiefs. The rats were driven into a field. The arrows were pointed with a long, carefully polished, sharp bone. The shaft was the stalk of a sugar cane tassel. Two of these arrows have been preserved in the British Museum, but no ancient bows have been preserved. They seem to have been 3 to 5 feet long and quite powerful. The Hawaiians shot at a mark and with great accuracy, whereas the Tahitians shot simply for distance.

BOXING (MOKOMOKO)

In Hawaii, boxing was more favored than wrestling. Great boxing tournaments were held during the Makahiki period. In the level space left clear by the crowd, the Makahiki god was set up at one end. When all was ready, a champion stepped forward, introduced by the boasts of his backers. The one who accepted his challenge stepped into the ring, and slowly approached his opponent. They glared at each other, clenched their fists, showed their teeth, and strutted about before coming to blows. While these preliminaries were going on, another might jump into the ring and take up the fight directly with one of the pair. They finally approached each other with both arms stretched out straight before them and when they struck, struck with the swing of the right arm and with the bare fist. They aimed their blows only at the head and avoided the blow by dodging or by warding it off with their fist. It is curious that they did not use the forearm as a guard. The moment a man was struck down or he stooped or shunned his antagonist, he was considered vanquished. The victorious side sent up shouts and the beaten man's place was immediately taken by another.

WRESTLING (HAKOKO)

Wrestling matches were held in the midst of a large assembly of people, as were the boxing matches. It seems to have been a more aristocratic sport than boxing, and much practiced about court. The principal aim was to throw an opponent by tripping with the foot.

Boxing Match at Kealakekua, Hawaii

NO'A

This was an extremely popular guessing game, and a favorite one of the chiefs. It frequently occupied them whole days together.

A small, smooth stone (no'a) was hidden under one of five crumpled pieces of kapa. One of the opposing side then guessed under which pile the stone lay. He indicated the pile by striking it with a maile, a small elastic rod, highly polished. Through a slit in the upper end of this rod a tuft of dog skin or a ti leaf was drawn. Each of the pieces of kapa was of a different color and each had its special name, Kihipuka, Pilimoe, Kau, Pilipuka, Kihimoe.

The opposing parties usually consisted of five each. The same party hid the stone 5 or 10 times, according to an agreement made at the beginning of the game. Whichever party came through with the fewest strokes was the winner. Sometimes they reversed this, and those who struck the most without finding the stone were considered the winners.

PUHENEHENE

A variation of the game no'a just described, was the game puhenehene, in which the stone, no'a, was hidden on the person instead of under a piece of kapa. This game was usually played in the house and at night time. It was open to all.

Two parties were made up of ten each, each party consisting of five men and five women placed alternately. A long sheet of kapa was stretched between them. When they were ready, the master of ceremonies called out "Puheoheo." The people answered, "Puheoheo." Then a man stood forth and chanted a gay and pleasing song, while three men picked up the kapa and covered or screened one party with it. One of this party then concealed the no'a on his person. The screen was removed and the members of the opposing side took turns in guessing who had the no'a. All the members of the party who had the no'a bent forward and down so that no one could look into their faces, for it was by studying the countenance that the only real clue could be found as to where the stone lay concealed. If the guess was right, it counted one point for the guessing side. If it was wrong, it counted one point for the opposite side. The first side to get ten points, won. Then some person on the winning side would start a hula.

KILU (QUOITS)

Kilu was an indoor game of quoits played only at night. It was a select game to which only alii were admitted. The men sat grouped at one end of the house, the women at the other. The kilu was a half coconut or gourd which had been split lengthwise. It was spun along a mat towards a pole or block and if it struck, it scored. One or more poles, or conical blocks of wood were set up on one side and an equal number on the other. Behind these posts sat the players, to the number of five or more. When all was ready, the master of ceremonies called out, "Puheoheo." The assembly responded, "Puheoheoheo," and all became quiet. The tally keeper of one side held up the kilu to be thrown and stated the forfeit demanded in case the kilu hit its mark. The tally keeper on the other side mentioned the name of the person on that side who would pay the forfeit. Each person chanted an oli before throwing his kilu. The play was kept up till morning and resumed the following night. When a player had scored ten he was declared the winner. This game seems not to have been practiced elsewhere in Polynesia.

KONANE

A game resembling checkers or the oriental game "gobang," was called konane. It was a favorite pastime of old men, but was played by chiefs and others. A man and woman might play together. Campbell, who was here between 1806 and 1812, saw Kamehameha at it for hours. He remarked that Kamehameha gave an occasional smile, but never uttered a word, and that no one could beat him.

The game was frequently played on a flat stone on the

house platform, although the chiefs had boards. The boards (papamu) were marked with rows of dots placed an inch from each other. There might be from 8 to 20 rows, and about the same number of transverse as of longitudinal rows. The checkers were an equal number of black and white pebbles. The board was entirely covered with these pebbles placed on the dots. They were laid down alternately black and white. When all was ready the player to pick first removed a stone from the center or a corner. Then the jumping continued, the stone jumped over being removed. It is not clear how the game was won. According to an old informant, when a person was blocked so he could not move he lost.

The game was sometimes played on the squares of a mat or on squares scratched in the ground. Konane was not played elsewhere in Polynesia, and is possibly an introduction from the west.

CONCLUSION

The games and sports which have been described are only a few of the more popular and characteristic pastimes of the Hawaiian adult. Of course the principal amusement or entertainment which was enjoyed by the grown-ups was the hula, but that is a subject in itself.

The children and young people were abundantly supplied with games and amusements: kite (lupe) flying, stilt (kukuluaeo) walking, top (hu) spinning, rope skipping (hakeokeo), and swinging. They had scores of string-figures or cats-cradles (hei), toy canoes, a game of jackstones (kimo), and another of cup and ball (palaie). Juggling balls was a favorite pastime, accompanied, as were so many others, by little jingles or chants.

The ancient Hawaiians need not be pitied over-much for having lived in the old unenlightened days. They had enough light to guide them along a path which frequently overflowed with laughter and song, and they paused long and often to enjoy in play their natural strength, skill, and grace.

CHAPTER 15

THE HAWAIIAN LANGUAGE

JOHN H. WISE and HENRY P. JUDD

The languages of Polynesia come from a common stock and naturally resemble each other. But in the course of the centuries, the language which was developed in Samoa and Tahiti, for instance, contained consonants unknown to the speech of the Hawaiians and of the Maoris of New Zealand. This was probably because Samoa and Tahiti were not so isolated from all outside influences as were Hawaii and New Zealand. As soon as Hawaii came into contact with these influences, harsher sounds gained a foothold in the language. "T" was used instead of the native Hawaiian "k" sound after foreigners entered the islands. However, when the missionaries reduced the language to writing in the 1820's, they put it into more or less permanent form and it did not continue to change.

Every word in the Hawaiian language ends in a vowel and no two consonants occur without a vowel between them. The one exception to this is the word "Kristo" meaning Christ, and this is of course not a native word. The soft musical sound of the language is partly due to this arrangement of vowels in the word. It is also caused by the softness of the Hawaiian consonants, and the absence of all harsh consonants. Only seven consonants, h, k, l, m, n, p, and w, appear in the Hawaiian language. The vowels are given a soft broad pronunciation, which contributes to the musical sound of the language.

The language has no inflections. There are no endings to indicate the plural, no changes in form of the word to indicate tense. In recent years many Hawaiian words in common use are given an "s" to indicate the plural. We speak of leis, of kapus, of kuleanas. Throughout this book, the reader will notice Hawaiian words which are given the plural to which we are accustomed. This is because the omission of the "s" creates a confusion. The addition of the "s" is, strictly speaking, not correct and not Hawaiian.

Intensity of expression in the language is accomplished by repetition of sound. For instance, "a" becomes "aa," "naki" becomes "nakiki," and "pulu" becomes "pulupulu." The language contains no relative pronouns. There are no verbs to express existing, having, possessing, being under obligation, or affirming. These ideas are expressed by articles of affirmation, as for instance, "he akamai kona," he is clever. This is translated literally, "his is the cleverness." Nouns may be placed anywhere in the sentence except at the beginning. Following is the order in which verbs and their adjuncts are placed:

1. The tense signs, as i, ua, e, etc.
2. The verb itself.
3. The qualifying adverb, as mau, wale, ole, pu, etc.
4. The passive sign, ia.
5. The verbal directives, as aku, mai, etc.
6. The locatives, nei or la, or the participles ana and ai.
7. The strengthening particle, no.
8. The subject.
9. The object or predicate noun.

There is fine distinction in the use of the words "a" and "o," both meaning "of." For example, "ka hale a Keawe" means "the house built by Keawe," and "ka hale o Keawe" means "the house in which Keawe lives."

The Hawaiian counted by fours: Kauna (four), kaau (forty), lau (four hundred), mano (four thousand), kini (forty thousand) and lehu (four hundred thousand.)

Oratory and poetry were characteristic forms of expression among the early Hawaiians. In their poetry there were several forms. Some of these were: (1) religious chants, (2) inoa or name songs, (3) funeral dirges, (4) ipo or love songs.

There were some twenty thousand words in the vocabulary, although the dictionaries contain only about fifteen thousand. Because of the relatively small size of the vocabulary, many words have several distinct meanings. We find the same thing true in the English language. Consider the word "fast." Immediately we think of such different meanings as "securely," in the expression "hold fast;" "rapid, quick," as in the expression "a fast horse;" a day when certain foods are not eaten, as in "a fast day;" indicating incorrect time, as in the expression "the watch is fast," "dissolute," as in the expression, "a fast man;" and so on. In the same manner single words carry many distinct meanings in the Hawaiian language. The translator needs to understand and know all the meanings and to fit in the one which was intended. Often the literal translation of an expression, while perfectly correct apparently, is not the intended meaning. Only a knowledge of all the possible meanings of a word and of the probable intent of the speaker, enables one to arrive at the corrrect interpretation.

Consider, for instance, this phase, "Ke kui mai la a'u keiki i na lehua o Kauai." Literally this means, "My sons are stringing the lehua flowers of Kauai." However, this apparently poetic and innocent statement is supposed to be a battle song. It was sung by Kawelo, a great chief, who was carried to Kauai wrapped in a bundle of mats in order that his arrival might not be known to the people of Kauai. Kawelo pulled aside the meshes of his mats and sang this song, "My sons are stringing the lehua of Kauai, the lehua partly eaten by birds." Surely Kawelo did not mean that his warriors had dropped their spears and fighting arms and had sat down to make leis! What did he mean? In the old-days, lehua was the personification of strength, of physical well-being. "Stringing the lehua," referred to the spearing of the strong young warriors of Kauai. "The lehua partly eaten by the birds," referred to the wounded who were being killed off as the humane way of dealing with them. The mele sounds beautiful. In its actual meaning, it is a war song describing the battle and the death of the enemy. The translator must know the story, the setting, the spirit of the composer, as well as the different meanings of words, when he puts a mele into another language.

The Hawaiians themselves did not always get the real meaning intended by the speaker. An instance of this is the story of a happening after the division of Hawaii between Kamehameha, Keoua, and Keawemauhili. An old man went to Keawemauhili, the chief of Hilo, and asked that he might have returned to him his calabash of food and calabash of fish. The chief asked what calabash he meant. "I have not your calabash of fish or your calabash of food," he said. The man answered, "Yes, you have them." The chief asked his attendants what the man meant. They said, "He wants Olaa, the great taro land, and Keaau, the great fish beach. These are his calabash of food and his calabash of fish." Another story of the misunderstandings which arose because words had several meanings, is the tale of two fishermen in a canoe. One was paddling in the bow, facing foward. The other was sitting in the stern facing toward land. The man in the stern, looking back at the island, said, "See how clear the land is." The fisherman in the bow, who was bald, thought the other man was referring to his baldness and insulting him. He answered, "Yes, it does appear to be clear and yet if you look at the red dirt being blown by the wind, you will see that it is windy on land." The man in the stern was watery-eyed and he thought that this remark was intended to insult him, so they fought. Finally the man in the bow said, "It is your fault. You said I was bald." The other man answered, "I did not mean that." These men were using common language, common terms, yet each misunderstood the other, because these words had more than one meaning. Some Hawaiian words have as many as five different meanings and there are endless possibilities of an error in use as well as of misunderstanding of the meanings. It is a good plan, unless you know Hawaiian very well indeed, to be quite careful in your use of Hawaiian expressions in any company where there are people who really know the language.

While the Hawaiian language has a relatively small vocabulary, it is rich in words pertaining to the ocean, the sky, the clouds, the surf, vegetation, and other concrete and objective terms. There is a name for every kind of wind and rain. Every day of the month has a special name. There are, however, very few words to express abstract ideas. The language is a concrete one, the language of a people who observed the things about them and sought to describe and identify them. And, though single words have many different meanings, it is interesting to note that there are a good many different words to express certain simple ideas. For instance, there are six different words to express the idea of "to carry," ten different words to express the idea of "to stand," and twenty different words describing the idea "to sit."

The Hawaiian language is not easy to learn. Often-times, "i's" and "o's" are used to express a whole word and it is impossible to get the meaning of these unless the context is known. Another difficulty which faces the learner is the matter of euphony or melodious sound. Much Hawaiian usage is based not upon rule, but upon sound. In the case of two expressions, the one which is correct is the one which gives the most musical sound. For instance, "ke" and "ka" are both articles. Sometimes one is the correct one to use and sometimes the other. "Ke pakau ko'u" is correct, while "ka pakau ko'u" is incorrect. Only the sound may be used as a guide. Again, "ke puka" is wrong, while "ka puka" is correct. There is no particular guide to the use of the personal pronouns, "kou, ko'u, nou, no'u, nau, na'u," except the sound in the phrase.

Poetic expressions in Hawaiian differ from those used to express the same idea in prose. This is true of most languages. Since however most of the old Hawaiian meles are poetry, we find that we are dealing with a language most of whose written expressions are figurative and not literal; poetic and not prosaic. Obtaining a real understanding of such a language demands insight and imagination as well as effort. Many of the Hawaiian names are drawn from poetic usage rather than from the everyday language. Though 'keakea'' is the common word for white, the mountain is known as "Mauna Kea" which is the poetic form. Many Hawaiian names in use at the present have these poetic forms and convey special meanings to those who understand them. All of the figurative names given to children are given because of something which happened in the past. They may be understood only through a rather complete understanding of the past event, and also of the language itself.

Many words and expressicns of the Hawaiian language have been taken over by the different people who have come here and they would be included in an English dictionary for the Hawaiian islands, as perfectly well recognized words. Any language attains richness and significance as it includes new terms and uses them for particular purposes. The word "lei" is known around the world. It is not only a recognized word in Hawaii, but it has been used to describe a particular form of decoration for evening dresses designed in Paris and sold in New York. "Aloha" has a warmth of meaning and a comprehensiveness of meaning not expressed by either the words "love" or "friendship." Aloha, as we all know, is something different from either of these. The word "hui" carries meaning which we can scarcely express without the use of several words in English. A great many of these expressive Hawaiian words are entering the language of the islands. They are known and used by all racial groups in Hawaii. It is inevitable that the Hawaiian language, as a language, will be used less and less, but many Hawaiian words and expressions will be retained in the speech of the islands.

CHAPTER 16

POLYNESIAN ORATORY

PETER H. BUCK

Oratory has been defined as the art of speaking in public eloquently or effectively. It was to the Greeks what the pulpit and press have been to modern Europe.

In Polynesia, owing to the lack of writing, there were no written records, no printed books, and no morning or evening newspapers. Thus mythology, traditions, history, customs, and ritual were all taught by word of mouth. The individual had to learn by ear and pass on information by speaking. All matters concerning the family and larger groups comprising subtribes and tribes were promulgated by speakers before the groups and much of the speaking was therefore public. Because public speaking was a common method of expression and because it was regarded as the usual thing, there was no shyness on the part of the speakers. There were thus no apologies and excuses to interfere with the flow of speech and the speakers were consequently eloquent. The leaders of the people who came from the upper class of chiefs and priests, maintained their prestige in part by the art of public speaking. As they were carefully taught the mythology, traditions, history, and pedigrees of their groups, they had a rich fund of material from which to quote both in ordinary speech and in matters of public importance. Speeches rich in metaphor and classical quotations stirred the people through the magic of appropriate words. They appealed to feelings of racial pride. They were effective and thus constituted oratory of a high standard.

In New Zealand, all chiefs, priests, and heads of families had the right of free speech in public meetings. A family which was not heard through its leader lost prestige, for silence was associated with inferiority. In the larger gatherings of several tribes only the leading chiefs spoke as representatives of their major groups.

In some regions, the high chiefs were represented on public occasions by an orator whose position was more or less hereditary. The official orator fully realized that the effectiveness of his position depended upon his power to use the richest words that the vocabulary provided. He was the exponent of the classical knowledge of his group. He trained for his position by acquiring from his father the correct procedure and etiquette in speech-making appropriate to the various occasions that arose in the culture of his people. He memorized a large number of chants, songs, and quotations with which to punctuate the speeches that different occasions demanded. He had to know the order of precedence between different chiefly families and family groups. He was thus one of the leading scholars of his group.

In the Cook Islands the orator of the ariki (high chief) was termed the va'a-tuatua (speaking mouth). In Tahiti the office was termed orero (speech). In both these regions, the orator spoke for his chief on public occasions. In Hawaii the orator was termed the kaka-olelo, which is similar to the Tahitian term. In Hawaii, however, the kaka-olelo seems to have had the additional function of relating historical stories for the entertainment of the chiefs. Specialization reached its highest in Samoa where a class of hereditary talking chiefs termed tulafale developed. In the course of time the tulafale created such a mass of observances in etiquette, precedence, and a special chiefs' language, that the high chiefs were unable to do without them. No high chief could travel to other villages without his official tulafale. Not only did the talking chiefs create increased ceremonial around the high chiefs, but they became administrative chiefs with regard to the distribution of food and presents and thus acquired a great deal of the power previously exercised by their superiors. In a few instances the alii (chiefs) retained the right to make their own speeches, which created the special title of alii-tulafale.

The occasions for oratory were numerous. All visitors from another tribe or district had to be welcomed officially with speeches, and they had to reply to their hosts. A member of a tribe who had been absent for some time was received back with welcoming speeches to which he replied. Owing to the social system which grouped people together into communities or tribes, the individual was regarded as representing his group. Thus no visitor could slip quietly into a village as an individual; etiquette demanded that he be welcomed officially by the chiefs of the community he visited. At feasts, marriages, and funerals, orations formed a necessary part of the procedure. In family and group discussions regarding economic matters such as food supplies, matters were formally thrashed out by the leaders delivering speeches. Other matters of public importance such as war were discussed in public either in the open village plaza or within the guest, or meeting, house. The chiefs and leaders spoke while the mass of the people formed their audience.

The procedure in welcoming guests varied in different regions. The ancient procedure in Hawaii, where matter-of-fact customs of Western civilization have replaced it, offers an interesting line of study for some student. New Zealand and Samoa retain today many of the old customs. In New Zealand, the whole village community gathers on the public plaza as the visitors approach. Women with good voices repeat at a high pitch some such phrase as "Come and weep for our dead." Both parties then weep for those who have recently died. After an appropriate interval the home chiefs make speeches of welcome to which the visiting chiefs make suitable reply. The greeting of pressing noses takes place and the visitors are free to mix with the local people. In Samoa, the demonstration is not so markedly public. The visitors are shown to the guest house in which they seat themselves beside the wall posts which denote their social status. The local chiefs enter, bringing presents of kava root. They seat themselves beside the appropriate wall posts at their end of the house. The kava presents are collected before the local talking chief, who in set phrases presents them to the visitors. The visiting talking chief also in set phrases acknowledges the gift and proceeds to divide the kava root among the visiting chiefs. Meanwhile kava is being prepared and the taupou (village hostess) takes up her position at the back of the house with the kava bowl before her. The local talking chief now formally welcomes the visitors and recites the fa'alupenga (order of prestige) of the visitors' village. The visiting talking chief replies in similar strain and recites the fa'alupenga of the local village. An eye is kept on the preparation of the kava and when it is ready the speeches are cut short. The serving of kava forms a necessary part of the welcoming ceremony.

The movements of orators during their orations are interesting for they tend to follow a regional pattern. In New Zealand, all speeches are made in the erect position and the orator walks or even trots over a short course which is either towards the visitors or parallel to them. As he approaches or walks to the left, he speaks with the appropriate force and gesture, coming to the end of a sentence as he reaches the limits of his course. He usually punctuates this by alighting on both feet at the same time. He then turns to his right and retraces his steps in silence. Arriving at his commencement point he takes a turn to the left and walking or trotting down the course he delivers another burst of eloquence. The correct turn at either end of the short course is important. To turn in the opposite manner to that indicated implies turning the back to the visitors and was regarded as a korapa or bad omen. The Maori technique is thus marked by movement and virility. In Samoa, movement and gesture are limited. The speeches delivered in the guest house are made from the cross-legged sitting position. In the open, the orator leans with both hands on a staff with the lower end fixed to the ground between the big and second toes of his right foot and hence his position is stationary. I was told in Tutuila that when trouble was brewing between two assembled groups, the talking chief waved his staff in accordance with prearranged signals to warn his group as to impending attack or defence.

The insignia of office of the Samoan talking chief is the to'oto'o (staff) and the fly whisk. The orator's staff can not be greater than his own height whereas that of an alii can exceed it. The orator's fly whisk differs from that of the high chief by having a shorter and thicker handle, while the strands of sennit braid are longer and more numerous. In any assembly, the talking chiefs can always be distinguished by the special fly whisks which mark their office. In a sitting speech, the orator may wave his fly whisk about. In a standing speech he usually holds his staff in his right hand and his fly whisk in the left. When he settles down to his speech, he balances his fly whisk over the left shoulder and holds his staff with both hands. On important occasions in the open a number of talking chiefs stand up together and perfunctorily argue amongst themselves as to which shall have the honor of welcoming or replying. This is regarded as a gesture conferring honor upon those to be addressed. In New Zealand, no orator will speak empty handed. Formerly, the orator always used a weapon to punctuate his remarks. The short club was the favorite symbol and when the speaker possessed a family weapon of whalebone or jade he always used it. A jade club from its value indicated that the speaker was of considerable social status. The long two-handed clubs were also used and their manipulation followed a set pattern. Thus while speaking the club was held horizontally in the right hand with the blade advanced. On turning to retire silently, the left hand relieved the right without turning the club. On turning to advance, the right hand again took charge. The wrong hold or the wrong position of the club were also regarded as korapa, mistakes that presaged disaster. In modern times, the functioning walking stick has replaced the weapon which has gone out of use. It is interesting on occasions to observe, even with a bent-handled walking stick of European manufacture, how punctilious the older men are in carrying it horizontally with the correct hold and the correct changes.

The speech pattern varied in different regions but unfortunately the incorporation of modern words and ideas has displaced the original pattern. In New Zealand, however, the old men have retained the old technique and the younger educated leaders have more or less followed it.

In funeral orations, the speaker directly addresses the soul of the deceased and speeds him on his way to the spirit land to join his ancestors and his people who rest in that region in their myriads. He uses figures of speech to indicate the disaster that has occurred. Some phrases are as follows:

> "The giant tree of the Forest of Tane, which sheltered the people beneath its branches, has fallen to the ground."
>
> "The peaks of the lofty mountains have been levelled."
>
> "The horn of the crescent moon has been severed."

The orator then addresses the relatives and tribe and conveys his sorrow and condolences. He enriches his speech with classical quotations from myth and tradition, usually dealing with death and disaster as appropriate to the occasion. He may sing one or more laments that have been composed on the death of chiefs. The following translation of a verse of a lament indicates the sentiment conveyed:

> "Alas! the bitter pain that gnaws within
> For the wrecked canoe—for my departed friend.
> My precious heron plume is cast on ocean's strand
> While the lightning, flashing in the heavens, salutes the dead.
> Where is authority in this world,
> Since thou hast passed by the slippery path,
> The sliding path to death?"

In addresses of welcome, the orator often commences with an introductory chant of which there is a rich assortment. One frequently used is as follows:

"Come hither, draw nigh,
Bring unto me the living waters of life.
Oh weary has been the rest of the aged at night,
But now, it is dawn, it is dawn,
It is light."

Such a chant, of course, conveys a compliment to the visitors. The orator goes on to welcome the visitors by alluding to their ancestral canoe, their tribe, and their individual chiefs who are present. He then refers to those who have recently died in the two tribes and sings an appropriate lament. If there is a relationship between the two tribes this is mentioned and stressed. Any particular topic of interest to both groups may here be introduced or it may be deferred to an evening meeting. He usually closes with the welcoming words of "haere mai," repeated thrice.

In speeches of reply, the speakers generally first chant the farewell to the dead, and then reply to the living. Chants and laments must be used for a speech which without them is considered unfinished.

It will be observed that public oratory by experts on so many occasions had an important educative effect upon the community. The orators were really lecturers who expounded the classical knowledge of the past and the assembled tribes formed their audiences. It is interesting to note that though the Maoris long ago embraced Christianity, they see no incongruity in quoting from their ancient mythology and rejected religious concepts. They rightly regard such patterns of speech as of literary value. They have therefore had a functional value in social relations and have thus survived to a greater extent than among Polynesian groups which had come to regard them as "heathen" practices. In a changing culture the mass of the people tenaciously cling to sentimental symbols which remind them of the glories of the past. Hence the old speech patterns with their classical quotations sound sweet to the ears of the people. The younger educated leaders were quick to realize that they could carry more conviction to the masses if they used old speech patterns to invest modern ideas with a sentimental setting. The people on their side felt that their young leaders were not revolutionists from an outside culture but were of their own flesh and blood who retained a pride in their past. Western culture has attempted to pull down the old house in order that it may erect a new one. In convincing the Polynesian of the inferiority of his own house, there has been the danger of forcing an inferiority complex upon him, and breaking down his spirit. Polynesian oratory based on old patterns has kept alight the lamp of the spirit. Polynesian orators, both old and young, can exercise an integrating effect upon the changing culture and by their efforts cause adjustments to take place gradually as an evolution from within and not as a revolution from without. This is taking place in New Zealand and it is possible in any Polynesian community, for Polynesian peoples all come of the same blood and are stirred by the same speech.

CHAPTER 17

POETRY *

EDITH RICE PLEWS

The subject "Hawaiian Poetry" is a very large one, and consequently cannot of course be treated comprehensively this evening; nevertheless I shall try to give you some idea tonight of the tremendous heritage of beautiful and interesting poetry that belongs to the Hawaiian race, and therefore to each one of you. I feel overwhelmed at being the one to tell you of it, for surely there are many older people in our islands who have a greater knowledge than mine, besides those like my friend Mr. John Wise, here, who have a profound and scholarly understanding of the Hawaiian tongue. Before I was as old as the youngest of you I found myself stirred by the classic poetry I read—that is, in the English tongue; then the new school of poetry interested me; next, when I was helping my grandfather, the late William Hyde Rice, in his preparation of his book on Hawaiian Legends, came the time when the subject of Hawaiian poetry opened before me. The translations of poetry here and there in the book fascinated me, and when he started work on translation of the prayer in the legend of the Menehune I found myself deeply stirred by the freshness of it, the vivdness of the images (that is, the comparisons, as you may have called them in school) and above all by the beauty of the thought.

I believe that the greater part of Hawaiian poetry can best be appreciated from the viewpoint of modern poetry. A knowledge of modern poetry and its tendencies intensifies our grasp and our understanding of it. As Padraic Colum has said, "The Hawaiian poet has anticipated effects that the cultivated poets of our tradition have

* This chapter is an unedited lecture.

been striving for; he is, for instance, more esoteric than Mallarme and more imagistic than Amy Lowell." A little explanation may be in order—you probably all know of Padraic Colum, the well-known Irish poet, who visited here about ten years ago, and put into very poetic prose form many of our more familiar Hawaiian legends, expressly for use in our schools. Mallarme is a famous French poet, and Amy Lowell, who died about two years ago, was among the foremost poets of our time. "Esoteric" means having an inner, or hidden, or secret meaning, that is, containing knowledge or a significance only to be grasped by those of superior understanding, or the initiated. "Imagistic" means figurative—you all understand what is meant by the phrase "figure of speech." For instance, "she sailed up the room." Now "she" did not actually sail up the room in a boat, but she walked across the room in such a dignified and sure manner that "she " reminded you of a ship in full sail—there is an image.

You all know that the Hawaiians had an interesting and advanced culture. The knowledge of some of it has been lost, but much still remains; some of it written down, and so preserved for those who will follow us, and some still uncollected. Your job and mine should be to make a record of all that still remains unwritten or inaccessible. Almost every Hawaiian family possesses a scrap book or copy book in which someone has written bits of meles and proverbs—"He mau olelo noeau Hawaii" or "Moolelo Hawaii." These are valuable sources and it should be our duty to our beloved birthplace, and our pleasure, to preserve and share them. There is also the tremendous work of translation, of which more later.

Now, to return to poetry: first, what is poetry? Poetry is a transfiguration of life, an imaginative presentation of it—that is, a picture of life—addressed to our nobler emotions, and expressed in language of appropriate rhythmic form. The music of the words and the beauty of the images they bring to mind move our feeling and give us delight. Poetry means a creation, literally, hence poet means a maker, a creator. Rhythm means a flowing, generally a flowing which conforms to a pattern of some sort, also. Rhythm, melody, and original, vivid images—pictures—cloaking a great thought, are necessary to true poetry.

Not only music or the magic music of words, which is another way of saying poetry, has rhythm and pattern. So have the other arts, the pictorial arts as well. For example, take this picture representing a kapa design, and these photographs of Hawaiian quilts, kapa apana. Note the balance, the repetition, the feeling, the rhythm, all making up the pattern, the design. It is the same with poetry, and also note, underlying all art, enfolded within, the thought, the idea, which quickens the whole to life.

The ancient Hawaiians were naturally a poetic race; their beautiful surroundings bred in them a feeling for the beauty and symbolism of life. Their liquid language was a flexible medium for its expression. As G. W. Stewart says, "Lovers of poetry, as well as poets, are born, not made." Since the people felt the poetic significance of all about them, there grew up naturally an expression of this feeling. Where poetry exists it cannot be suppressed.

As to time, the poetry of Hawaii can be thrust roughly into three groups, which all dovetail and overlap.

First: The great body of ancient poetry. The very ancient and that of a hundred years ago are of about the same quality. There is no marked difference. Some of the meles we possess are several hundreds of years old.

Second: The period between 1820 and 1900. Running almost parallel to the Victorian era. This consists of poems in the old manner, translations of old poetry, and also various adaptations of English forms, influenced often by hymns.

Third: The newer poetry. 1900 to the present time. Quite recently the old Hawaiian forms have proved the foundation for new renderings in English.

What chiefly concerns us is the old, the true poetry of the Hawaiian people. Of course they had no exact word for so abstract a term as our "poetry." Mele, their equivalent, means a song. And all meles were sung, or rather chanted, or cantillated. This is equally true of all early poetry of whatever race.

The mele is interwoven in Hawaiian culture with the hula and the kaao—that is, poetry is interwoven with the dance and with mythology. Rhythm of utterance, music and motion are the three things that express and rule the emotions. This is likewise true of early Greek and Hebrew poetry, and also in a large degree of ancient Chinese poetry. Although poetry and prose are often interwoven, they are easily differentiated by the ear. Of course, where there is no written language, all ideas must be conveyed orally. The trained memories of the ancient Hawaiian poets were retentive to a remarkable degree. While we have a literary education and training that reaches us through the eye, as we read, the literary training and perception in old Hawaii was all through the ear. As I have said, in the introduction to Wm. Hyde Rice's "Hawaiian Legends," there was an honored class of men attached to the courts of the high chiefs, made up of the poets, genealogists, story-tellers, etc., similar to the bards, minstrels, and story-tellers of medievel Europe or Asia. Sometimes these men were wanderers, going from place to place, plying their trade. The old-time Hawaiians, belonging to this class, were skilled in the art of the apo, that is, "catching" literally; trained to receive and hold the spoken word, that is, to memorize instantly, at first hearing. One man would recite or chant for two or three hours at a stretch, and when he had finished, the auditor would start at the beginning of the chant and go through the whole mele without missing or changing a word. Fornander speaks of one instance when the recital took six hours—equivalent to several books of Homer! These tráined men received through their ears as we do through our eyes, and in that way the Hawaiians had a spoken literature much as we have a written one.

It is now conceded that the Greek epics were handed down from generation to generation for centuries before Homer, in this same way. There are many other points of similarity to Greek poetry, some of which I will point out.

As I have said, mele means song, or words so arranged that they may be chanted. To arrange words in order is termed haku. Haku originally meant "to sort out feathers of different qualities and colors, and to arrange them into bundles to be used for feather cloaks." A secondary idea was to regulate, to put in order, to compose, or to put words in order. This is also the meaning of the Greek word word poieo, whence comes our English word poet.

Therefore a poet is called, in Hawaiian, a haku mele—"one who arranges words into a song." Among Hawaiians the skill of the poet has been honored since time immemorial. They classed the worth of their poets in several grades—those exceedingly skillful, those of medium worth, and last the makers of vulgar songs. Discrimination and appreciation were among their attributes.

There were three usual methods of composing poetry. The first was that a poet (either a man or a woman) would go off alone and think out the ideas and words for a mele, and afterwards repeat them in public. These were generally short poems, and were afterwards committed to memory by other bards. Most long or epic poems were composed by a conclave of poets, who met together, and decided on a subject. Then one poet would begin the first line; after he had recited it, it was criticized and corrected by the gathering, and then the next line was begun, and so on. Judge Andrews says that the remarkable part was that the corrected version was fixed in the memories of all, even to the particles. Still another way was for a high chief to select his most able chiefs and warriors, and propose the subject of the mele and appoint each one to furnish what he would call a line or a verse, while the others acted as critics and correctors.

As you see, the poetry of the Hawaiians resembled that of the Ancient Greeks. It is also like the old Arabic poetry, in quality, and expression, and there are points of resemblance between it and ancient Hebrew poetry.

It is hard for us to read intelligently, or to translate Hawaiian poetry, as we are ignorant in such great measure of its tremendous background of mythology, tradition, and history. What would the Iliad or the Odyssey mean to us without some knowledge of Greek mythology and history? It is not that Hawaiian poetry is more obscure, but that we are less familiar with its background.

You remember my quotation from Padraic Colum about Hawaiian poetry—"more esoteric that Mallarme, more imagistic than Amy Lowell." Let me quote him further:

> "Every Hawaiian poem has at least four meanings: (1) the ostensible meaning of the words; (2) a vulgar double meaning; (3) a mythological-historical-topographical import; and (4) the Kauna or deeply-hidden meaning. I have sat gasping while, in a poem of twelve or twenty lines, meaning under meaning was revealed to me by some scholar, Hawaiian or Haole, who knew something of the esoteric Hawaiian tradition.
>
> "But the main thing that Hawaiian poetry has to offer an outsider is the clear and flashing images that it is in its power to produce. The languages of the Pacific, it should be noted first, have no abstract terms. If an Hawaiian wants to refer to my ignorance he speaks of me as having the entrails of night; if he wants to speak of someone's blindness he will bring in eyes of night. Abstractions become images in the Polynesian language. The people themselves have an extraordinary sense of the visible things in their world; they have, for in-

stance, a dozen words to tell of the shades of difference in the sea as it spreads between them and the horizon. And their language forces them to an imagistic expression. Their poetry, then, when it is at all descriptive, is full of clear and definite images. I open Nathaniel Emerson's Unwritten Literature of Hawaii, a book upon the hula that is also a great anthology of Hawaiian poetry, and I find:

'Heaven-magic, fetch a Hilo pour from heaven!
Morn's cloud-buds, look! they swell in the East.
The rain-cloud parts, Hilo is deluged with rain,
The Hilo of King Hana-kahi.

Surf breaks, stirs the mire of Pii-lani;
The bones of Hilo are broken
By the blows of the rain.
Ghostly the rain-scud of Hilo in heaven.

The cloud-forms of Pua-lani grow and thicken.
The rain-priest bestirs him now to go forth,
Forth to observe the stab and thrust of the rain,
The rain that clings to the roof of Hilo'."

Translation by N. E.

MAHELE-HELE

"Hi'u-o-lani, kii ka ua o Hilo i ka lani;
Ke hookiikii mai la ke ao o Pua-lani;
O mahele ana, pulu Hilo i ka ua—
O Hilo Hana-kahi.

Ha'i ka nalu, wai kaka lepo o Pii-lani;
Hai'na ka iwi o Hilo,
I ke ku ia e ka wai.
Oni'o lele a ka ua o Hilo i ka lani.

Ke hookiikii mai la ke ao o Pua-lani,
Ke holuholu a'e la e puka,
Puka e nana ke kiki a ka ua,
Ka nonoho a ka ua i ka hale o Hilo."

As to the structure of Hawaiian poetry, Judge Andrews

says they have "no measure of feet as dactyl, spondee anapest, etc." However I find they measured by sound, not feet. In other words our modern poets would call it cadenced. Sometimes, however, one finds perfect rhythms, or several successive lines of iambic, trochaic, or dactylic meter. These the poets recognized as good, and often repeated them as refrains. Could this have been purely accidental? Rather, have they not anticipated our modern tendencies? However, Hawaiian poetry does not generally rhyme; in fact Hawaiians (another anticipation) are not particularly impressed with rhymed endings—they see no special beauty in it. They do use internal rhyme, assonance, and such subtle forms very often, and find pleasure in them. Proportion was strictly adhered to, (the pattern or design idea, again) and one of the principal points was the expression of a thought in a short, terse, carefully adjusted sentence. Anything that could be eliminated was thrown out, so that the main idea might make a vivid impression. "Great abruptness or suddenness of introduction is a quality of Hawaiian poetry," writes Judge Andrews. "The poet seldom prepares or warns his hearers of what is coming." He rushes at once into the midst of his subject. Lines need have no definite length, each is generally complete as to sense. They observe "a rhythm of proportion and a harmony of sentences" and they were aware of the effective value of a refrain. There are also often distinct parts for solo and chorus.

Now for a word concerning translations and translators. Judge Andrews is, to my mind, the most gifted. He has a true poetic feeling. Much very valuable work has been done by such scholars as Nathaniel Emerson, Fornander, and Bingham, but they were more interested in the ethnological value of the meles than in their poetry. In addition these scholars probably did not consider themselves poets, though Emerson particularly flashes into vivid, memorable phrases. We must remember the times and ideas which influenced these men. Perhaps the Victorian era, with all that it stands for in poetry and phraseology, as well as in ideas, was the most alien period as far as the English language is concerned, in which Hawaiian poetry could have been translated. Therefore, do not expect too much of these translations as far as the freshness of diction, vividness of imagery, and fullness of flavor are concerned. All that is in the originals is not expressed in many, if not most, of the translations. On the other hand, these scholars, immersed as they were in the traditions of mid-Victorianism, had a tremendous background of reading, that of the King James' version of the Bible and of Shakespeare, the twin perfect flowerings of the English tongue. There is an old Hawaiian proverb—"If you would learn to sing, go listen to the running water." Likewise, if you would learn to write English with a living feeling for its words and use, or to translate into English from Hawaiian, go to the fountain head—the living waters—of that tongue; that is, go steep yourselves in the Bible—the King James' version I mean—and in Shakespeare. The Psalms are among the finest poems in the English language; read over the 137th Psalm and you will understand me. "By the waters of Babylon there we sat down, yea, we wept, when we remembered Zion." That is pure spoken music.

There were at least nine classes of Hawaiian poetry. As I recount them to you, I shall in most cases give you an illustration, Mr. Wise reading the original Hawaiian version, and I following with the translation.

First: We have the mele kaua, the war songs.

Now these are generally included in longer poems, as is this example, from the story in poetic form of the hero, Kawelo. This is a rather literal translation made by Wm. Hyde Rice, in his "Hawaiian Legends."

"I remember the days when we were young.
Swelled now is the limu of Hanalei.
Swelled above the eyes is the cloud of morning.
In vain is the battle at the hands of children.
The great battle will follow
As the deep sea follows the shallow water.

In vain are the clouds dispersed.
O Kauahoa, the strong one of Hanalei!
Awake, O Kamalama, the strong one of Kualoa!
Awake, Kawelo, the strong one of Waikiki!
Awake, Kaelehapuna, the strong one of Ewa!
Awake, Kalaumeki, the strong one of Waimea!
We will all gather together at noonday.
Postpone the battle, my brother. Leave me.
This is not the day for us to give a mock battle,
Friend of my boyhood days, with whom I made lehua leis
At Waikaee for our lord and older brothers.
Awake, O Hanalei, the land of chill and rain,
The land where the clouds hover!
Awake O Kauahoa, the handsome one of Hanalei!"

W. H. R.

KAWELO

"Pehu kaha ka limu o Hanalei
Pehu ka luna i ka maka o ka opua
Hai hewa ka lima i ke kaua kamalii
E i aku ke kaua i ka hope
Me he ku la na ke kai hohonu
Me ka hiwehiwe a Kauakahi
He opua oe, he kakala kela
Na ka ole ka hue a ke aki-e
E a Kauahoa ka ui o Hanalei
Ala o Kamalama ka ui o Kualoa
Ala o Kawelo ka ui o Waikiki
Ala o Kaelehapuna ka ui o Ewa
Ala o Kalaumeki ka ui o Waianae
Huhue aku kaua moe i ke awakea.
Kapae ke kaua e ka hoahanau
Ewaiho ia'u i kou hoahanau.
Aole hoe na la o kuu hoike
Kuu hoa hele o ka wa kamalii
Hoa kui lehua o Waikaee
A kaua e kui kane ai
I lei no ke kaikuaana haku o kaua.
E ala e Hanalei

Hanalei aina anuanu
Aina koekoe
Aina a ka pea i noho ai
E-a Kauahoa
Ka meeui o Hanalei-a."

Second: The mele koihonua, which detail and celebrate the genealogies and exploits of the famous chiefs and legendary heroes. The epic you have studied is the Odyssey. I suppose that the whole of "Kawelo" should be considered a mele koihonua. However, my example is from the "Haui ka Lani," perhaps the most famous Hawaiian poem, which is a prophesy as well as an epic, as the first canto was composed by Keaulumoku eight years before the defeat of Keoua by Kamehameha. We have two translations, one by Judge Andrews and one by Mr. Thrum, but as Andrews' is far better both as poetry and as a literal translation, I have chosen his to give you.

"Fallen is the Chief; overthrown is the kingdom,
Gasping in death, scattered in flight;
An overthrow throughout the land;—
A hard panting from the rapid flight;
Countless the numbers from the universal rout.
The night declares the slaughter.
There extended lay my conquering night,—
Mine own night, dark and blinded,
Falling on the road, falling on the sand;
The sovereignty and the land
United in the Chief, are passed away.
The royal dignity and glory of the Chiefs are lost.
The many also in high places,
There are they now, humiliated.
They are shaken, scattered abroad, impoverished, crushed:
Their women mercilessly slain.
Two signs appear of the great slaughter;
The house of death with them, the house of safety here,
Here triumph for him, there destruction for them.
The land is conquered, its Chiefs are overthrown;

The day of Hoku is arisen on the land:
The mountain tops are bare,
Blasted by the hot whirlwinds of Heaven, they stand
Withering up. The stench rises to Heaven;
The stench of the night, struggles with the burning
heat of the day,
The scent overcometh. The bluffs are scorched.
The mountains are covered with pointed, rushing clouds
bearing stormy winds.
The glory of the land is fled.
The spirit of the island has flown upward,
(The pebbles of Palila appear)
Cast aside into the place of death: Kau is dead!
Kau is slain by these.
The ghosts approach, weak and staggering.
Even the enlarged ghosts of the land—
The three ghosts of the lands of Kau, of Puna, of Hilo.
Not lately they fled, long ago were they vanquished
by the Chief.
Then was finished the sacrifice offered by Ku,
The ghosts are crowded together,—they are dead,
Flown to the pit of oblivion, to the pit where regret
cometh not.

Alas for them, now grieving in sadness!
Everywhere mourning their losses!
They sit constantly with heads bowed down;
They sit with hands beneath their chins;
They feed upon their sadness and grief.
Sweet is the food of men; their constant food is flight.
The fire of death rages among them; O thou Kalani-
makua;
Puna is dead! Puna is dead! Puna is thrice dead!
They are dying, gasping for breath;
They catch the breath, they hiccough; the hiccough
ends the breathing;
The breath and the breathing are over, the spirit has
fled.
They have forsaken the sunlight,—the place of warmth;
They have gone down to darkness, the place of the cold;

They have leaped into darkness, the place of shivering.
The light is lost; the warmth is for desolation;
The day hath passed over to the Chief,—the father and his people.
Only one father is over the island now.
Let the Chief live forevermore;
Let him live a chief till the coming of death;
Till the coming of the death of his land;
Till the coming of the death of his district of Hilo.
Hilo is as dead; even Waiakea;
Hilo is cast down the precipice of death;
Death bursts forth on Hilo, the dying of Hilo is twisted as a cord;
The mountain part of Hilo is dead, the other part wails in dying;
Even now dead; Hilo is utterly destroyed, lost in darkness."

L. A.

HAUI KA LANI

"He wanana no ka make ana o na aina ia Kamehameha

Na Keaulumoku

PAUKU I

Haui ka lani, ka mauli au honua,
He mauli hau lani, malolo auhee—
He malolo auhee hulimoku keia;
He ana hanui keia no ke auhee la!

Ke hai mai nei ka po i ka hee,
Ua ka ilaila kuu po auhee—
Kuu po maoli, makole, ka ala,
Hina wale i ke ala kapapa, ke one;
Ke au me ka honua,
Ua lilo, eia la ia ka lani,
Ua hele kino alii, ka hanohano.

O ke kini hoi i kahi kiekie,
Aia hoe i kahi haahaa;

Ua luia, ua helelei, ua hune, ua make,
Ua pepehi wale ia kana wahine,
Ke ku la na kii elua i ka paupau make,
Ka hale make ia lakou, ka hale ola ia ia nei;
Ka lanakila ia ia nei, ke auhee ia lakou.

Ua hee kela aina he alii make,
He malama aina i o Hoku,
Ua omea ia ke kuahiwi
Ku kamaehu owela uluwela ka lani.
Ua kamae, ke ku nei ka maea lani,

Hakoko maea ka po hahana koehana ke ao,
Ua maea lani, wela ke kuahiwi,
Ua kaiopua kaiawe na mauna,
Ua lele ka hoaka o ka aina,
Ka uhane o ka moku eia iluna,
Ua ikea na iliili a Palila.
Ua hoolei ia i kahi make,—Kau make la,
Make Kau e lakou nei,
Ke newa mai nei ka uhane,
Ka uhane kinowailua o ka aina,

Ke kinowailua o na kolu o Kau, o Puna, o Hilo,
E oe kala i hee ai, he luahi kahiko, na ka lani,
Ua noa i ka hai ia e Ku.
Ua laumiloia na uhane, ua make,
Ua lele i ka lua pau aia i ka lua mihi ole.

PAUKU II

Nani lakou e mimimihi nei,
Ua mihi aku ua mihi mai,
Ua haakulou wale ka noho ana,
Ua kalele na lima i ka auwae,
Ua ai i ke ana i ke kenaa,

Inai i ka ia o kanaka, o ka ia mau no ka hee;
Ua hoaa ia no ka make, e Kalanimakua e.
Make Puna e! make Puna!! Makemake Puna ! ! !
Ua na ka noho ana, ke kaili nei ka nae,
Ua kaahiki mauliawa, ua kona mauliawa ke ea,

Ua lilo ke ea me ka hanu, ua haalele loa ke aho:
Haalele lakou i na la, i kahi mehana,
Lilo lakou i ka po i kahi anu;
Kaa i ka hakapo i kahi koekoe,
Lilo ka la, ka mehana ia mehameha,

Lilo ke ao ia Kalanimakua ma;
Noho hookahi makua i luna o ka moku;
Kau i ka puaneane ola ke alii,
Ola ka lani i kona haili make,

I ka haili make o kona aina,

I ka haili make o kona moku o Hilo;
He ano make o Hilo—Waiakea;
Lumia Hilo i kaulu o ka make,
Lele make Hilo, hilo ka make ana o Hilo,
Make Hilopaliku, ke uwe mai o Hilo, nei make,
Aia make-a make loa Hilo, nalo i ka polioia."

Third: We have the mele kuo—paeans, songs of praise. The 100th Psalm which you studied in school is also a paean.

The examples I have for you of mele kuo are:

First: The 4th Canto of "Haui ka Lani."

"To the chief belongs the whole land;
To the Chief belongs the ocean and the land;
The night is his; the day is his;
For him are the seasons,—the winter, the summer,
The month, the seven stars of heaven now risen.
The property of the Chiefs, above and below,
All things that float ashore, the bird driven upon the land,
The thick-shelled, broad-backed turtle, the dead whale is cut up;
The yearly Uhu of the sea.
Let the Chief live forever! Evermore a Chief!
Let him be borne forth gloriously with the short gods and the long gods.
Let him go forth fearlessly, the Chief holding the Island.

Let the dance begin, dancing on the dancing ground.
Let the dancers rise and fall in ranks throughout the land;
The rising of this one and that one like the tiresome road to Hilo,
Passing on from ridge to ridge." L. A.

PAUKU IV

"No ka lani ka moku, ka honua,
Ka uka, ka moana no ka lani;
Nona ka po, nona ke ao,
A, nona ke kau, ka hooilo, ka makalii,
Ka malama, ka huihui hoku lani e kau nei.
Ke kapolapilau oluna olalo;

No ke alii ka ukana kikoola;
O ka haopae, o ka manu pae i ka honua,
O ka ea makaulii me ka palaoa,
Ka uhu kai o ka makahiki.
Niaupio ka lani, ke kupa ai au,

Kaa niau ka lana, ke 'kuapoko, ke 'kualoa;
Holo kapapa, a he aliiaimoku o ka lani;
Ku ka hula, haa ka papa haa,
Ulu papa mahimahi na moku,
I ka pii, i kana pii, pii ke ala o ana Hilo."

Second: The beginning of "Maikai Kauai."

"Beautiful is Kauai beyond compare,
She sends forth a bud in the summit of Waialeale,
She flowers in the heights of Kawaikini,
Her strength radiates in awful splendor from the Alakai;
Though I weary, though I faint, she renews my strength in her soft petals:
I have myself beheld Maunahina!
Beautiful, serene, all surpassing, here is Hihimanu!
The imprint of her hand is all-embracing, far-reaching, tantalizing:
For none other do I yearn; she is all that is good, none other can compare.
Hear me, Light of my Eyes, as I cry—You are like a young

green fern, spangled with dew.
I am ensnared, I can not turn in the sands of Mahamoku.
I slip on the seaweed, I fall; overcome is the man of Maunakepa.
Splashing upward is the rain of Hanalei,
Brandished again are the hala of Haena by the wind,
None other is your peer, O Hoohila!
As resistless as the sea, so is my desire, strong as the sucking wind.
Life-Protected by the Heavens, my heavenly one, this is your name!
Borne to the heights are the fires of Kalalau
You surpass the flaming torches of Mahuaiki,
I cling fast, asking no return, to the flame flung from Kamaile
Licking up the dry brands, the proud torches of Napali,
The water cools the consuming flames of Kaholanui
The brands make a cloak of shining feathers for the sea at Nualolo."
E. R. P.

MAIKAI KAUAI HEMOLELE I KA MALIE

"Maikai Kauai hemolele i ka malie,
Kupu kelakela ke poo o Waialeale,
Kela i ka lani kilakila Kawaikini,
Ka no ka helekua linohau Alakai,
Maloeloe ka laau huli e mai ka pua,
Ke ike iho ia Maunahina.
He makai, he nani, he hemolele ke alo o Hihimanu,
I ana kapuai lima ia ka nui, ka loa, ka laula, ka hene o na kuahiwi,
Aole a'u mea maikai ole olaila
He makamaka ke oho o ka palai lipolipo i ka ua,
Ke hopu aku i ke one o Mahamoku,
Pahee i ka limu kaha kanaka o Munakepa.
Kapekupeku iluna ka ua o Hanalei,
Owala lua na hala o Haena i ka makani,
Aole wahi hemahema o Hoohila,
Miki ke kai miki kaupale, miki ka apo'na a ka makani,
O Keolaokalani ke'lii nona ia inoa,

Auamo iluna ke ahi o Kalalau,
I'i ka welo'na a ke ahi komo i Makuaiki,
Pipili mamau ke ahi hele i Kamaile
Miki maloo ke ahi haaheo i Napali
I hooma'u wai ia ke ahi komo i Kaholanui
Kuehu ka laau me ka mamo kukupa'u ke kai o Nualolo."

In this poem we have a very good example of an inner meaning, as it is obviously a love song, as well as a paean as it ostensibly purports to be in praise of the island of Kauai. It might be classed as an ode, also.

Fourth: The mele olioli, which are lyrics and odes. In the poems you have studied in English, Ben Jonson's "To the Memory of my Beloved Master, William Shakespeare" and his "Song to Celia" are lyrical odes. Also in "As You Like It," Jacques' song, "Blow, Blow Thou Winter Wind" is a lyric. Like it my example is taken from a larger work—again from our "Kawelo," Wm. Hyde Rice's translation.

"Hanalei, the land of cold and wet,
Hanalei, the land where the clouds hover!
The Ukiukiu, the northerly storm, of Hanakoa,
The cliffs of Kalehuaweki are in vain.
The lama and wiliwili are in flower.
The rain that flies beyond Mamalahoa
Is like Kauahoa, the man that Kamalama will defeat."

W. H. R.

"O Hanalei aina ua
Aina anuanu
Aina koekoe
Aina a ka pea i noho ai
Noho ana ka ukiuki o Honokoa
I ka pali o Kalehuawehe
Pua ke lama me ka wiliwili.
O ka ua lele mawaho o Mamalahoa
O Kauahoa ka Meeui o Hanalei
O ke kanaka a Kamalama i hopo ai o Kauahoa
He mea e ka nui--e--a
Eia ka hoi ua kanaka nui o Kauai o Kauahoa."

Fifth: The mele paeaea—provocative songs, of a vulgar sort, which we need not take up.

Sixth: Mele inoa, name songs, panegyrics, songs in praise of some person. There are many examples of these, but I have chosen to give you the mele inoa of Nahie, translated by Emerson.

A NAME-SONG, A EULOGY (FOR NAIHE)

"The huge roller, roller that surges from Kona,
Makes loin-cloth fit for a lord;
Far-reaching swell, my malo streams in the wind;
Shape the crescent malo to the loins—
The loin-cloth the sea, cloth for king's girding,
Stand, gird fast the loin-cloth!

Let the sun guide the board Halepo,
Till Halepo lifts on the swell.
It mounts the swell that rolls from Kahiki,
From Wakea's age onrolling.
The roller plumes and ruffles its crest.

Here comes the champion surf-man,
While wave-ridden wave beats the island,
A fringe of mountain-high waves.
Spume lashes the Hiki-au altar—
A surf this to ride at noontide.

The coral, horned coral, it sweeps far ashore.
We gaze at the surf at Ka-kuhi-hewa.
The surf-board snags, is shivered;
Maui splits with a crash,
Trembles, dissolves into slime.

Glossy the skin of the surf-man;
Undrenched the skin of the expert;
Wave-feathers fan the wave-rider.
You've seen the grand surf of Puna, of Hilo." N. E.

HE NELE INOA (NO NAIHE)

"Ka nalu nui, a ku ka nalu mai Kona,
Ka malo a ka mahiehie,
Ka onaulu-loa a lele ka'u malo.

O kakai malo hoaka,
O ka malo kai, malo o ke alii.
E ku, e hume a paa i ka malo.

E ka'ika'i ka la i ka papa o Kalepo;
A pae o Halepo i ka nalu.
Ho-e'e i ka nalu mai Kahiki;
He nalu Wakea, nalu ho'ohua.
Haki opu'u ka nalu, haki kua-pa.

Ea mai ka makakai he'e-nalu,
Kai he'e kakala o ka moku,
Kai-ka o ka nalu nui,
Ka hu'a o ka nalu o Hiki-au.
Kai he'e-nalu i ke awakea.

Ku ka puna, ke ko'a i-uka.
Ka makaha o ka nalu o Kuhihewa.
Ua o ia, noha ka papa!
Noha Maui, nauweuwe,
Nauweuwe, nakelekele.

Nakele ka ili o ka i he'e-kai.
Lalilali ole ka ili o ke akamai;
Kahilihili ke kai a ka he'e-nalu.
Ike'a ka nalu nui o Puna, o Hilo."

Seventh: The mele ipo, love songs. I have chosen an example translated by Emerson of a song used in the hula. I also give my own more literal translation.

First Translation

"Fragrant the grasses of high Kane-hoa.
Bind on the anklets, bind!
Bind with finger deft as the wind
That cools the air of this bower.
Lehua blooms pale at my flower,
O sweetheart of mine,

Bud that I pluck and wear in my wreath,
If thou wert but a flower!" N. E.

Second Translation

"Fragrant is the grass of upland Kane-hoa,
Bind on the anklets, bind!
Bind with the hand of the soughing wind, Wai-kaloa.
Balmy Wai-kaloa, wind cooling Lihue,
Blemished is the lehua before my cloud from the sea,
My loved one, my flower—
Flower I yearn to bind in my lei,
O, that you were as near as my lei—be my lei!" E.R.P.

MELE KU-PE'E

"Aala kupukupu ka uka o Kane-hoa.
E ho-a!
Hoa na lima o ka makani, he Wai-kaloa.
He Wai-kaloa ka makani anu Lihue.
Alina lehua i kau ka opua—
Ku'u pua,
Ku'u pua i'ini e ku-i a lei.
Ina ia oe ke lei 'a mai la."

The lei is another form of the oldest love symbol, the ring. As you can see, these mele ipo are highly figurative.

Eighth: The mele Kanikau, dirges or laments. An example of a dirge that you have had in school is Milton's Lycidas—"Yet once more, O ye Laurels, and once more, ye myrtles brown with Ivy never sear"—The sound of it alone conveys the lament.

My examples are, first, Kamamalu's lament as she left Hawaii with her husband, Kamehameha the Second, never to return:

"Ye skies, ye plains, ye mountains and great sea,
Ye toilers, ye people of the soil, my love embraces you,
To this soil, farewell!
Yea, land for whose sake my father was eaten by deep
sorrow—farewell! alas! farewell!" E.R.P.

KAMAMALU'S LAMENT

"E ka lani, e ka honua, e ka mauna, e ka moana,
E ka hu, e ka makaainana, aloha oukou;

E ka lepo, aloha oe.
E ka mea a kuu makuakane i eha ai, auwe oe!"

Another beautiful dirge is this, preserved by Ellis. have kept the old spelling in the Hawaiian version.

"Alas, alas, dead is my chief,
Dead is my lord and my friend;
My friend in the season of famine,
My friend in the time of drought,
My friend in my poverty,
My friend in the rain and the wind,
My friend in the heat and the sun,
My friend in the cold from the mountain,
My friend in the storm,
My friend in the calm,
My friend in the eight seas;
Alas, alas, gone is my friend,
And no more will return." Ellis.

"Ne, Ne, ua mate tuu Arii
Na mate tuu hatu e tuu hoa
Tuu hoa i ta wa o ta wi,
Tuu hoa i paa ta aina
Tuu hoa i tuu ili hune
Tuu hoa i ta ua e ta matani
Tuu hoa i ta uera o ta la
Tuu hoa i ta anu o ta mauna
Tuu hoa i ta ino
Tuu hoa i ta marie
Tuu hoa i mau tai awaru
Ne, ne, ua hala tuu hoa
Aohe e hoi hou mai."

In connection with this old spelling of the consonants, the "t" instead of the "k" sound was much used in poetry.

Ninth: The mele pule or prayers. Sometimes these also took the form of responsive prayers, spoken first by the priest, and then by the people.

Here is an English adaptation of the form, a poem "Hawaiian Fisherman's Prayer" written by my sister, Juliet Rice Wichman.

"To you, the Great Sea, and the Small Sea,
The Sea at Morning and the Sea at Night,
To you the Father of all waters,
My nets are light.

Haven of little snub nosed fishes,
The Great Shark's lair,
To you I offer my libation,
Grant me my prayer.

Grant me full waters for my fishing,
Grant me a flecking sea,
A thousand thousandth of your plenty,
The word is spoken—it is free." J. R. W.

And last of my examples is this beautiful prayer, translated very literally by Wm. Hyde Rice in his "Hawaiian Legends." He says: "This is the prayer used by the kahuna ana-ana, who can pray to death, and who can also defend from death, when they pray in these words to ward off the evil that is keeping the sick one down:"

"To You, who are the breath of the Eighth Night:
To You, Kane, the Yellow Edge of Night:
To You, Kane, the Thunder that Rumbles at Night:
To You, Kane, Kamohoalii, Brother of Pele, Sea of Forgiveness:
To You, Ku, Kane, and all the other Gods that hold up the Heavens:
And likewise the Ku, the Goddess women that hold up the night:
To You, Kane, Who is bristling, to Ku, and to Lono:
To You, Lono, Who is awakening as the sun rises:
To All of You in the Night: Stand up!
Let the Night pass, and Daylight come to me, the Kahuna.
Look at our sick one: If he be dying from food eaten in

the day,
Or from tapa, or from what he has said,
Or from pleasures he has had a part in,
Or from walking on the highway,
From walking, or from sitting down,
Or from the bait that has been taken,
Or from parts of food that he has left,
Or from his evil thoughts of others,
Or from finding fault, or from evils within,
From all deaths: Deliver and forgive!
Take away all great faults, and all small faults,
Throw them all into Moana-nui-kai-oo, the great ocean!
If Ku is there, or Hina: Hold back death!
Let out the big life, the small life,
Let out the long life, for all time:
That is the life from the Gods.
This is the ending of my prayer
It is finished; Amama ua noa." W. H. R.

HE MOOLELO NO KA POE MANEHUNE

"Ia oe e Ku-i-ke-olo-walu i ka po
Ia Kane-i-ka-pua-lana i ka po
Ia Kane-i-ka-poha-kaa i ka po
Ia Kane Kamoholii i kai kala e
Ina Ku Kane no apu o ka paa iluna
Pela no na ku wahine apau o ka po
Ia Kane-i-ko-kala, ku e lono e
E Lono-i-ka-uweke i ka haikala la e
Ia oukou no apu i ka po ku mai
Pale ka po, pukai i ke ao, ia'u nei la
(Inoa o ke Kahuna)
E nana ia mai ka ma'i a kakou
Ina he make i ka ai i ka la
I ke kapa, i ka olelo, i ka lealea e,
I ke kaha mana alanui la
I ka hele ana, i ka noho ana,
I ka maunu lilo, hakina mea ai la,
Ka ohumu, ke keemoa, ka nonohua,
I na make no apau, e uweke, e kala ia.

Lawe ia aku na hala nui, na hala liilii
A kiola, hoolei loa i Moana-nui-kai-oo.
Ina ilaila o Ku, me Hina, paa ia ka make
Kuu ia mai ke ola nui, ke ola iki,
Ke ola loa no, i ka pua aneane,
Ke ola ka hoi ia a ke Akua,
Elieli kapu, elieli noa, noa loa no."

I wish I had time to tell you of several other forms of poems, serenades to Royalty, songs to awaken a high chief, and so on, also something of the censoring done to prevent any words or thoughts of evil omen entering a mele, especially mele inoa, but time does not permit.

In conclusion, I hope I have shown you what a beautiful and precious inheritance you possess in your Hawaiian culture—and remember I have talked about only one part of it.

BIBLIOGRAPHY

1 The Islander: Articles and translations by Judge Lorrin Andrews.

2 The Unwritten Literature of Hawaii: Nathaniel Emerson.

3 Pele and Hiiaka: Nathaniel Emerson.

4 Hawaiian Legends: William Hyde Rice.

5 La Hanau o Ka Moi: King Kalakaua.

6 The Fornander Collection.

7 The Dial—April 1924—Article and Poems by Padriac Colum.

8 New York Herald Tribune: Review of "Hawaiian Legends" by William Hyde Rice, written by Padraic Colum.

Other material was from direct sources and unpublished manuscripts and collections of poems.

CHAPTER 18

MUSIC

JANE LATHROP WINNE

Music, generally speaking, includes both melody and harmony. Vocal music implies poetic expression. Rhythm is an element of both instrumental and vocal music, and when we think of instrumental music we have before us all the range of instruments of orchestra and band. The music of ancient Hawaii was not characterized by what we call melody and harmony. It was almost entirely vocal, a natural expression of poetical and rhythmical impulses. Let us consider first some modern songs which contain survivals of old forms.

SURVIVALS OF OLD FORMS IN MUSIC TODAY

The words of many familiar modern songs have been adapted from the old poetry or meles. Even today certain composers depend very largely upon the old meles for the texts of their songs. If, for instance, a selection in honor of Queen Emma were desired, a tune might be composed for one of the Queen's chants. Of this type is "Wahine Hele La O Kaiona," dedicated to the High Chiefess Bernice Pauahiokalani (Mrs. C. R. Bishop) and composed by Prince Leleiohoku. The chorus and second stanzas are old; the rest, describing Mrs. Bishop's trip to Niagara is of course of later composition.

WAHINE HELE LA O KAIONA

"Honi ana i ke anu, i ka mea huihui,
Hui hewa e ka ili, i ka ua Poaihala,
Lei ana i ka mokihana ka wewehi o Kaiona,
Lihau pue ike anu hauoki o Kaleponi.

Hiaai aku welina, ka nenee a ka ohelo papa,
Puapua i ka noe, mohaha i ke anu,
Noho no me ka anoi ka manao ia loko,
Oloko hana nui pau ole i ke ana ia.

A ka wailele o Niakala, ike i ka wai anunue,
I ka poaiai a ka ohu halii paa ilaila,
Pue ana i ka ehu wai pupuu i ke koekoe,
Eia iho ka mehana o ka poli o Hiilei.

Chorus-

E o e ka wahine, hele la o Kaiona,
Alualu wailiula o ke kaha pua ohái,
O ka ua lani polua po anu o ke Koolau,
Kuu hoa o ka malu ki malu kukui o Kahoiwai."

This Hawaiian version is recorded in the Bishop Museum and is given here through the kindness of Mrs. Lahilahi Webb.

Mrs. Mary Kawena Pukui has translated it into English as follows;

"Braving the cold and all things which chill,
A pelting cold, like that of the rain of Poaihala,
She wears a wreath of mokihana, the adornment of Kaiona,
As she shivers in the icy cold snow of Kaleponi.

We extend to her our love, like the ohelo plants that
Snuggle close in the mist and thrive in the cold.
There she stays enfolded in love, possessed with thoughts
That are exalted and unfathomable.

At the falls of Niagara where she saw the rainbow's arch,
In the all-surrounding mists, spreading tightly about,
Chilled was she with the wet sprays, shivered she in the cold,
Here warmth could be found in the bosom of Hiilei.

Answer to your name song, O Lady of the sunshine of Kaiona,
Where the mirage is seen amongst the ohai of the plain.
In the shifting rains of the heavens, the cold rains of the Koolau.
My companion of the sheltering ki and kukui shade of Kahoiwai."

The song "Hole Waimea" composed by Prince Leleiohoku is another illustration of this same method, that is, of setting an old mele to modern music. Still another example is "Waipio" which is in origin a very old chant. In its melodic setting of more modern times, its hula-like tune and the suggestion of hoaeae in the prolonged ending of each line might be considered imitations of old forms. This song is printed in King's Collection of Hawaiian Melodies.

WAIPIO

Aia i Waipio Pakaalana,
Paepae kapu ia o Liloa.

He aloha ka wahine pii i ka pali,
Puili ana i ka hua ulei.

I ka ai mo'a i ka lau laau,
Hoolaau mai o ka welowelo,
E ola o Kukaikeolaewa e.

The simple tune and characteristic rhythms of the hula have persisted and may be perceived in songs other than the regular dance melodies. The hula mele, sometimes very old in origin, always closed with the conventional phrase, "Haina ia mai ana ka puana" (thus ends my song"), or some one of its variations. Likewise in the popular modern song, "Na Lei O Hawaii," we note the same traditional phrase at the close.

Highly figurative expression, characteristic of the ancient mele, is also typical of modern Hawaiian songs. The words of these songs are seemingly descriptive of nature, as of flowers or places; in reality, they refer to persons and emotions.

The old poetry and the more modern song alike show tendencies to emphasize euphony and rhythm. One feature which produced harmony of line and couplet was a form of repetition called by some authorities, "linked assonance." In the following mele quoted from Roberts' Ancient Hawaiian Music,the end of each couplet is repeated exactly or in similar sounds at the beginning of the next couplet.

"Onaona na maka o Leialoha
Ua pulu i ka wai lohi o Maleka.

Ma ka leka kuu ike lihi ana iho
Hoopulu i ka welelau lihilihi.

A he lihi kuleana ko'u ilaila
Eia ka iini i ka puuwai.

Waiwai ke aloha hiipoi nei
A na'u a nau no kekahi.

Hookahi hoi au, hookahi oe
A i kolu i ke aheahe makani.

Ke aheahe kehau na ke ahe lauae
A i lawe mai ke elele waha ole."

The same form of euphony occurs frequently between successive lines. In the modern songs of David Nape and Charles Hopkins we may find survivals of this same feature, as noted in these lines from various songs:

O ka lei o Kamakaeha
No Kamakaeha ka lei na lia wahine,
Na wahine kihene pua.

A pili na kuu puuwai
Waiwai nui oe na'u.

O ka honehone mai a ka wai
Wai poai olu o Punalau.

Honi ana ike ala
He ala kupaoa.

Ike ia Eka inu wai
O ka wai no ia pono kaua.

Ko aniani mai nei e ke ahe
Ahea oe hoolono mai.

I luna o Wailana
Lana ae ka manao e kii.

Ua hookohu ka ua iuka, noho mai la i Nuuanu
Anuanu makehewa au, i ke kali ana ilaila.

The last illustration just given is from the well known song, "Alekoki."

Composers in the old days considered well the kaona of a song. This term refers to the significant power believed to lie in the inner meaning of words which would affect the person concerned in the song. Some modern composers still regard this belief.

These then are some of the characteristics which tie the modern song to the days of the old poetry: (1) the actual use of the old mele in the new song; (2) the survival of certain old phrases; (3) the survival of melodic and rhythmic forms, especially in the hula; (4) highly figurative expression; (5) dominant rhythm and euphony frequently expresed in definite forms of repetition; (5) regard for kaona.

OLD FORMS

Numerous selections may be found in Roberts' Ancient Hawaiian Music which is an authoritative and detailed study of old forms. The early music may be considered in two general classifications,—(1) chant or oli; (2) dance or hula. The dance movement naturally suggested vocal movement, hence we find in the hula an approach to real melody with marked rhythmic accompaniment. Oli was a chant or intonation, a solo performance, unaccompanied. Under this term are therefore included all meles not intended for dancing.

The most usual styles of chanting were known as kepakepa, oli and hoaeae. The kepakepa was the simplest form. It was given in rhythmical conversational tone. The oli, with its deep chest quality, demanded natural vocal ability and superior breath control to sustain the excessively long phrases. Throughout the rapid movement of syllables the pitch was maintained on a general level.

Drops and inflections of voice occurred naturally at breathing places and a modified trill was usual at the end of a phrase. The hoaeae was more regular in form and more emotional. Each couplet ended with the prolonging of the vowel producing an effect similar to trilling. According to some authorities this form was used only for hooipoipo, or love chants.

THE MELE

The mele was the poetry of the chant In the elaborate system of ancient days life was a continuous ceremony and there was an appropriate mele for every occasion. The following classes of meles may be noted. A more detailed list may be found in Roberts' Ancient Hawaiian Music.

1. Pule and wanana (prayers and prophecies) for planting, fishing, building, etc.
2. Mele inoa (name chants) lauded the chief, the heroic deeds of ancestors, etc.
3. Ko'ihonua (genealogies)
4. Kanikau (dirges)
5. Hooipoipo (love songs)
6. Mele kaua (war poems)
7. Mele haku-kole (in derogation of an individual.)
8. Miscellaneous or topical, as for contests, clothing, etc.

These chants had certain elements found in all music, though they did not sound tuneful. Prehaps we should call it dynamic form. Throughout Hawaiian literature, we find persistent balance and proportion, word against against word, line against line, repetition, contrast. Through such means, form is built up. While there was not a great variation of tone, there was beauty of language and fine distinction in voice inflection. The people enjoyed meles, not only because of the story, but because they appreciated the rhythm and harmony of the phrases. In the examples which follow, both the Hawaiian and English versions may be studied in the reference volumes here noted:

"Fallen is the Chief; overthrown is the kingdom,
Gasping in death, scattered in flight.

To the Chief belongs the whole land;
To the Chief belongs the ocean and the land;
The night is his; the day is his;
For him are the seasons,—the winter, the summer,
The month, the seven stars of heaven now risen."

This illustration just given is from Keaulumoku's great prophecy of twelve cantos, "Haui Ka Lani." It foretold the ascendency of Kamehameha I. Further detail may be found in The Islander, Vol. 1, 1875, and in Volume VI of the Fornander Collection of Folklore.

Lines from the canoe chant, in the story of Kana, Fornander Collection of Folklore Vol. IV, part 3, give a good example of balance through repetition of phrases. There is also in lines 4-7, a very nice rhythmical climax through a word series.

"Get the canoe!	"E kii i ka waa!
Get the canoe!	E kii i ka waa!
From your grandmother's	I ko kupuna wahine
To Hoanuiikamapu,	Ia Hoanuiikamapu,
To Hoanuiwaalau,	Ia Hoanuiwaalau,
To Hoanuiwiliwiliwaa,	Ia Hoanuiwiliwiliwaa
To Hoanuihoonohowaa."	Ia Hoanuihoonohowaa."

After 8 lines there is this variation:

"E kii, e kii, e kii ka waa!
E kii ka waa Kaimu a Kainalu."

From a mele in the story of Kamapuaa, the use of couplets and contrasts may be noted in these lines:

"The small god is mine,
The large god is mine,
The long god is mine,
The short god is mine."

Later in the same mele, we find this illustration of repetition and contrast:

"The small night,
The large night,
The long night,
The short night,
The small cloud is here,
The large cloud is here,
The long cloud is here,
The short cloud is here."

A mele in the story of Kuapakaa, in Fornander's Folklore, Vol. V, part 1, contains these lines:

"Over the great waves, the little waves,
Over the long waves, the short waves,
Over the long-backed waves of the ocean."

"That block of wood, this block of wood (the waves),
That rope is drawn, this rope is drawn;
Some will rush there, some will rush here,
The large wave will rise,
The small wave will break,
The sticks at the bow will fly off,
The sticks at the stern will fly off."

Kuapakaa tries to save his father in flight from the king by swamping the king's canoes. He chants all the names of the winds and rains of each district on every island. Here is a short descriptive portion.

"There they are! There they are! There they are!
The apaapaa is of Kohala,
The naulu is of Kawaihae,
The kipuupuu is of Waimea,
The olauniu is of Kekaha,
The pili-a is of Kaniku,
The ae is of Kiholo,
The pohu is of Kona,
The maaakualapu is of Kahaluu,
The pilihala is of Kaawaloa,
The kehau is of Kapalilua,
The puahiohio is of Kau,
The hoolapa is of Kamaoa,

The kuehulepo is of Naalehu,
The uwahipele is of Kilauea,
The awa is of Leleiwi,
The puulena is of Waiakea,
The uluau is of the cliffs of Hilo,
The koholalele is of Hamakua,
The holopoopoo is of Waipio,
The end of that wind,
The end of this wind,
Join and cause a whirlwind."

Couplets are very frequent, as noted in the following:

"Na aumakua i ka po,
Na aumakua i ke ao,
Ia pale i ka po,
A puka i ke ao."

THE LAND SHELL MELE

"Kahuli aku,
Kahuli mai,
Kahuli lei ula,
Lei akolea,
Kolea, kolea,
Hoi ka wai,
Wai akolea,
Kolea, kolea."

The chant then, had no tune, but the rhythm and form of the poetry itself gave it dynamic form, a recognized essential in all musical composition.

The art of the composer or haku mele was highly respected and was, like other Hawaiian skills, handed down from generation to generation. The haku mele himself was by nature a master of language and chanting, and besides had (1) an extensive knowledge of traditions and genealogies; (2) an inexhaustible store of geographical names, as of places, winds, rains, surf, etc.; (3) phenomenal memory, for a lapse or wrong word was an ill omen; (4) understanding of kaona, the power of the inner meaning of words.

THE HULA

The hula was of fundamental significance in ancient Hawaii and must be understood from the point of view of its place in the old culture. The strict training and the ceremonies attending graduation at the completion of the instruction are described in another chapter. Although some very ancient hula meles have been preserved, little is known of the oldest dance forms. More than thirty different kinds of hulas are recorded by Dr. N. B. Emerson in "Unwritten Literature of Hawaii." It has already been noted that in hulas there was more tonal and rhythmic variety than in any of the chant forms. The most frequent intervals in its very simple tunes were the major second above the general level, and below the level the minor third and the perfect fourth. Two-part measure was usual, although other forms occurred. Phrases in pairs naturally followed the couplet forms of the mele. Suggestion of modulation extension and inversion may be occasionally noted.

MUSICAL INSTRUMENTS

Some of the instruments used as accompaniment for the hula have survived. We hear in the dance of today the ipu or gourd drum, the uliuli or coconut rattle, the puili or fringed bamboo rattle. On the other hand, the pu-niu, small coconut drum, and pahu, wooden kettle drum, are no longer used and rarely seen except in collections. These two drums were sometines used simutaneously as hula accompaniment. In this case the small drum was tied to the left thigh just above the knee and played with a fibre thong in the left hand, while the big pahu was slapped with the right hand. According to tradition the pahu was brought from Kahiki by Laa, the son of Kauai. Laa was also an expert in the hula and instructed the Hawaiians in his art. The many interesting episodes in the extensive voyages of Moikeha and his sons are told in "More Hawaiian Folk Tales" by Thrum and in "The Bright Islands" by Colum.

Besides these hula instruments there were two others

which are now only relics. The ukeke, a form of musical bow, was the only stringed instument. It was about an inch in width and varied in length from fourteen inches to two feet. Some instruments had two strings, others three. With the bow held horizontally between the lips the singer articulated the sounds of the chant, at the same time strumming the strings with the finger or with a fibre plectrum. The ohe ihu or nose flute had from one to three finger holes. Except for certain whistles and the conch shell the nose flute was the only wind instrument. The conch shell or ceremonial trumpet might be included in this list. All of these instruments may be studied at the Bishop Museum or from plates in Ancient Hawaiian Music.

MODERN FORMS

Since there were no real tunes in Hawaii before the coming of foreigners and since most of the early residents were missionaries we find that the hymn set the type for Hawaiian songs of the nineteenth century. Bible stories were often told in song. The story of Noah is here given as sung and translated by Mrs. Mary Kawena Pukui who learned it from her mother.

NOAH

Pane mai o Jehovah ia Noa me ka nahenahe
"E hana oe i hale nou no ke kai a ka Hinalii
Hookahi no mea nui o oe me ka ohana
Na holoholona maemae a pau loa o ke kula."

Hookomo papahiku o Noa ia lakou
A hele papalua na mea maemae ole
Hookahi no mea nui, o ke kauoha a Jehovah
I kane i wahine i mea hoolaha no ka honua apau.

A komo akula o Noa ame kona ohana
E hooko i na kauoha a Jehovah
Hookahi kanaha la ame na po pu hoi
Ka iliki a ka ua a hana mao ole, i ke kai a ka Hinalii.

Translation

Jehovah said to Noah in a gentle voice,

"Make yourself a house to withstand the flood.
This is very important for you and your family
And all the clean beasts of the fields."

Noah put them in in groups of seven,
While the unclean beasts went in in pairs.
One thing was important, that was Jehovah's command
That there be a male and a female to replenish the earth.

Then Noah and his family went into the house
In obedience to the comand of Jehovah.
Fully forty days and forty nights too
The rain poured in ceaseless torrents, making a flood.

These religious songs are not heard today to any extent, but they were a characteristic form of earlier composition. Whaling days left something of a stamp upon songs "heard about town," but only fragments of these seem to have survived.

Modern songs which had been gradually emerging expanded greatly during the regime of the Kalakaua dynasty. King Kalakaua, Queen Liliuokalani, Princess Likelike and Prince Leleiohoku were all singers and composers. With notable contemporaries they form the highlight of modern composition. Foreign instruments had found their way to Hawaii, among them the ukulele and guitar prototypes of which came with the Portuguese immigration. The influence of Captain Henry Berger who had come from Germany at the request of King Kalakaua was naturally a dominant one. Under his leadership the Royal Hawaiian Band was organized and disciplined in the rendering of the best classical music. He, too, was the one who arranged and harmonized Hawaiian songs. The ability attained by the Hawaiian band in its prime was quite remarkable. For nearly a half century Captain Berger rendered a most unusual and devoted community service.

The art of the oli is now known only to a few. Throughout Hawaii the harmonies of part songs dominate. Survivals of hula accompaniment mingle with the ukulele, guitar and all the instruments of the modern orchestra. The innate musical qualities of the Hawaiian were already evidenced in the first half of the century which followed foreign instruction. During that time the people achieved a phenomenal musical development, from chant to part-singing. At the present time there are many Hawaiian persons, who with a minimum of training, are contributing much to the musical life of these islands.

REFERENCES

Beckwith, Hawaiian Romance of Laieikawai, see Introduction.

Emerson, N. B. Unwritten Literature of Hawaii.

Fornander, Collection of Folklore, Bishop Museum Memoirs.

Roberts, Ancient Hawaiian Music.

CHAPTER 19

RIDDLES AND PROVERBS

HENRY P. JUDD

The Hawaiian language is musical and is very beautiful when it is spoken by those who pronounce it clearly and distinctly. Even if a person does not understand Hawaiian, he cannot help being interested by a fine Hawaiian orator who always is a master of graceful gesture as well as of fluent and musical speech.

We are going to examine some old expressions of wisdom among the Hawaiians, which illustrate their point of view. They show that the Hawaiian was a man who used his eyes and saw the interesting and significant things in the world of nature about him. He was clever in making comparisons between nature and human beings. He was always on the lookout for natural beauty and for interesting things. His old sayings contain considerable humor, which is a trait rare in "primitive" peoples. These expressions which follow are divided into groups, under topics which indicate the nature of the content.

NATURE AND NATURAL PHENOMENA

"Pua ke ko, ku mai ka hee"
When the sugar cane tassels, then the squid comes in. (This refers to the time in November when the cane tassels and indicates that this is the time to go for squid.)

"Pua ka wiliwili, nanahu ka mano"
When the wiliwili blossoms that is the time of the shark's bite.

"Kau ka iwa, he la makani"
When the frigate bird is flying, it is a windy day. (The Hawaiian says that is always a sure sign it is a windy day.)

"Uwe ka lani, ola ka honua"

When the heaven is crying, then the land is living. (This refers to the rain or a rainy time)

"Aia i ka maka o ka opua, ka wai"

If you see opua clouds at ten in the morning as you look from Kealakekua, it is a sure sign it will rain by afternoon.

"Ona hoku no na kiu o ka lani"

The stars are the spies of heaven. The stars are looking down to see what the people are doing on earth.

"Kukulu kalaihi a ka la i Mana"

This may be used when a person is boastful—an old expression about a man not telling the truth—a mirage.

"He kiu ka pua kukui na ka makani"

When the kukui blossoms fall down it is a sign of a strong wind that is coming.

"Kakai ka pua puaa i ka malie, he ino"

A storm is coming when you see pigs go single file up the trail; in fair weather they go up the trail in twos or threes but when a storm is coming they go one by one.

FISHING INDUSTRY OR THE OCEAN

We find a great many expressions pertaining to the ocean or fishing. As the Hawaiians came thousands of miles across the ocean, they steered by the stars, knew how to sail their canoes, to fish, to dive; they knew much about the ocean. There are 250 or more recorded sayings about the ocean, about the fishing, and about the fishing industry.

"Moe waa"—Canoe dream. A dream about a canoe was thought to be an unlucky sign.

"Pao'o lehei, aole kaheka komo ole"

This old Hawaiian saying applies to persons jumping from place to place, like politicians. These people jump from one salt pond to another.

"E wahi ka maka-ha, i pii ka ia"

Break away from bad habits, then you'll have good

friends. Or, you break open the soil at the maka-ha (fish pond) to let fish out; you break away from bad habits and then you will get good friends because if you keep bad habits you cannot hold good friends.

"Ua hewa ka ia a Umiamaka, he okea oloko"
Something is wrong with Umiamaka's fish; it is white inside.

"Hawawa ka heenalu, ha'i ka papa"
An inexperienced person.

"Aole loea i ka wai oopu"
It is no trouble at all to get the oopu; in other words, easy matters can be handled by anybody without brains; a smart man is not needed to get oopu, it is a simple matter.

"He mahoe he i'a hololua"
A two faced person.

"He ula, ka i'a noho i ka hapapa"
A person of limited means is like a lobster. He is usually near the shore.

"Ka ulua kapapa o ke kai loa"
A man of means is like the ulua; a very fine fish that is hard to catch and gives a good fight before you can get him in.

"Hoi hou no i ka ehu, me he moi"
Returning to former habits.

"Ahu ka alaala palu"
You have gathered a lot of ink bags, you have nothing.

"Aole e hiki i ka ia liilii ke ala i ka nui"
A low person cannot contend with a man of rank. Literally, a little fish cannot absorb a big fish.

"Aole make ka waa i ka ale o waho, aia no i ke ale oloko o ka waa"
We have more danger from internal trouble than from external trouble; the wave near at hand, not outside,

is the one that will give trouble.

"Nana kee ka ia i ka maunu ekaeka; he papai ka i'a e hoi ai"

The fish will look askance at poor bait and the only thing you will bring back is a crab; in other words, if you don't take good bait you can't expect big fish. Bad methods will bring only things easy to get.

"Hamama ka waha, he po i'a ole"

A sleepy person will not catch fish.

"I kahi e ka malie, hana e i ka makau"

Get ready for the fish in good weather.

"Ale kualoloa o ka moana"

A fighter's boast—back like long waves.

"Aohe hana a Kauhikoa, ua kau ka waa i ke aki"

When a man marries well, he takes it easy, he rests.

"Ola ka lawaia i kahi poo maunu"

Unlucky fishermen can eat the head of the bait. This is another way of saying you have not had good results.

ANIMALS AND PLANTS

"Pupuhi ka ulu o Keei, ua koe ka aaiole"

Breadfruit of Keei are gone, only windblown are left, or, the best men are gone, cripples left.

"He liilii aalii, aole e hina i ka makani"

He is a small person but he will not fall down, he will stand up and do his work.

"Mai lou i ka ulu iluna lilo, o lou hewa i ka ulu aaiole, eia iho no ka ulu i ke alo"

Don't marry a stranger, but one you know. In other words, don't reach for the breadfruit that is far off as it may not be as good as the one in front of you.

"Mai nana i ka laau maloo, aole mea loaa malaila"

Don't look at the dead limbs or branches of the tree, you will get nothing from it; a dead tree is like dead hopes, nothing is obtained therefrom.

"Lele aku ka manu hulu"
A rich person is a bird in full feathers or groomed nicely.

"Aohe nana, he mauu Hilo" (modern)
Never mind, it is Hilo grass. (Worthless)

"He hihi wale no ka ke kaunaoa iluna, aohe kumu, hookahi kumu o ka laau e hihi ana ke kaunaoa"
A parasite. It spreads upon the top, it crawls along in hedges, it has no trunk, it only spreads around, it is a parasite and lives off another bush.

"Haahaa haka, pau i ka iole"
An insignificant person. A low shelf is reached by the rat.

"I ka moa i hanai ia i ka la i oi aku mamua o ka moa i hanai ia i ka malu"
To make him strong, bring up your son in the sun. This is not a commonly known Hawaiian expression; it was found in an old mele.

"Ina e loaa ka punana o ke kolea, alaila loaa au ia oe"
Impossible to find. When you get the plover's nest, then I'll get you.

"Kikaha ka iwa i na pali"
Well-dressed man. The man-of-war bird dashes by the cliffs.

"Haehae ka manu, ke ale nei ka wai"
Hasten, no time for niceties. Tear the bird; the water is rippling.

DOMESTIC AND SOCIAL LIFE

"Hae ka ilio, alala ka puaa, kani ka moa, uwe ke keiki"
A noisy household is described as follows: the dogs bark, the pigs grunt, the rooster crows, the children are crying.

"Aole hale i piha i ka hoihoi; haawi ia mai, lawe mai no"

There is no house that is completely filled with joy because things are given, things are taken out; there is no household that has not expressed sorrow because of the uncertainties of life.

"I Kahiki ka ua, ako e ka hale"
Always prepared. While the rain is still far off, thatch your house.

"Ua pau ka wai oia punawai, ke pii mai la ka huahu'a lepo"
When there are no good arguments, there is abuse.

"He palupalu na hewa liilii i ka wa kolo, lolelua i ka wa kamalii; oolea i ka wa u'i; loli ole i ka wa oo; oni paa i ka wa elemakule"
Do not allow sins to get started.

"Pua ke ko, nee i ka hee holua"
After the first day you must work.

"Aohe i pau ka ike i kau halau"
Other sources of knowledge.

PERSONAL APPEARANCE

"Ka luahine moe nono o papa enaena Pele"
Describes Pele. The old woman who snores on the lava rocks.

"Ua ulu ke ko-kea"
Getting old.

"Lulu ka hee"
Long-legged man.

"Ku paku ka pali o Nihoa i ka makani"
Tall man. The cliff of Nihoa stands as a wind break.

"Mahina ke alo, pali ke kua"
Physically fit. Front like the moon, back like the cliff.

ETIQUETTE, MORALS, AND RELIGION

"Pau Pele, pau mano"
An oath. Consumed by Pele, consumed by sharks.

"Umi ia, i nui ke aho"

Hold on and take a long breath. An encouragement.

WARFARE, CHIEFS

"Imua e na pokii, a inu i ka wai awaawa, aohe hope e hoi mai ai"

Kamehameha's words before Iao. Forward, brethren, till ye drink the bitter waters; there is no means of retreat.

"He kii kanaka noho wale o kahi alii"

Everyone at the royal place must work. An image is the only thing that does not work in a king's household.

"Hana ka iwi a kanaka, hoohoa mai"

Let your bones mature, then attack me. A challenge.

MISCELLANEOUS

"Ku ka eha o na wahi auwaa liilii"

How the spray dashes up before the fleet of small canoes. Little people fuss more than big people.

"Liiliii ka ohiki, loloa ka lua"

Size does not limit accomplishments.

"Uala liilii o Kalepolepo"

Insignificant person. Small potatoes of Kalepolepo.

"Hu ka alaala"

The secret is out. The ink from the squid is exuding.

"I lele no ka lupe i ka pola"

Do not ignore small things.

"I pae mua oe, pao oe i ka wahie "

First man to shore attends to the fire.

SAYINGS ABOUT PLACES

"Paakiki kanaka o Kauai." (Niihau saying.) The Kauai men are hard.

This refers to the driving out of the spirits from Niihau. When a man came over in a canoe from Waimea the spirits sat up on the Pali. They saw the canoe come and land. There was an idol in the canoe house so they waited until the god went to sleep. The man hid behind the door and waited until the spirits came into the house. Then he set fire to the building and burned them all up.

"No Hanamaulu ka ipu puehu"
Implies stinginess. From Hanamaulu comes the empty gourd.

"Wawa ka menehune i Puukapele ma Kauai, puoho ka manu o ka loko o Kawainui, ma Koolaupoko, Oahu."
Murmurings can be heard far off. The hum of the voices at Puukapele, Kauai, startled the birds of Oahu.

"Aole au he kalai hoe no Puukapele"
I'm no fool. I am no paddlemaker from Puukapele.

"Hoi hou ka paakai i Waimea"
Coals to Newcastle. The salt is carried back to Waimea.

"Lewa i ke alahaka o Nualolo"
Destitute. Hanging on the rope ladder of Nualolo.

"Nani Leahi, he maka ia no Kahiki"
Beautiful Leahi pointing the road to Kahiki.

"Oahu maka ewaewa"
Unfriendly the eyes of the people of Oahu.

"A ka lae o ka Laau, pau ka pono a Kakina"
At Kalae, the right living taught by Mr.Thurston is gone.

"Maui poo hakahaka"
Maui of the empty head.

"Ka poe unaunahi hee o Kula"
Kula people know nothing about squid.

"O kula ka aina piha i ka eepe"
Kula, the land full of fools.

"Hawaii kua uli"
Verdure clad Hawaii.

"Kohala ka unupaa"
Kohala of the solid step.

"Hele poala i ke anu o Waimea"
Going in a circle in the cold of Waimea.

"Kawaihae—kai hawanawana"
Whispering sea.

"Hilo ka ua kani lehua"
The rain patters down and the lehua blossoms fall.

"Kalapana—ka niu moe"
Kalapana, the lying coconut.

"Lohiau Puna i ke akua wahine"
Puna is backward because of the Goddess of Fire.

"Punaluu kai haa i ka malihini"
Punaluu, the sea where the stranger dances (stranger standing in a canoe.)

"Kau-aina kipi"
The rebel land of Kau.

"Kau niu kua makalepo"
Great Kau of the dirty eyes.

"Keahou-kai nehe i ka iliili"
Keauhou, where the sea nestles in the pebbles.

"Kalaoa-ai poeleele"
Stingy. The people of Kalaoa eat in the dark.

"E Kona-kai opua i ka lai"
Kona of the calm seas.

RIDDLES

"Kuu Wahi loko. Hookahi no ia o loko. He ekolu makaha."
Pane: Niu.
My little fish-pond. It contains one fish. It has three outlets. A. A young coconut.

"Kuu punawai kau i ka pali" Pane: Niu.
My spring up on the cliff. A. A coconut.

"Ekolu pa a loaa ka wai." Pane: Niu.
Three walls and you reach water. A. Coconut.

"Hanau mai ua poohina." Pane: Pua-ko.

When it is born, it has gray hairs. A. Flower of the sugar cane.

"A lau a lau ke alinalina, hookahi no opihi koele."
Pane: Hoku ame ka mahina.
Many small shellfish, one large shellfish. A. Moon and stars.

"Kuu ia nona ka honua." Pane: Honu.
My fish which owns the earth. A. The turtle. (A play on "honu" in honua.)

"Kuu wahi kua kani mau, aohe wa hoomaha."
Pane: Ke Kai koo.
My kapa log that is always sounding without rest.
A. The sea beating in surf.

"Kuu wahi ia nona ka maka." Pane: Omaka.
My little fish for which is the eye. A. The omaka fish. (A play on "maka," eye)

"Kakahiaka eha wawae, awakea elua wawae, ahiahi ekolu wawae." Pane: Kanaka.
In the morning four legs, at noon two legs, at evening three legs: A. A man. (In youth, crawling; in maturity, walking; in old age, with a cane.)

"Kuu wahi manu, noho no a moe pu me kanaka. Aole ai i ka ai, aole no hoi inu i ka wai, ola no nae a elemakule. Owai ka inoa o ka manu?" Pane: Pueo.
My bird dwells and sleeps with men. Eats no food, drinks no water, but lives nevertheless to a ripe old age. What is the name of the bird? A. The pueo batten of the Hawaiian house. (A play on the word pueo, meaning owl or batten.)

"Kuu alii, hoi no a ka maka o ka honu, make."
Pane: Kamehameha.
My chief who returned to the eye of the turtle and died. A. Kamehameha the Great. He died at Kamakahonu (the eye of the turtle).

"Kuu wahi kanaka, moku ole ke oki ia." Pane: Aka.

My man that cannot be cut. A. Shadow.

"Kuu wahi hale—halau—loa, hookahi pou, elua puka." Pane: Ihu.
My little canoe house that has one post and two gates. A. The nose.

"Kuu mau waa kaulua, holo i ke ao, holo no i ka po, he umi ihu, elua hope." Pane: Na kapuai.
My canoes, going day and night, ten bowspirits, two sterns. A. The feet.

"Kuu ana ula, ku lalani na koa kapa keokeo." Pane: Na niho.
My red cave, white soldiers standing in line.
A. The teeth.

"Kuu wahi kanaka uwe ana i ka po ame ke ao, a puni ka makahiki." Pane: Kai.
My man crying day and night, all through the year. A. Sea.

"Kuu lei hala." Pane: Kohala.
My hala wreath. A. Kohala.

"Ia oe e ala ana i ke kakahiaka a hele, ehia olua?"
Pane: Elua—kino, aka.
When you get up in the morning and go, how many are there?
A. Two—body, shadow.

"Ka ele i uka, ka ele i kai, ka ele iwaena, ka ele-ke." Pane: Elepaio, elemihi, elemakule, elelu.
The "ele" in the upland, the "ele" in the lowland, the "ele" in the middle, the"ele" on the shore.
A: The elepaio bird, the black crab (elemihi), the old man (elemakule), the cockroach (elelu). (A play on the word "ele").

"Kuu kapa halii mau." Pane: Ke one (kai).
My cloak always spread. A: The sand (ocean).

CHAPTER 20

CARVING

HUC M. LUQUIENS

The Hawaiians were notable craftsmen. Whatever they could do with their hands and their primitive tools, they did well. The decorative kapa that they made for their chiefs was not only the finest kapa made by any Polynesians, but it compares favorably with other textiles in other places. The weaving that they did with the pandanus leaf, their use of fibers in general, showed the same excellence of workmanship. Their featherwork impressed all early visitors as possessing a unique beauty. Without machinery or tools of any modern sort, they produced many articles, for daily and ceremonial use, that amply testified to their thorough-going primitive skill.

Behind their craftsmanship, there existed a well advanced primitive culture. The Hawaiians possessed a wealth of poetic legend that reminds us of the legends and mythology of the ancient Greeks. With them the dance and ceremonial observance were fine arts. Their social system was a finely developed feudalism, which not only gave continuity to their existence, but which made courtesy and dignity ordinary amenities of their daily life.

With this background, we should expect to find some well established art of the sort that is possible to primitive peoples. Such an art is to be found in their wood carving.

The Polynesians in general, and the Hawaiians in particular, were adept workers in wood. It is true that the old Hawaiian utensils and the images they made of their gods have seemed rather crude, even ugly when the images are in question, to many casual observers, but a second look reveals many admirable qualities. To sense these qualities, we must first understand just what the old Hawaiian had to work with, and what he wished to accomplish.

We use the word "primitive" pretty freely in speaking of the old Hawaiian culture. It may easily become an exaggeration. The Hawaiians, of course, had no machinery such as we are used to now. They had no writing. Their poetry was passed down by word of mouth, depending for its existence on the accurate memories of trained kahunas. More particularly still we call the Hawaiians primitive, because they had neither metals nor pottery, two aids to existence which have been considered essential to civilized culture. It is supposed that at about the beginning of our era the migrations of the peoples who have become the Polynesians started out from Asia into the Pacific. It hardly seems possible that they could have set out without having known something of metal and pottery, but when they came into the islands of the Pacific which we now know as Polynesia, they found there no clay suitable for pottery, and they found no metals at all. If they had ever known such things they now necessarily forgot them. When Captain Cook landed in Hawaii in 1778, it is certain that he found the Hawaiians living without either substance. The people used wood or coconut shells or gourds to make their dishes and containers, and they made everything they used with stone tools. They were living in a stone age, and our interest in their carving is closely related to this fact.

ANCIENT HAWAIIAN TOOLS

The stone adze was the chief wood-working implement. Polished to a nicely shaped edge and mounted on a wooden handle, it was a well made tool, though it is hard for us to imagine using it very effectively. It was made of hard volcanic clinkstone found in certain favored quarries throughout the islands. The locations of two of these quarries, on Mauna Kea and Haleakala, are still well known. The Hawaiians naturally turned to the use of steel tools when the white man brought them, because they cut more easily. Nevertheless, the stone implement lingered for special purposes. William T. Brigham, former director of the Bishop Museum, writes of seeing an old Hawaiian using a stone adze in making a canoe. He used steel tools for the first shaping and hollowing out but for finishing, returned to the stone adze, with which he took off fine shavings of the hard koa, never going too deep, as he might have done with steel. Mr. Brigham closes his account, however, by stating his belief that a good deal of skill was necessary. When he tried to use the adze himself, he succeeded only in making dents in the wood.

Other tools were used with the adze. Let us examine the simplest kind of carving, that of the wooden umeke or poi bowls. In New Zealand, the Marquesas, or Samoa, such objects would have been ornamented with elaborate designs in low relief carving, but in Hawaii they were usually without decoration, their beauty lying in the handsome shape and finish alone. Mr. Brigham gives a good description of the methods used in making them. First, they were roughly shaped with the adze and hollowed out in steps with the adze or stone chisels. Further work with the same tools removed the steps inside and approximated the final shape. The surfaces were rubbed down with a piece of rough coral, and with sand and water. The final polish was accomplished with a leaf or a piece of kapa, with fine earth and with kukui nut oil. This procedure is not as strange as it seems. The tools correspond to our hatchet, chisel, rasp, sand paper, pumice stone, and rag with linseed oil. The strangeness lies simply in the fact that the tools themselves were of stone, with cutting edges that we should consider hardly usable. The results achieved were certainly as perfect as they could well be, and the shapes of the bowls are invariably more interesting and less mechanical than they would have been if they had been made with a modern lathe.

Not all Hawaiian bowls, however, are so devoid of ornament. Although the Hawaiians used little low relief carving, some utensils, for special purposes, were decorated with figures carved in the full round. There is an amusing platter preserved in the Bishop Museum, which is supported by two such grotesque figures, supposed to represent Kahahana, King of Oahu and his wife Kekuapoi, who were conquered in battle by the King of Maui and carved on the latter's meat platter as a mark of disdain. For such carving, found not only in ornamented bowls of this sort, but also in the characteristic images of the gods, the adze alone would hardly suffice. The Hawaiians had still another important cutting tool in the shark tooth knife. This was a handy and effective tool, acording to Mr. Brigham, quite capable of elaborate carving.

RELIGIOUS ART AND ITS SYMBOLISM

The bowls, which we have examined as specimens of the simplest Hawaiian carving, constitute an applied or utilitarian art. The finest artistic effort of the Hawaiians, as has often been true with other peoples in other places, is to be found in the images which they made of their gods. These idols represented their religion, and to them they applied the best skill they posessed. The very artists who made them were kahunas or priests, trained in the art of wood carving. The idols have often been called ugly, but whatever we may think of the characteristic forms used, many of the figures must be considered handsome achievements in wood sculpture.

It is very probable that these statues were intended to be ugly. They were meant to look ferocious, and to inspire fear in all beholders. The Hawaiians began their wars by shouting insult at the enemy and by making fierce grimaces as a preliminary challenge. Sticking the tongue out was a common Polynesian gesture of defiance. Naturally, the gods, who were supernatural leaders in war, were given the ideal expressions of the human warrior plunging into battle. There is more to it than that, however. The decorated headdresses of the idols, the staring eyes, the big heads and the scowling mouths, with tongues sticking out, have undoubted symoblic significance, though we can not interpret the full meaning. These features are common throughout the Pacific, being found in China, Japan, India, through all the Islands, and in Alaska, and in Mexico. Fenollosa, a well known writer on Chinese and Japanese art, calls the staring eyes "spirit eyes" and believes them symbols of demonic force or power. In China today and in Alaska, you will see these eyes on the prows of boats. If one asks a Chinese fisherman why his boat has eyes, he is likely to answer that the boat needs eyes to see where to go. But this answer is not quite accurate. The eyes are really good luck symbols, invoking the god or demon who has power to give good or bad fortune. At any rate, in Hawaii, we may be sure the idol's staring eyes were the symbol of the god's power.

There are not many of the old Hawaiian idols left. When Captain Cook first came to the islands, the Hawaiians were living their own life completely isolated from the rest of the world. From then on, however, as Vancouver and other explorers came, they began to see a great deal of the European. They heard something of his religion. They found the European extraordinarily powerful, with his big ships and his guns, and they became gradually doubtful about their own religion. In 1819, after the death of Kamehameha the Great, Liholiho, the new king, decided to destroy the old religion. He broke the most sacred kapu, by sitting down to a meal with his wife and her women, and by offering them bananas and pig, foods which had always been kapu to women. His revolutionary action was the end of the old religious system, and when, shortly after, the first American missionaries came to the islands, the Hawaiians found themselves adopting Christianity. From then on, with the zeal of new converts, they made it a virtue to destroy the old idols. They burned them up - there are several half-burned images in the Bishop Museum - or they hid them in caves, if they were hostile to the new reform. There are not many left, and there is not much chance that many more will be found.

The word "idol" is commonly used, but we must remember that the Hawaiians probably did not worship their idols, any more than the Catholics worship statues of the Virgin Mary. The images were shrines which the gods could be induced to enter on occasions, to be consulted or asked for help. Naturally the priests gave the figures such symbolic form as their artistic ability permitted. That the idols themselves were not gods is evidenced by the common custom of making a new image for every ceremony of importance, even though the old one might be kept as still retaining some of the sacredness it had previously possessed.

The best of the idols are the big temple images that were set up on the platforms of the temples, or on the walls of the heiaus to keep the enemies away. We have a number of pictures made by the early explorers which show the images in place in the heiaus, grouped like grim conclaves of chiefs, deciding some momentous question of state. The Bishop Museum has several fine specimens. There is one characteristic example of the larger gods, very grotesque and very old, and there are two well carved fence posts from heiau walls, complete as to the heads but without legs. Perhaps the most striking in our collection here is a smaller statue, the so-called Bloxam idol. It is one of a pair found at Hale o Keawe, Honaunau, by Andrew Bloxam, naturalist of the "Blonde," which brought Liholiho's body back from London in 1825. The two images were taken to England, and this one, after a hundred years, finally found its way back to the Museum here. The statue is crested with the warrior's helmet. It has the staring eyes and the snarling mouth, showing the teeth and tongue. It has the customary lively pose. The workmanship is excellent. The man who made it was a wood carver in every sense, using his adze boldly and vigorously, with a skill that made any final polishing unnecessary. We can hardly say which god the figure represents. It might have been Ku, the war god, since he has the warrior's crest. But in general, though we know much of Hawaiian religion and its many gods, it is impossible to give specific names to the idols. The larger images might naturally represent any of the four major gods, Ku, the war god, Kane and Kanaloa, creator gods of heaven and earth, or Lono, god of seasons and games, for whom Cook was mistaken.

In addition to the larger temple images, the Hawaiians made many smaller wooden idols for household or family use. These were the aumakua or protective spirits belonging to individuals or families—in many cases ancestors turned into gods. They could be conveniently carried around and set up in houses or small places for private worship. The collection of the Bishop Museum contains a large number of these small images, whose variety in form demonstrates that the Hawaiian artist was not bound to any one convention. The most striking, perhaps, are two small stick gods found in a cave near Kawaihae, very ornate in workmanship. They have, in miniature, all the symbolic features of the largest temple images, with even more elaborate head-dresses than appear in any of the large figures. Another interesting statuette is said to be the poison god Kalaipahoa. His image was supposed to have been made of a very poisonous wood, and he himself was a god of special malignancy. The idol that we have amply demonstrates the Hawaiian artist's ability in representing such malignancy in sculptured form.

Most of the small gods, however, are more definitely realistic than the images already discussed, as if they represented real men and women turned demigods. There is one such realistic female figure in the Museum here which must rate as one of the best of the Hawaiian carvings. It is one of three, evidently made at the same time by the same artist, whose quality is so naturalistic that they might have been meant as portraits, father, mother, and daughter. It is the daughter that we have in the Bishop Museum. It is a handsome piece of wood carving, very finished in workmanship. The adze marks have been polished out, and the figure has a soft sheen which beautifully enhances the grain of the carefully chosen wood. In spite of its successful realism, however, we notice immediately that the eyes are staring disks of pearl shell. This brings us back to the symbolism of Pacific art. We must not suppose that the artist was trying to imitate human eyes when he made this little statue. Portrait or not, the figure is a god, and the artist gave it "spirit eyes," the customary symbols of superhuman power.

STONE CARVING

The Hawaiians made a great number of stone tools and utensils, but did little successful carving in that medium. They were not naturally sculptors in stone. On occasion, a Hawaiian found a rock which resembled a man or an animal; with a little chipping he added to the resemblance and set the image up as a god. Such were the stone fishing gods which were sometimes set on a hill overlooking the fishing ground to bring the fisherman good luck. But these images are too crude to attract our attention long as carving. On Necker Island, however, some small stone images of an interesting sort were found. In some ways they seem like stone imitations of carving that would more naturally be done in wood. It is believed that they were the work of the earliest immigrants to Hawaii, the people who have now become the legendary menehunes. Later, in the 12th and 13th centuries, when the Hawaiians that we know came along, these earlier people were driven into the mountains, to Kauai and even to the smaller islands to the northwest. There, on Necker Island, finding no trees, and consequently no wood for carving, they made their images as best they could in stone. These idols are amusing little figures, very interesting, though crude.

THE REAL ART OF THE HAWAIIANS

The wooden gods constitute the real art of the Hawaiians. All the Polynesians were wood carvers. The Samoans and the Marquesans carved profusely in low relief. The Maoris in New Zealand carved almost everything they used, both in relief and in the full round. Our Hawaiian carving, meager in quantity and restrained in ornament, is hardly comparable with the profuse art of the Maoris. The New Zealanders lived in a large country, with plenty of soft woods suitable for easy sculpture, and they had much better stone for tools. They achieved a luxuriant decorative art of the greatest interest. Still, it must be remarked that they never destroyed the best of their old sculpture in a wave of religious reform. In Hawaii, we know that we have lost much of what existed before 1819. We also know that what we have was made before 1819, before the ancient Hawaiian culture was much touched by outside influence. A few of the remaining idols may certainly be considered to be among the finest things produced in Polynesian art, and splendid examples of true primitive carving with Stone Age tools.

CHAPTER 21

WARFARE

KENNETH P. EMORY

Kamehameha's long and bloody struggle to gain possession of the island of Hawaii, his later conquest of Maui and Molokai, and then of Oahu, ended the last and greatest of the Hawaiian wars which had been going on for many years. For centuries before the time of Kamehameha, the chiefs of the different islands were frequently engaged in contests for the possession of the soil, or in carrying out expeditions of revenge. Chiefs of Hawaii often tried to get a hold on Maui, and in fact, Hana was several times completely under their control. Maui chiefs fought against those of Oahu for the control of Molokai. Although Kauai successfully warded off all comers, she had her share of internal strife. Warfare, therefore, was an art to which much attention had to be given. War offered such scope for the ambitions of the chiefs that they devoted much of their time to training and preparation for it. But no standing army was ever kept. While there was no standing army in Hawaii there were standing warriors, koa, individuals who made fighting their profession and who were the champions on the field of battle. They often engaged in single combat while both sides watched and awaited the outcome.

TRAINING IN WARFARE

How, then, given a few days notice, were thousands of men put into action in special formations adapted to the circumstances and calling for no small degree of coordination? The answer is that the whole adult male population was in times of peace a reserve army, each individual of which kept his weapons in readiness in his house. Training in group fighting was given by the staging of sham battles on those fairly frequent occasions when the people from all the surrounding districts were gathered for some festivity. The chiefs from adolescence received individual training in the use of various arms from the older men about them. Having much of their time free to devote to this training, they naturally became the proficient class in fighting. All those about the king's court received much training. The district chiefs saw to the training of the men about them, but the mass of the people were left to themselves to pick up instruction from each other in the use of their own weapons. Much of the training in the use of weapons took the form of sport or amusement, or entertainment. For this reason, in Samoa, Fiji, and the Tuamotus, drills and exercises with spears or clubs are still to be observed.

The Kalaimoku, or those skilled in the management of the affairs of government, made it their business to master the technique of mobilization and direction of armies. They were the right hand men of the king.

Nearly all fighting was done in broad daylight, in open country, and in a very straightforward manner. Warfare was under the regulation of some very curious customs and codes of conduct. Between the first of June and the end of the year, war was even kapu, a most remarkable custom. The place and time of battle and even the method of fighting were not infrequently agreed upon in advance by the opposing parties. It is related in the story of Kawelo of Kauai, that when he returned from Oahu to give battle to his cousin, he and his warriors, as was the custom, were allowed to land unmolested and prepare for the fight.

POLYNESIAN WEAPONS AND EQUIPMENT

What characterized Polynesian fighting more than anything else is that it was hand-to-hand fighting and that it was the aim to come directly to blows. This explains the types of weapons used. The sling and javelin served for the short interval when the people were marching upon each other but within striking distance with these weapons.

The sling took the place of the bow in Polynesian warfare, not because of ignorance of the bow, but because the sling had certain great advantages over the bow in their method of warfare. It could, for instance, be tucked in the belt during the hand-to-hand fighting and the missiles could usually be secured on the spot. Worked slingstones were quite symmetrical and oval in shape; most of them were pointed at each end. They were hurled with great force and precision in a sling made of human hair, coconut fibre, or plaited pandanus leaf. After the stone was placed in the pocket of the sling it was laid over the shoulder and gripped in the left hand behind the back. Stretched tight, it was then released by the left hand, swung with the right once around the head, and released. The stone was made to travel as low to the ground as possible so that it would be difficult to dodge.

The javelin, ihe, was five to six feet long and was made of kauila or some such hard wood. Some were notched at one end in a series of dull barbs. Men were trained in catching and returning, dodging, or warding off these ihe thrown through the air. You know Vancouver's description of Kamehameha in a sham battle, catching three flying spears in his right hand, warding off two others by a parry with his spear in his left hand, and avoiding the sixth spear by a dexterous twist of the body. Spear throwing as a sport training was called lono-maka-ihe.

The long pololu spear was held in the highest esteem as an offensive and defensive weapon. It ran up to twenty feet in length. It was used for thrusting and tripping, in giving chase, and even for pole vaulting.

The spear club, laau palau, about eight or nine feet long, was perhaps the most efficient all-around weapon. It could be used as a club, sword, and spear. To fence with these weapons in sport was called kaka laau.

Clubs were as indispensable as spears. All clubs were short. There was a club shaped like a policeman's billet, only fuller, and this might be of stone in place of wood. The commonest club, however, was an ugly knobbed club; the knobs of some were round and smooth, of others, rough. The best clubs were stone headed. A lobbed stone was lashed to a short handle. All these clubs were called newa. Club heads or very short clubs were sometimes tied to a cord and swung so as to trip up an antagonist. Such were called piikoi. A stone held in the hand served the purpose of a club. Long wooden daggers, pahoa, were used as final weapons. Hafted stone adzes, shark tooth knives, and strangling cords were also used.

Men went to battle as little encumbered with clothing as possible. A narrow malo was all most wore. Some had their heads done up in kapa, like turbans. The chiefs frequently wore their helmets and capes. Canoemen seem to have worn gourd masks as protection against sling stones.

THE DECLARATION OF WAR

A chief declared war after consulting with his advisors and sub-chiefs and after the priests at the heiau had pronounced the will of the gods favorable. The kahuna slept in the temple and learned the will of the god by vision or dream, or went into a trance whereby the gods spoke through him. The poe kilo, diviners, sacrificed hogs and fowls, and by observing the manner in which they expired and the twitching of the entrails, predicted the future of undertakings. Kukailimoku was Kamehameha's famous war god; to him alone human sacrifices were offered. Images representing this dread god are in the Bishop Museum. The king and warrior chiefs fixed the time of mobilization and the manner of carrying on the war. It was not uncommon to allow months for preparation.

COLLECTING THE ARMY

When it was desired to call the people to war, messengers, lele, were sent to districts and villages to inform the chiefs of the numbers of men required for the expedition. The chiefs saw that the men came with their weapons, kukui nuts for torches, calabashes of water, dried fish, and other portable provisions. As arms were always kept in readiness, they came quickly, and upon their arrival their numbers were reported to the chief. They camped about their own chief in huts of coconut leaves or ti leaves (hale pai) or in large sheds (auroro). Slackers were rounded up, their ears were slit, and they were led into camp by a rope tied to their waists.

The warriors frequently encamped by a river or on the edge of a ravine. No artificial barriers were thrown up. Pickets were stationed at passes. Wives who did not go, children and old men, were left at a natural or artificial fortress in the mountains to which all fled if their side was vanquished. Or they were put in the puuhonua, or city of refuge. When the mountain fortresses were attacked, stones were rolled down upon the enemy. In Kona, at Kahaluu, miles of underground lava tubes served as refugee caves or hiding places in times of war.

Before going into battle the poe kilo were again consulted for the portents. Clouds before the sun, rainbows, the appearance of the heavens at night, all had signs for those who could read them. If all seemed well, the image of the principal war god was brought out before the whole army and placed near the king. The priests addressed the gods, then the king or commander-in-chief addressed the assembled warriors. A fire might be built and a pig sacrificed. They marched to battle without trumpets, drums, or flags, as did the Tahitians, but they carried their images with them. The national war god, Kukailimoku, was elevated above the ranks. The image was fixed on a pedestal or pillar, carried by the priests, or set up on the ground and defended. The priests let out diabolical yells to assure the people the god was there.

SETTING THE ORDER OF BATTLE (HOONOHO KA KAUA)

If there was a large body of warriors and the ground was level and open, the fighters were marshalled in a great crescent, the commander-in-chief in the middle. This formation was called Kahului. Doubtless it took the name from the plain of Kahului on Maui. If the ground was obstructed by irregularities or clumps of trees, the fighters were divided into groups which advanced together, a formation called makawalu. Sometimes the opposing forces, by prearrangement, drew up in two solid lines facing each other, an order of battle called kukulu. A small army, however, was likely to be arranged in this order: skirmishers in front called the huna lewa, backed by a larger body called the huna paa. Behind these came the waa kaua, literally "war canoes." These were groups of perhaps a thousand each. Last of all came the poe kaua, the mass of soldiery. In their midst or in the midst of the waa kaua stood the king surrounded by his dearest friends and his gods. They were encircled by the guard called papa-kaua armed with the pololu spears.

THE BATTLE

Skirmishing might be started by a single warrior advancing and challenging someone to meet him. In general, however, it was started by the slingers on each wing harassing the enemy. When the forces were near enough, showers of spears were cast forth. The first person to be killed was called a lehua. If he could be secured by his victors and dragged to sacrifice, it was considered an omen of great favor for that side. The first, ulukoko, the second, makawai, and the third, helu one, victims were offered as sacrifices to the war god.

Women often accompanied their husbands, carrying water and food to refresh them and attending to their wounds. Some bore weapons and fought side by side with their men. When their husbands were killed they were almost certain to be killed also. Others of the women stayed behind the lines ready to lend succor.

Naval battles sometimes took place. Upwards of one hundred canoes on each side might be engaged. At a distance they fought with slings and javelins; at close quarters, with spear and club. Canoes were smashed by heavy stones swung by a cord.

RESULTS OF DEFEAT AND VICTORY

When an army was routed, they were pursued and cut down without mercy. The fugitives who did not reach the fortress or city of refuge were hunted for days and even months and cruelly dispatched when found. Occasionally pleas for mercy were heard and the person spared to become a slave or made a captive to be saved for a future human sacrifice. A friend of the conquered chief might evade the hunting parties and succeed in getting into the presence of the chief. None could touch him in the king's enclosure without his orders. The fugitive would address the king in those words, "E mako paha, e ora paha,—iluna ke alo, ilalo ke alo?" (Is it life or death, —is the countenance uplifted or is it cast down?) If the chief said nothing, or did not look up, the pleader was immediately killed or dragged away to be executed.

Victors buried their dead. The bodies of the vanquished were left to be devoured by dogs and hogs, or to rot. Stones were sometimes piled over them as a memorial of the victory.

When the vanquished were completely overcome, their country was reapportioned among the chiefs and warriors who had been the companions of the king. The women and children of the conquered people were made slaves and, with the male captives, were attached to the soil for its cultivation.

When both sides found they were equally matched or had mutually suffered great losses, sometimes a truce was called by one side sending an ambassador with a young banana tree and a green ti leaf branch. If he was received and the plea to call off the quarrel entertained, arrangements were made for the meeting of chiefs and priests.

Peace treaties, when they had been agreed to, were ratified at the temple. A pig was slain, its blood caught in a vessel and poured on the ground. This was perhaps a symbol of the blood the gods would cause to spill if the treaty were broken. A wreath of maile was then woven by the leading chiefs of both sides and deposited in the heiau. Feasting, dancing, and public games then followed. Irreconcilable differences and hatreds were soon swallowed up in sympathy and in joy over being delivered from the burdens and brutalities of war.

Warfare in Hawaii was marked, as is all warfare, by cruelty and misery, but war as it was conducted in ancient Hawaii has one interesting aspect. It was definitely not the warfare of savages, rushing out to destroy or capture. It was rather the warfare of feudalism, with its recognized rules and formalities, its prayers, invocations, and ceremonial preparation. While the constant wars of Hawaii caused much misery particularly among the common people, we cannot expect that these people could have had a more humanitarian attitude toward suffering and dispensed with some of their unnecessary wars, for even civilized people of the present have not come to this stage as yet. It was natural that the Hawaiians should have engaged in war to the extent that they did, for it afforded them an outlet otherwise lacking in their lives. But it is interesting that the warfare itself was highly developed and so far removed from savagery in its conduct and regulations. Hawaiian warfare is another proof of the high degree of development of many aspects of life in old Hawaii.

CHAPTER 22

NAVIGATION

KENNETH P. EMORY

There is no one with Hawaiian blood in his veins who would be here if it had not been for the knowledge, skill, hardihood, and adventurous spirit of his Polynesian ancestors. They traversed the Pacific, the greatest of all oceans, and came to the hundreds of lovely islands which they first discovered and colonized. They did this at a time when the English were being Christianized and introduced to civilization. Let us consider how they accomplished this, an enterprise that properly should rank among the great achievements of human history, and one that must have been flooded with human drama.

Fortunately, through the researches of the Bishop Museum and other institutions, we do know something of how these islands were peopled. We are sure that the Polynesians are not descendants of survivors of a people who clung to the tops of a sinking continent or sinking archipelagoes, nor is their culture a remnant of a great and ancient civilization that once occupied the middle of the Pacific. They are recent arrivals on the last bits of fair earth to be occupied by man, and they brought with them a heritage of an ancient continental civilization, which they adapted to their new life in the island environment.

The Hawaiians were evidently quite satisfied with their new home, for they gave up long ocean voyaging probably five centuries ago. It became more or less of a lost art with them. Their canoes were descendants of the canoes in which they came originally, and their inter-island travel embodied some of the ancient art of ocean travel. But we have only to go to a very intimately related branch of the Polynesians, the Tahitians and their neighbors, who were making fairly distant voyages up until a few years ago, to judge how the ancestors of the Hawaiian people performed them. Let us consider first the vessels in which the voyages were made, and their equipment; then the preparation for a long voyage, and finally, how the canoes were guided over the ocean.

VESSELS

The Hawaiian outrigger canoes you see today differ very little from canoes seen by Captain Cook. The only difference is that the fore and end pieces of the canoe, manu, are now made out of one solid piece instead of two, and that these end pieces and the board, moo, attached on each side, are now nailed on instead of being lashed on. The lashings of the outrigger of modern canoes are not nearly so neat as those made in the old days. In Cook's day there were much larger canoes, and also double canoes rigged with the Hawaiian sail which went out of existence more than one hundred years ago. The large double canoes, rigged with a mat sail, were quite suitable for inter-island travel. Some very large Hawaiian canoes were made from great California redwood logs which drifted to these shores. The rotting hull of one 108 feet long was still to be seen in the 1870's. The hulls of Hawaiian canoes were always in one piece. The trees, when not redwoods, were carefully selected by the kahuna kalai wa'a who slept in a house in a heiau for a vision to guide him in his choice. A sacrifice of a red fish, of coconuts, and awa, was made before the felling of the tree. Ceremonies were performed at every stage in the shaping of the log, of its dragging to the shore, of its building in the canoe shed, and finally at its launching. The canoe was smoothly finished off by rubbing with sand caught in the meshes of coconut husk fiber, or by shark skin. It was then painted black with burnt kukui nut mixed with oil. The trimmings of a royal canoe were painted red.

In Tahiti, hulls of large canoes were made of several sections of hollowed-out log joined together. The stern rose high out of the water and the bow was fitted with a projecting plank. In the outrigger, the forward boom was not attached directly to the float, but indirectly by means of pegs. The double seagoing canoes were, most commonly, twin canoes. Each was built up of planks carefully fitted and secured in place by sewing with sennit. The seams were caulked with coconut fibre, perhaps soaked with breadfruit gum, and the seams were covered with battens held firmly in place by the sewing. By this means, canoes could be built up to almost any size and could be varied as to shape. The space between the canoes was decked over, and on this deck were set

A Double Sailing Canoe from the Tuamotus

(Model made in 1854, of a canoe then in existence. It was 60 feet long, 14 feet wide, 5 feet 8 inches deep, and carried 60 passengers.)

one or two masts and a deck house thatched with pandanus leaf. The sails were narrower and higher than the Hawaiian sail but embodied the same principles.

The Tuamotu double canoes were the finest vessels in the Southeast. They were also built up of small pieces sewn together. They differed from the Tahitian and Hawaiian canoes in being equal-ended so that they could sail in either direction without tacking. This also enabled them to have a permanent cabin in one canoe which would always be on the windward side. The sails were wider than the Tahitian sails and could be lowered and furled. This was a real ship, accomodating comfortably sixty to one hundred persons. Great steering oars or paddles were necessary to hold it on its course.

The Tongan canoes were the finest sailing ships in Polynesia when the Europeans first came upon the scene. They reached the enormous length of 150 feet, nearly twice the size of the trading schooners in the South Seas today. The Tonga double canoe had one canoe very much smaller than the other. The sail, though a lateen, or in other words, a triangular sail, was suspended from the mast by the middle of one side. The end of the mast was fixed on the deck or front of the canoe and when it came to tacking, the sail, not the canoe, was reversed. The Tongan canoe was modeled after the Fijian, the Tongans improving on the Fijian. This Tongan-Fijian canoe was perfected in about the 16th century when the Tongans were securing the central Pacific and penetrating north even as far as Fanning, 1000 miles from Hawaii, where they left two tombs of chiefs.

Canoes were equipped with ordinary paddles, steering paddles, bailers, seats, mat sails, and tassels of feathers or pennants of kapa flying from the masthead or outer end of the sail. Most old Hawaiian paddles were tipped at the end with a midrib on one side. Stone anchors were carried, although in the Tuamotus the usual method of anchoring a canoe was by diving and fastening the anchor to a coral head.

PREPARATION

It is altogether likely that at the height of the colonization period when whole families with their retinues, their household property, their domesticated animals and plants were to be transported, that canoes were built for the purpose. They were undoubtedly larger and better than any Polynesian craft Europeans have seen in our times, centuries after the period of colonization had come to an end. In preparing for a long voyage, canoes were carefully gone over. They were recaulked and relashed on all weak points and the rigging was overhauled. If the canoes were especially built for the voyage, preparations might extend over many months.

The stores of food and water were the next most important things to attend to. Water was stored in bamboo joints or in gourds or in coconut bottles. Of these, the bamboo could be most conveniently packed away on board. Sweet potatoes, taro, bananas, young drinking coconuts, and breadfruit would last a week or ten days and a supply for this period was put in. Yams would last two months. Among other lasting foods were mature coconuts and several prepared foods, such as fermented breadfruit, dried taro, dried sweet potato, and dried bananas. Pandanus food was another concentrated lasting preparation taken on a voyage. It was a yellow dough the consistency of putty, and was made by scraping the starch from the base of .the keys, mixing it with coconut milk, and baking it. Fresh fish could be kept alive in bamboo aquaria, and shell fish would keep alive a few days. Dried fish was one of the staples of the long voyage. Pigs and chickens were kept alive on copra and the dogs were fed the remains of the pigs, chickens, and scraps of fish. A few birds and fish might be caught at sea to round off the menu. Sand, earth, stones, and firewood were carried for the imu.

The Tahitians and the Tuamotuans rarely took more than twenty days' provisions. The Polynesian canoe is a fairly fast sailing vessel. With favorable winds it makes eight or nine knots. It has been estimated that with a fair following wind the great voyage from Tahiti to New Zealand could have been covered in about 11 days, and the Polynesians most carefully chose their weather. Tuamotu natives have been known to wait months at

Tahiti for the right season of the year to return home. In addition to waiting for a perfect day for the start, all omens must be right on that day, and the religious rites attending the departure must be completed.

NAVIGATION

Now, how were the great stretches of water between islands navigated? How was the way back to land found when canoes had been driven away from their islands, or out of their course by storms? We have our best information in answer to these questions from the natives of the Tuamotus. When the natives of Anaa in the Tuamotus set out for Tahiti, 250 miles distant, they dragged their fine twin ships from their neat canoe sheds and hauled them to the edge of the reef flat over the butts of coconut leaves amid their lively hauling chanties. The canoes were lined up with points on shore which gave the exact direction for them to pick up Matavai point on Tahiti and at sunset they took final leave of their friends and launched their canoes. They fixed on the first bright star directly ahead near the western horizon. When it began to sink into the horizon haze they guided on the star following this one. If you stop to think you will realize this is not so easy. The second star would not be directly above the first but slightly off to one side or the other. Here is where the lore of the Tuamotu astronomer came in. He was aware that all the fixed stars which sink on one spot on the horizon arise from one spot on the eastern horizon, and that these two spots never change as long as he remains in one place. These stars follow the same curved course through the sky and are said to belong to the same rua, or pit. The principal stars which follow a number of courses in both the northern and southern parts of the heavens were known by name. The Polynesian navigator could recognize and give the name of 150 or more stars and, furthermore, what was of the greatest importance, he knew which belonged to the same parallel of latitude. He did not express it that way, of course, but said instead that they all issued from the same pit.

If on this voyage to Tahiti, clouds suddenly began to obscure the western sky, a man would be stationed in front and keep a back sight on a star on the eastern horizon, and on the stars following it. If the whole sky became overcast, he fell back temporarily on the slants of the wind and waves. If the heavens cleared he would search for stars on the western horizon known to belong to the same series as the stars guided on when they started.

In black weather or rainy weather at night, a change in the winds would be immediately noted because the waves would not change their direction right away. Winds, also, were recognized as much by their character as by the direction from which they came, so that a native baffled as to his directions could often re-orient himself by recognizing a certain wind. In the knowledge of winds the Tuamotuans were most expert.

In the day time, the sun became the principal guide, supplemented by waves and winds, and in addition, currents. The rippling of the current could be detected by the eyes, and the general trend of currents in particular regions is fairly constant. The direction from which came sea birds roosting on land, or to which they returned at night, was a guide

Every intelligent Polynesian had a very clear notion of the cardinal points, N., S., E., and W., and of the points midway, and as soon as he could find a wind, or celestial body on which he could right himself, he would know if he was going in the likely direction of his island. A string in which knots were tied each day enabled him to keep good track of the days passed. As Tahiti was neared, usually great piles of clouds indicated where it stood long before it could be seen.

The return from Tahiti to Anaa was a much more difficult matter. The island is not very wide and is so low that a canoe can pass within eight miles in clear weather and not see it. Much greater care had to be exercised in choosing the weather, for Anaa lay to windward and the favorable winds were rare and occurred only in one season. The shallow lagoon of Anaa in the daytime casts a reflection of a peculiar greenish color on any clouds that pass overhead. We saw this light at a distance of twenty miles and it acted as a beacon to us. I have been told that in rainy weather when coral islands are easily passed by, that a pig on board would be carefully watched. If he got a whiff of land his nose would turn landward. Many such tricks must have been used by the Polynesians.

This story illustrates how the Polynesian navigator made his way back when he was blown far from his island, or course. In 1821, three double canoes left Anaa with 150 natives to pay their respects to the new Tahitian king. Two days out on their course they were met by a gale which scattered them and drove them in the opposite direction for a day and then left them in a calm. When the wind sprang up again one canoe felt its way back to the course but was then surprised by a storm which drove it several hundred miles eastward. The people in this canoe then found themselves becalmed for more than a week during hot, dry days. Their two weeks provisions of water and food gave out and they were exhausted. Seventeen of the twenty-three men, fifteen women, and ten children who sailed on this vessel, died. A rainstorm put a temporary end to their misery. Further heartened by a catch of three sharks, they hunted for land. They finally discovered the tiny atoll of Vanavana, which they found uninhabited. They stayed here ten months preparing for the return voyage. On their way home they stopped at another island and in attempting to land they damaged their canoe. They remained here eight months, repairing the damage and laying in stores of dried fish and pandanus cakes. They were about to embark when Captain Beechey came by and so learned of their adventure. They were well and happy and taking their time to insure a safe return in their unusually small vessel, a double canoe of thirty feet in length.

In exploring for new lands, a fleet of canoes, according to Maori tradition, would spread out in line, each canoe just in sight of another. With land birds ranging fifty miles out to sea, the chances of discovery of an island, by a fleet of five canoes, were very good, if they came within fifty or sixty miles on any side of it, even if it was a very low island.

Knowledge of Polynesian voyages helps us to appreciate the skill and daring of these first explorers and colonizers of the Pacific. At a time when our European ancestors knew little more than the world about the sheltered Mediterranean, our Polynesian ancestors were navigating the greatest of the oceans. And while Columbus and the European navigators of a much later date launched out with fear and trembling into the unknown, these earlier Polynesian navigators knew where they were going and how they were going to get there.

CHAPTER 23

ASTRONOMY AND THE CALENDAR

E. H. BRYAN, JR.

Astronomy was an important subject to the Hawaiians of long ago. Nearly all people, from very early times, have had some knowledge of the heavenly bodies and their movements. Few made more practical use of this knowledge than did the ancient Hawaiians. Not only did they use the movements of the sun, moon, stars, and planets as their timepiece and calendar, but also much of their skill as deep sea navigators was due to their knowledge of these objects and their movements.

Over 120 Hawaiian names of stars and planets have been preserved. The fact that in many cases we do not know to what objects these names referred is the fault, not of the Hawaiian astronomers, but of the haole recorders, most of whom knew far less about the subject than did their informants.

THE PLANETS

The Hawaiians readily distinguished between the planets (called "hoku-aea" or "hoku-hele") and the fixed stars (called "hoku-paa"). The planets were given various names according to their position in the eastern or western sky, much as we speak of "morning star" and "evening star". The eastern or morning star was generally called "iao" or "manalo". The evening star was called "na-holo-holo". Some of the planets also had names of their own, regardless of their position in the sky. Mercury was called "ukali", because it followed close after the sun. It was also known as "kawela." Venus was called "mananalo," as well as "hokuloa" when in the morning sky, and "naholoholo" when in the evening sky. Mars, like other red stars, was called "hoku-ula;" also more specifically, "holo-holopinae." Jupiter was called "kaawela;" and also, because of its brightness, "ikaika."

The movement of the stars across the sky, from east to west, both nightly and throughout the year, was quite familiar to the Hawaiians. Whether or not they suspected that the nightly movement was due to the rotation of the earth on its axis, and the yearly movement to its revolution around the sun, we do not know. They probably did not. However, they based their measurement of time and their calendar upon these movements with considerable accuracy.

THE STAR GROUPS

To the Hawaiians, one of the most familiar groups of stars was "huihui" or "makali'i," the Pleiades or "seven little sisters." Its first appearance in the eastern evening sky, in November, marked the beginning of the year, a season of great festivity. "Makali'i" was also the name for the "twins," Castor and Pollux, the two stars being called "Nana-mua" (the one going ahead) and "Nana-hope" (the one following). The familiar belt and sword of Orion together were called "Na Kao." The Big Dipper was called "Na Hiku."

The north star, Polaris, was called "hoku-paa" (fixed star) and "hoku-ho'o-kele-waa" (the steering or guiding star). The Milky Way was called "ka'u" (something stretching across overhead). This name was also given to the summer season, as distinguished from "ho'o-ilo," the winter season. When voyagers went south they used a group of stars to steer by, called "newe," which might have been the Southern Cross.

THE CALENDAR

Very early in the history of mankind the day became the unit of time. The sun, whose presence or absence produced day and night, was the most important heavenly body. The Hawaiian name for the sun was "la." The same word was very naturally applied to the day. Next to the sun in prominence was the moon, called "mahina." The nightly movement of the position of the moon across the sky from west to east, changing its shape from slender crescent to full moon and back to crescent, in a period of between 29 and 30 days, furnished another unit of time, the month. The Hawaiians used the name of the moon, "mahina" to signify a month. Each day of the moon's change was given a separate name (see Table 1), from "Hilo," the day after the appearance of the new moon, low in the west, to "hoku," the day after the full of the moon, and on to Hilo again. There were thirty names in all, but in some months only twenty-nine were used.

The third unit of time, the year, commenced when the Pleiades first made their appearance in the eastern evening sky. This would happen in Hawaii at the present time on November 18th. In other latitudes and in other eras the date would be different. Thus, about the year 1000 A. D. it would have risen at sundown in Hawaii on November 5th; and 2000 years ago, on October 20th. Likewise, it would be seen to rise at the present time in Rarotonga and Tahiti on about November 21st or 22nd, and in New Zealand on the 24th. The year was called "Makahiki" after the period of festivities which marked its beginning. It was made up of twelve lunar months and a bit left over. The names of the twelve months are given in Table 2. The first commenced with the new moon immediately after the Makahiki. The length of the extra period varied in length, depending upon the number of days between the end of the last month and the new moon after the rising of the Pleiades.

Making the day, the month, and the year agree with each other has been the bugbear of all calendar makers. It is too bad that these three units of time do not have a common divisor. The month contains 29 days, 12 hours, 44 minutes, and 2.8 seconds. In the year there are 365.24218979+ days. As you can calculate for yourself, the number of days in the month goes into the number of days in the year twelve times with 10.875142+ days left over. Hawaiian calendar makers must have been puzzled by the problem of what to do with the days between the end of the twelfth month and the first new moon after the Makahiki, when the first month could begin.

We do not know exactly how the Hawaiian astronomers managed the details of this problem. The method apparently was not understood or recorded by the first haoles who came here. Now, the Hawaiians themselves have forgotten. We do know, however, how certain other Polynesian peoples worked out their calendars. Dr. Peter H. Buck has recorded it for the people of Manihiki (Cook Islands) as follows: They had twelve named months of 29 or 30 days, from new moon to new moon, and the extra period. They had a cycle of 19 years, in which the 3rd, 5th, 8th, 11th, 13th, 16th, and 19th years were allowed to have an extra (or 13th) lunar month In the intervening years they lumped the extra days with the 12th month, until the coming of the first new moon after the appearance of the Pleiades made it possible to start the first month of the new year.

It may be that the Hawaiian Kilo-hoku, or astronomers of olden days, had some such arrangement for keeping their calendar straight. It is interesting to note that the Greeks, who also regulated their months by the moon, had the same system. One of their astronomers, named Meton, worked out this cycle of 12 years with 12 months and 7 with 13, which has ever since been called the "Metonic cycle" in his honor.

Some Polynesian peoples used the rising of the Pleiades in the eastern evening sky to mark the beginning of the year; others used their first appearance in the morning sky. For this latter group the year began about June 4th.

The great skill exhibited by the Hawaiians and other Polynesian people in navigating by the stars is discussed in another chapter.

Table I: Nights of the Moon, after which the Days Following Received their Names.

	HAWAIIAN	MAORI	TAHITIAN
1	Hilo (New moon)	Whiro	Tirio or Teriere
2	Hoaka	Tirea	Hirohiti
3	Ku-kahi	Hoata	Hoata
4	Ku-lua	Oue	Hami-ama-mua
5	Ku-kolu	Okoro	Hami-ama-roto
6	Ku-pau	Tamatea-akiri	Hami-ama-muri
7	Ole-ku-kahi	Tamatea-a-ngana	'Ore' ore-mua
8	Ole-ku-lua	Tamatea-aio	Ore' ore-muri
9	Ole-ku-kolu	Tamatea-whakapau	Tamatea
10	Ole-ku-pau	Huna	Huna
11	Huna	Ari-roa	Rapu or Ari
12	Mohalu	Mahwharu	Maharu
13	Hua	Maurea	Hu'a
14	Akua	Atua-whakahaehae	Maitu
15	Hoku (full moon)	Turu	Motu
16	Mahealani	Rakau-nui	Mara'i
17	Kulu	Rakau-matohi	Turu or Turutea
18	La'au-ku-kahi	Takirau	Ra'au-mua
19	La'au-ku-lua	Oika	Ra'au-roto
20	La'au-pau	Korekore	Ra'au-muri
21	Ole-ku-kahi	Korekore-tutua	'Ore' ore-mua
22	Ole-ku-lua	Korekore-piri-ki-tangaroa	'Ore' ore-roto
23	Ole-pau	Tangaroa-a-mua	'Ore' ore-muri
24	Kaloa-ku-kahi*	Tangaroa-a-roto	Ta'aroa-mua
25	Kaloa-ku-lua	Tangaroa-kiokio	Ta'aroa-roto
26	Kaloa-pau	O-Tane	Ta'aroa-muri
27	Kane	O-Rongo-nui	Tane
28	Lono	Mauri	Ro'o-nui
29	Mauli	O-Mutu	Ro'o-mauri
30	Muku	Mutuwhenua	Mutu or Mauri-mate

(*Shortened from Ka'aloa—etc.)

Note: There are similar lists of "Nights of the Moon" for almost every Polynesian island. Although the similar names do not apply to exactly the same night, the general sequence is the same, suggesting that the differences are only due to tricks of memory, and that all these different lists are part of one great system of keeping track of time, used by different, but closely related members of the great Polynesian race. In the samples given above, you can see that the addition of another name between the 5th and 6th in the Maori list will make the agreement very much closer.

Table 2: Names of Hawaiian Lunar Months.

1 Makalii	5 Welo	9 Hilinaehu
2 Kaelo	6 Ikiiki	10 Hilinama
3 Kaulua	7 Kaaona	11 Ikuwa
4 Nana	8 Hinaiaeleele	12 Walehu

CHAPTER 24

MEDICINE

I

ANCIENT HAWAIIAN REMEDIES KNOWN TODAY

JOHN H. WISE

The ancient Hawaiians had a considerable reputation for their use of herbs in medicine. Some of the knowledge of the old days has come down to the present, though by far the larger part of it has been lost. Probably in the old days the effect, use, and preparation of some three hundred plants and herbs were known to the kahunas who were the herb doctors of those days. Very careful training was given to the young men who were to be the herb doctors of that day. While they were very young, they were taken into the family of a specially trained kahuna and carefully instructed in the appearance of the different herbs, in their uses and effects, in the way to find them and gather and prepare them for use. The student remained in the home of the kahuna for fifteen or twenty years, and when he left this home, his training was complete and he was ready to enter upon his life work as a kahuna, expert in what was then known of drugs and medicines.

Some of the herbs and plants whose uses were known to the Hawaiian people, and which are still used today to some extent, were:

Noni—Reputed to have healing powers. Leaf used for boils and other injuries.
Laukahi—Used as a poultice for boils.
Pohe—Used in the same way as laukahi.
Kokea—White sugar cane for colds.
Lau flowers—A remedy for "sour stomach."
Ohia bark—Used for sore throat.
Banana ends—The juice was extracted from the part of

the bunch just below the fruit and used as a remedy for colic.

Puakala root—Used for sores.

Kowali juice was extracted from the roots and prepared with starch. Used as a laxative.

Pia—Starch was extracted from the dried roots and used as a remedy in dysentery.

Uhaloa—Bark was removed from the roots of this plant and chewed as a remedy for sore throat.

Popolo—For hundreds of years, the Hawaiians knew and used this plant. Burbank, the man who perfected so many varieties of plant life in California, "discovered" a plant which is exactly like the Hawaiian popolo.

Hinahina—This was cooked, pounded with salt, and used as a poultice for a broken bone. The Hawaiians did not use splints, as we know them, for broken bones, but they did wrap the injured part in ti leaf and kapa.

The Hawaiians knew about the medicinal properties of salt. After a severe injury, a large dose of salt and water was administered internally. Salt was used externally as well. Hot applications of a strong salt solution were made in the case of injuries. Poultices of salt were placed over bruises. Salt pounded with coconut bark was rubbed on wounds, sprains, or broken bones. In connection with this medicinal use of salt, it is interesting to note that the old Hawaiians, alone among the great Polynesian peoples, used salt as a seasoning. The Samoans of today do not use salt in their food; Tahitians use very little salt; and the Maoris never used it before the British went there and showed them that food tastes better when it is prepared with salt.

A form of treatment known as apu is still common among the Hawaiian people today. This treatment was known for its beneficial results. It was a combination of rest, of mental relaxation brought about by reciting the prescribed prayers, and of medical treatment. The medicines administered differed but the rest and the prayers were always a part of the treatment. The treatment was especially beneficial in the case of people who were thin and run down physically. The apu has been known to be harmful when it has been given to diabetic patients, for instance, for the medicine administered was very frequently compounded of starches and sugars which are of course forbidden to the diabetic. Providing the illness is correctly diagnosed, the apu is generally beneficial.

These common remedies of old Hawaii are known to many Hawaiians today, but the present-day knowledge is much less exact and far less comprehensive than the information possessed by the trained kahunas of the old days. Every now and then we hear very interesting stories of the effects of a Hawaiian medicine. This is to be expected, for there are in Hawaii many efficacious native plants whose medicinal properties are known.

Boiling was the process used in preparing many of these Hawaiian medicines. It is interesting to know how the Hawaiians managed to boil anything, when they had no fire-proof pots or containers. In order to bring liquids to a boil, the Hawaiians cleaned and heated rocks. The very hot rocks were dropped into the container. In a short time, the liquid began to boil. Stones used for this purpose were kept in a basket and used from time to time.

Something else survives to the present, besides the knowledge of some of the Hawaiian remedies. This is knowledge of ways of controlling pain through the personal influence of another person. In the old days, the trained kahuna had this power over people. There are people today who have it, and there are many stories to show this. It is a thing which is difficult to explain. It sounds like "magic" but there is nothing magic about it. People today are only just beginning to explain, and to understand, the power of suggestion in relieving pain and curing illness. The old Hawaiians perhaps did not understand how this happened, but they knew it did happen, and they developed this art in the kahunas.

II

ANCIENT HAWAIIAN MEDICAL PRACTICE VIEWED BY A DOCTOR

NILS P. LARSEN

An understanding of the medical practice of a people helps us to interpret their civilization. The reputation of the Hawaiians in the field of medicine was based on their knowledge of herbs, which was extensive. It is apparent to the student that the Hawaiians possessed other medical knowledge as well, just as important as the use of herbs. Among these may be mentioned forms of physio-therapy—for instance, lomilomi, the use of steam baths, the use of ti-leaf wrappings—and forms of psycho-therapy, labelled "magic" by the uninformed. Another significant aspect of Hawaiian medical practice was its place in the social scheme.

Behind the social organization of old Hawaii were the kahunas who were experts in their chosen fields. Very frequently the older writers, seeing ancient customs with a prejudiced eye, did not give this interpretation to the kahuna, but instead, made such remarks as these, "Heathenism now has full sway and in every village each missionary has a kahuna to combat." Such a remark indicates a partial and incorrect interpretation of the meaning and function of the kahuna. The kahuna, actually, might be a judge, or a doctor, or the head of the church. In any case, he was the expert in that particular field. The kahunas were intelligent trained men, the power behind the chiefs.

The kahuna nui was the community high priest. The kahuna makaula was the prophet, the seer. He read and interpreted, for instance, the signs of nature, in a manner which may be compared to the way in which our present-day weather prophets make their forecasts. The kahuna kilo studied the heavens and forecast events. There are astrologers today who do much what the kahuna kilo did. The kahuna puuone was the engineer. He laid out the village, made arrangements concerning water rights, and planned the use of water in the taro patches. Old Hawaii also had the kahuna po'iuhane, who may be compared to the modern spiritualist. The kahuna lua was a master in boxing and wrestling; he knew how to tie up the muscles of an antagonist, and the secrets of releasing the incapacitated muscle, which made Hawaiian wrestling so skilled. The kahuna hookelewa brought the canoes through dark and wide oceans; he was the skilled navigator. The kahuna kalaiwaa directed the building of the great canoes. The kahuna kuauhau recounted genealogies. The kahuna paaoao was master of the art of averting evil from unborn children. The kahuna hanaaloha arranged love affairs. We often see a person belittle the peculiar incantations and beliefs of barbarians. But we see these same people seriously tapping wood after a boast, or refusing to light a third cigarette with the same match, or refusing to put on a left stocking first, or becoming upset because they need to return for a forgotten article, or depending on a charm hung around the neck, to preserve them from accident. Superstition exists in any age; it is characteristic of many so-called educated people today, and it was of course found in ancient Hawaii.

Many of us at the present time have heard only about the kahuna anaana, who prayed people to death. This kahuna was only one among a large class of specially trained people. He had at his command not only the power of suggestion, but knowledge of poisons. The Hawaiians were informed about three powerful poisons—akia, a plant poison, auhuhu, a fish plant poison, and oopuhue, a deadly fish poison. Very frequently all the Hawaiian medical lore is confused with the activities of the kahuna anaana, but these were in reality only one part of Hawaiian medical practice.

There were many different skilled kahunas who may be compared to present-day specialists. The kahuna ha'iha'i iwi may be compared with the old bone setter who is still found in many communities; he made adjustments to relieve pain. The kahuna lapaau laau was the herb doctor. The kahuna lomilomi was the expert in the field of massage. The kahuna ha ha was the diagnostician. He felt the patient to determine what was wrong. If he could determine no bodily ailment, he might send the patient to the kahuna nui for spiritual aid. Otherwise, the patient was sent to the kahuna lapaau laau. The kahuna hoohanau attended women in childbirth and functioned much as the obstetrician does today.

The old Hawaiian had an interesting drug therapy. Some of the Hawaiian remedies have been shown to be effective. It is interesting to notice that the Hawaiians knew the effect of single drugs and administered simple doses as well as strange combinations. European medicine in the early 1820's relied on wierd prescriptions. In a reputable book published in 1828 in America, formulas like this are found:

> Take one armful of Thorough Wort
> One peck of White Ash Bark
> One armful of Celendyne
> Half bushel of Butternut bark
> Four pounds of Sweet Elder bark
> Four pounds of Dog Mackimus
> Six pounds of Sarsaparilla
> Four large Wake Robins
> One pound of Blood Root
> Two pounds of Balsam bark
> Two handfulls of Gill go by the ground
> One peck of Burdock roots
> Two armfulls of Arsmart
> One peck of Cuckoo Ash
> One pound of Snake root
> Two pounds of Spruce bark
> One peck of Tamerack bark

The directions state, "Boil these separately, until the strength is out; then throw out the herbs and barks; settle the liquors, and boil them together to the consistency of tar. Take White Ash bark, and burn it to ashes. With the above mentioned gum make pills by rolling it in the ashes as large as a pea. The proper dose is from seven to twelve for an adult. These give relief in pain in the stomach, jaundice, and bilious complaint, all kind of inflammatory and chronical disorders, and a safe and efficacious remedy in all cases where physic is necessary."

Such practice prevailed in Europe and America a hundred years ago. The old Hawaiians used mixtures like these, but they did not rely on them exclusively. Through trial and observation, the Hawaiians developed their pharmacopeia. They learned, for instance, to use pia. Pia is one of the finest powders which can be found. It was used for hemorrhage either of stomach or bowel, and for dysentery. Today, we use a fine powder to coat the intestine, and it is more than likely that pia is just as good for this purpose as any of the modern preparations. Kowali, used as a laxative, was no less effective than the hundreds of medicines prepared and sold today for this purpose. Uhaloa, used for sore throat and colds, has an effect very similar to that produced by aspirin. Noni, used to bring a boil to a head, acts much as magnesium sulphate which is used today. Awa was used to induce sleep and to dry up secretions; this drug was used even in Germany before the war. In modern medical practice, most of the thousands of prescriptions which were formerly used as specifics or curatives, are now known to be merely alleviative. The basis of modern drug therapy is knowledge of the use and effect of relatively few drugs. Drug therapy is a comparatively small part of the cure and prevention of disease, and although the Hawaiians often believed there was some magic curing power in their herbs and though many people today still believe this, we now recognize their alleviative rather than their curative effect.

The Hawaiians were quite abreast of modern practice in some of their ways of handling certain types of injury. If a man fell, or was hit on the head, the first thing the kahuna did was to bring him a whole calabash full of sea water or any salt solution, to drink. If the patient vomited, it was known that he was seriously ill, and that a bad turn might be expected within twenty-four hours. Today, we call this "delayed shock." The kahuna showed good observation and excellent treatment. Today, salt with sugar is administered through the veins rather than through the mouth. The underlying idea in both treatments is the same. The ancient Hawaiians treated wounds in a sound manner. They used a strong salt solution, mixed often with coconut or taro, which probably were good astringents. They left wounds open to the sun; they did not close in the infection and thereby endanger the patient.

While the Hawaiians had a relatively sound drug therapy, we must not forget that much of that knowledge has been lost. Certainly, there are at the present no persons who have been as intensively trained in the recognition of the plants, in their uses, in their effects, and in their preparation, as were the kahuna lapaau. However, though this is true, there are many people today who tend to rely on Hawaiian medicines prescribed by a friend or relative. This has been known to cause serious results, because the treatment is often given without first finding out the cause of the complaint. The fault does not lie in the Hawaiian drug therapy, but in the ignorance of the person attempting to apply it. Sometimes the patient tends to believe that the Hawaiian medicine has a peculiar magic and will surely prove effective. As a matter of fact, many Hawaiian drugs are simple and effective. In some cases they are quite as good as better known medicines, but they should be administered, as should all medicines, on the advice of some one who knows, and never under any other circumstances. The kahuna lapaau, was, in my opinion, just as scientific as the old pharmacologist with his thousands of prescriptions. For at least fifteen years, the kahuna lapaau studied nothing but herbs and plants and their effects and their preparation. No Hawaiian of the present time has had this training, or has command of this information. The herbs themselves have no magic power. It is dangerous to believe that any grandmother can prescribe for any ailment, just as it is dangerous to rely upon castor oil for every stomach ache. Each of these practices has placed many a victim in the cemetery with a ruptured appendix.

Reliance on patent and proprietary medicines, taken on anyone's recommendation, is just as unwise as reliance on some Hawaiian remedy suggested by a friend or relative. Patent medicines are peculiarly dangerous, because they are so widely distributed and advertised. A worker in a drug house made this statement to me, "We shoot through a little mixture of the coal tar products and make it into good looking pills. We give it a nice South American name, and then plaster the country with advertisements announcing that this will cure everything from a headache to a broken toe nail. We sell a lot. We can keep on selling for about three years. Then the sales begin to dwindle. When this happens, we color the compound blue, give it a new name, and stage another advertising campaign." Last year the United States drug bill for patent medicines amounted to three hundred and eighty million dollars, and for home remedies, to one hundred and sixty-five million dollars. In Hawaii in one month we spend thirty thousand dollars for a highly advertised medicine which has been proved to have no more effect than kowali. Fraud and deceit exist at any time and in any age; credulity is perhaps more characteristic of these times we call civilized and are at the mercy of any advertising talk or campaign directed by the unscrupulous, than it was of those times when there were no radios and no newspapers and no advertising circulars to spread information abroad.

Among the Hawaiian kahunas were those who were expert in the field of massage or lomilomi. They knew just how to manipulate and massage and pound sore and stiff muscles, and to bring relief. They were skilled in the arts of what is known as physio-therapy today.

In addition to their sound drug therapy and their knowledge of physio-therapy, the Hawaiians possessed knowledge of effective psycho-therapy, as we should call it today. The kahuna kahea relieved pain through the influence of his prayers, or, as we might explain it, through his powers of suggestion. To whatever cause we ascribe it, it is a fact that suffering and pain can be relieved through "suggestion" or whatever we choose to call this power. These powers were made very effective in the old days because the patient believed implicitly in the skill of the kahuna, whom he had respected and looked up to from his earliest years. Today, modern medicine is recognizing this field of psycho-therapy, which is so widely misunderstood and misinterpreted. Deceit and fraud may operate in this field perhaps even more readily than in the field of medicine itself, but certainly not more widely than it operates in the patent medicine field today.

While the Hawaiians did not possess knowledge of what we call preventive medicine today, many of their kapus operated as preventive measures, and preserved the health and secured the integrity of the ancient stock. The rigid regulations regarding intermarriage of classes, the measures taken to insure purity of stock, the penalties for breaking these regulations, helped to keep the health of the Hawaiians at a high level. Kapus having to do with sex relationships had the same effect. When these, and other, kapus were broken, and at the same time, venereal disease was introduced, the Hawaiians died in great numbers, and the health of many of those surviving was affected. There is no doubt that the ancient kapus would have served as a barrier against the inroads of new disease, if they had been kept, but they were thrown away, and the Hawaiian people were left unprotected. Their long isolation from foreign diseases had prevented them from developing within themselves any immunity; their kapus which would have helped to save them, were cast aside, and the people which had numbered some 400,000 at the time of the coming of Captain Cook, were reduced to 180,000 in the early 1800's. Today Hawaiians of pure descent number less than 20,000, while those of part-Hawaiian blood number perhaps 40,000. The decrease may be attributed not only to the inroads of disease, and the intermarriage with other peoples, but also to the fact that the Hawaiian people as a whole have not adopted modern preventive measures to take the place of the old kapus discarded more than a hundred years ago. This disastrous rate of decrease still exists. Last year, out of every thousand Hawaiian mothers who gave birth to children, 37 died, while during the same period out of each thousand haole mothers, 2.5 died. Two hundred twelve out of every thousand Hawaiian babies born last year died, while only 40 out of every thousand haole babies died. The death rate among Hawaiian babies is high, but it is decreasing as a result of education. It will continue to decrease as modern knowledge of preventive measures is applied, and if there is not too great a tendency to rely on the medical lore of the past about which no one today is fully informed.

CHAPTER 25

NATURE'S BALANCE IN HAWAII

E. H. BRYAN, JR.

There are a few general interesting facts about the plants and animals of the Hawaiian islands which everyone here should know and understand. These facts explain the "why" of many things which seem puzzling. It is not necessary to learn a lot of long tongue-twisting names. Names are only handles for objects, by which we can pick them up. Unless we intend to do a lot of "picking-up," it is quite a waste of effort to learn a lot of names. But we should have some understanding of these general ideas and relationships which explain so much about the plant and animal life of the islands.

There are three words which are used by scientists to indicate the relationship of a plant or animal to a region. These are "endemic", "indigenous," and "introduced." Endemic means that the kind of organism is found in that region and nowhere else. Indigenous means that it is at home in the region, but got there naturally from somewhere else. Introduced means that it got to the region accidentally or on purpose, directly or indirectly, through the help of man. The distinctions between the three are sometimes a little hard to determine. For instance, if a weed seed reaches Hawaii floating on a log, and the seed is cast up on the beach and sprouts, you would have to call the plant indigenous; certainly its descendants would be. But if the seed arrived in a packing case, on a ship, even if the man who owned the case did not know it was there, the resulting plant would be called introduced. However, the general distinction between these three terms is plain.

A surprisingly large percentage of the plants and animals which occurred here before the coming of man are found nowhere else in the world. We say "before the coming of man" because man has accidentally or intentionally brought into these islands a great many foreign plants, birds, insects, domestic animals, and other forms of life, which would probably not otherwise have found their way here.

There are about 2500 different kinds of flowering plants known in these islands. About 1500 of them have been introduced, either accidentally or on purpose, through the agency of man. This leaves 1000 which are native. Of these approximately 900 are endemic and 100 indigenous. In round numbers, 90 per cent of the native plants are endemic, or found in no other part of the world. There are about 150 different species of birds which have been recorded as living in the Hawaiian islands. About 40 of these should be classed as introduced. Of the remaining 110 species, some 88 are endemic in these islands. But some of the remaining 22 are migratory birds which fly down from the far north, so that again we can say that between 80 and 90 per cent of the native birds are endemic. How about the insects? The Bishop Museum's card catalogue shows about 4600 different species in the islands. Of these about 800 are introduced species. Of the remainder, 3700 species are endemic, 100 species indigenous. This gives 95 per cent of the native insects as endemic.

The same proportion is found for the famous Hawaiian land snails, and for various other forms of life in these islands, but these few examples should be enough to indicate that the fauna and flora of Hawaii are very specialized, with a very high percentage of the species which were not brought here in quite recent times in man's shipping found nowhere in the world except in these islands. You naturally ask, "What causes that?" Let us see if the answer is not brought out later.

Another interesting thing about Hawaii's plant and animal life is the fact that most of the serious insect pests are not native insects, but introduced species. This might be expected in the case of cultivated crops nearly all of which are introduced. But it is also equally true for the native plants of the forest, whose chief insect enemies are introduced species. The native insects seem to do little or no damage. Consider just one of many examples of this. There are about 150 different species of leafhoppers, which are native to the islands, and are found in the mountain forests. Not one of these does any particular damage to the plants with which it associates. But three species of introduced leafhoppers cause an immense amount of damage: one to the sugar cane, one to corn, and one, the "torpedo bug," to both ornamental and forest trees. Again you ask, "Why?" Again let us wait and see!

If we ask why the native birds are so rare, we are again led back to the reason underlying the effect of native and introduced insects. We hear it said that the birds are scarce because of the Hawaiian feather gatherers; because the mynah birds have driven them all away; because they have been killed by the mongoose. Thousands of birds must have been snared, and, no doubt, a few were killed by the men who were employed as professional feather gatherers. Still this is not the reason why native birds of the forests became extinct. The feather gatherers commonly captured only three kinds of birds, the mamo, the oo, and the iiwi. Of these, the one which was most generally killed, the iiwi, is one of the few native forest birds which is at all common in the forests today. The mynah is a pugnacious, quarrelsome fellow, but one can hardly blame him for the extinction of birds in the dense forest where he seldom, if ever, goes. It is true that the mongoose has been the downfall of several kinds of ground-nesting birds. But the forest birds on Kauai, where there is no mongoose, are little better off than those on the other islands. No, we will have to look to the subject of nature's balance, again, to answer this question.

The underlying reasons for all these conditions, the answers to all these questions, are the same: Nature's balance in Hawaii has been upset. What is this balance of nature? The story is a long and somewhat complicated one, but it is so fundamental to the study of Hawaiian natural history that everyone should try to understand it. To understand it, we need to appreciate the isolation of Hawaii, the balance which was established here, and the way in which this balance has been upset.

HAWAII'S ISOLATION

The Hawaiian islands are the summits of a great range of volcanic mountains which rises 18,000 feet above the floor of the ocean in order to reach the surface of the sea. Were the water to be removed, Mauna Kea and Mauna Loa would be found to be the highest mountains in the world, nearly 32,000 feet high, with a continuous slope. This chain of islands is separated from other masses of land by broad stretches of deep ocean. It is over 2000 miles to North America; over 4000 miles to Japan and the Philippines. To the south are only small scattered islands, the nearest of which are 900 miles away. The Hawaiian islands are among the most isolated areas in the world.

Having been built up by successive outpourings of lava, flow upon flow, these islands were not always covered with plants and animals. The plants and animals which are native to these islands today are the descendants of others which found their way here at some time in the past. Some people think that they came here floating on the ocean, blown by the wind, or associated with flying birds or floating logs. Other people think that the islands of our group were once connected with other island groups, or perhaps the mainland, by areas or ridges of land, which they called "land bridges," along which the plants and animals spread. We do not know which explanation is true, for it is hard to see how some of our plants and animals could have gotten here by wind, sea, logs, or birds; and, on the other hand, the islands are surrounded by great stretches of very deep water, giving no hint of former "land bridges."

NATURE'S BALANCE AND HOW IT WAS ESTABLISHED IN HAWAII

In any event, the plants and animals came slowly, over a long period of time. Those which could not get along with the others either perished or were forced to become modified so that they could get along. Thus, the native plants and animals reached a state of harmony with each other and with their environment, which we call a "balance of nature." If an insect arrived in the islands which was a serious pest of some plant, one of two things happened: either the plant became killed off until it no longer served to support the insect, which in turn, through this loss of food, became reduced in numbers until it no longer destroyed all the plants of that kind, and a balance was formed; or else the insect was preyed upon or parasitized by another insect, which kept it under control. Thus, by strife, all lived in a seeming harmony; and in the native forest, as well as elsewhere, there was established a "balance in nature."

As the ancestors of the present plants and animals arrived, they gradually became spread throughout the different islands, and became isolated from each other, even as they were isolated from their original homeland. Hawaii is noted for its great range of environmental conditions. Within a few miles one can find rainfall varying from almost none at all to huge quantities. As one goes up Manoa Valley from Moiliili to Konahuanui, the rainfall increases from 25 inches or so to 150 inches a year. The greatest range within a limited area is found on Kauai, where Waialeale has a rainfall of about 500 inches a year, and a few miles away, Mana has only a dozen inches. Thus, plants and animals, isolated in different environments, tended to become different; and in the course of thousands of years they formed new species, different from their ancestors. Many of the ancestral species may have died off, because they were not too well suited to their environment. This would account for the great number of endemic forms, found nowhere else in the world.

Although the forests were formerly much more extensive than they are today, they probably did not cover all of the islands. There were dry or lava-covered areas where forests could not grow. The physical environment played a very large part in nature's balance. But the fresh lava flows gradually weathered, and on them a succession of plants followed one another. Lichens, mosses, grasses, hardy shrubs and tree ferns, lehua trees, vines and undergrowth, gradually turned porous rock into fertile soil, in which luxuriant rainforests could grow.

But at every stage there was harmony. The ferns, mosses, and undergrowth caught and conserved the moisture about the bases of the trees. The trees, in turn, shaded and protected the moisture-loving undergrowth. The insects were not destructive, but lived in happy, though seemingly harsh, association with the plants. The native birds ate the insects or sipped the nectar from the flowers. Excess was soon put down by its very excessiveness; that is, by keen, but harmonious, competition. There was balance in nature.

HOW THIS BALANCE WAS UPSET

Then came influences which upset this balance. For instance, there was the Polynesian with his gardens, his foreign plants, his pigs, and his dogs, and later his greed which led to the gathering of sandalwood for the foreigner. There was the haole, with his cattle, sheep, goats, cultivation, roads and trails, along which spread the foreign weeds and insects which came with his shipping. The cattle, first introduced by Captain Vancouver in 1792, soon ran wild in the forest. Goats, a present from Captain Cook, may have been progenitors of those which we have to kill off today to keep them from making all our mountains as barren as Kahoolawe. These and other introduced animals trampled down the protecting undergrowth. Strange plants, inharmonious to these surroundings, such as uluhi fern, lantana, and foreign grasses, took the place of the undergrowth which had died off and prevented the native trees and shrubs from propagating themselves.

As the vegetation went, so went the insects, the land shells, and the birds. Our old men of Hawaii in their youth gathered land shells from sturdy trees where only grassland and pineapple fields are found today.

The extinction of the birds may not have been wholly due to the dying back of the forests, but both were victims of the advance of "civilization," the upsetting of nature's balance. Mr. George Munroe has pointed out that many birds died off on Lanai at a time when, and in a region where, the forests were not dying back. He thinks the cause was some bird disease, introduced with foreign birds and poultry. Even this was an upsetting of nature's balance. The arrival of the mongoose might also be so considered. Domestic cats and other animals that have gone wild are also terribly destructive of birds.

We are able to understand most of the curious and interesting facts about the plant and animal life of these islands by a knowledge of nature's balance and its upset in Hawaii.

CHAPTER 26

TREES AND PLANTS

ALBERT F. JUDD

NOTE: This lecture on plants was given in the old Hawaiian style, during observation of the objects discussed. This chapter is the material presented for study prior to the lecture in the arboretum of The Kamehameha Schools. It is not a formal inclusive treatise on the subject but is rather a practical talk on the plants of Hawaii, their characteristics and their ancient and possibly modern uses.

The Hawaiians were intimate with the botanical world. They were close observers of nature. They brought certain plants of these islands to a high degree of development. They knew every plant and tree of the mountains and of the lowlands; they discovered the value of every useful root, bark, fruit, wood and leaf. From the trees and plants came much of their food; every material which went into the building of the house; every article which furnished the house—the calabash, the gourd, the mat, the kapas; most of the clothing and many of the ornamental leis; nearly all of the medicines in common use; the soap and the dyes, the lights,—all of these things and many others, the Hawaiians obtained from the plants and trees of the islands.

The Hawaiians were good agriculturists. The sweet potatoes which they cultivated are among the most delicious in the world. They developed numbers of varieties of taros and bananas. Among the best eating sugar canes are those which have been here from early times. The Hawaiians were good botanists. They classified some of their plants. For instance, they named the ohia ai, ohia ha, ohia lehua, ohia lehua makanoe, and many more. They made these classifications long before the great botanist Linnaeus was born.

The house building and furnishing, the clothing, utensils, and fishing gear, showed the Hawaiian's knowledge of and dependence on, the plant life of the islands. The corner posts were, when possible, made of the durable uhiuhi, the thatch of pili grass. Calabashes were made of kou, milo and kamani, for these woods contained no tannic acid to spoil the flavor of the poi. Koa furnished the timber for the canoes; hau and wiliwili the material for the outriggers and the floats for the fish nets. Long withes of ulei kept open the fish nets of certain types. Olona was the strongest fibre. The barks of akolea, wauke and mamake were made into kapa. Dyes came from many plants; the gray-green came from the mao; the yellow from the olena, the seeds of the nanu and the roots of the noni; the pink from the alaea; from the kukui came the dark stain used on the new fish nets. Akia and auhuhu, pounded to paste, made easier certain types of fishing and did not damage the fish as food. Kukui furnished light at night, while the nuts when cooked furnished the relish called inamona. Leis were made of many things—maile, seaweed, mokihana, hala fruit, lehua and ilima blooms, and such ferns as palapalai and pala. Medicines were obtained almost entirely from herbs. The Hawaiians possessed considerable accurate knowledge of the medicinal qualities of the plants of the islands and used this knowledge to good effect. The Hawaiians kept their persons clean; bathing was necessary for their comfort. Their soap was anapanapa. Coconut oil was used to keep the skin smooth and the scalp soft. The coconut palm gave the Hawaiian his broom which was made from the midrib of the coconut leaf. The coconut bole, with its hard exterior and pithy interior, was easily fashioned into the hula drum. Niu hauhau was the perfect drink. A confection was the root of the ti, baked in the big imu for forty-eight hours. Green ti leaves were used as wrappers for the food to be cooked and for bundles of things to be kept fresh. Dried ti leaves were used on the hukilau nets and for the making of sandals. Ieie and halapepe furnished their tops to decorate the heiau and the lanai during feasts. The fragrant awapuhi and palapalai were strewn on the floor of iliili. From the hala came the materials for the common mats, while the finer mats were made from makaloa. The aerial roots of the ieie furnished material for baskets, while the large gourd provided the containers for kapa and the smaller gourds were made into water bottles. These are only a few illustrations to show the dependence of the Hawaiian on the plant life of the islands, and the expert knowledge he must have possessed of the peculiar properties and values of these plants.

The following list is not a complete inventory of the trees and plants which existed in Hawaii before the coming of Captain Cook. It contains only those trees and plants which may be found in the Kamehameha Schools' Hawaiian Forest. Some of these were planted; others grew there naturally, but all may be found and identified by the interested observer. The uses listed are only those which are known to the writer; doubtless there are other uses which may be added.

NATIVE NAME	BOTANICAL NAME	USED IN OLDEN DAYS	Page reference in Neal and Metzger "In Honolulu Gardens"
Aalii, aalii kumakua	Dodonaea eriocarpa		
Aalii, aalii kumakani	Dodonaea viscosa	Wood dark, heavy and hard.	
Aheahea or Aweoweo	Chenopodium sandwicheum	Leaves for pot herb.	
Akia	Wikstroemia oahuensis	Fish poison; inner bark for rope.	
Akolea	Boehmeria stipularis	Bark for kapa.	
Alahee or walahee	Plectronia odorata	Hard, durable wood, used for agricultural implements.	
Alaea	Bixa orellana	Seed for red dye.	
Anapanapa	Colubrina asiatica	Leaves for soap.	
Aulu or kaulu	Sapindus oahuensis	(Indigenous to Oahu and Kauai.) (See Manele.)	
Hala (screw pine)	Pandanus odoratissimus	Wood of female tree soft. Wood of male tree hard, beautiful; used for many things; seeds for leis and for brushes for applying kapa dye; leaves for mats, baskets, fans, etc.	20, 21
Halapepe	Dracaena aurea	Soft wood used for carving idols. Sometimes confused with ieie which is a vine—Halapepe is a tree.	

NATIVE NAME	BOTANICAL NAME	USED IN OLDEN DAYS	Page reference in Neal and Metzger "In Honolulu Gardens"
Hau	Hibiscus tiliaceus	Light wood used for canoe outriggers; bark for rope.	195, 196
Hoawa Aawa hua kukui	Pittosporum Hosmeri		
Iliahi (Sandalwood)	Santalum ellipticum Santalum cuneatum	Leaves and bark used in mixture for destroying lice and removing dandruff.	
Iliau	Wilkesia gymnoxiphium	(Resembles small halapepe.)	
Ilima	Sida spp.	Flowers for leis.	195
Kalamona	Cassia Gaudichaudii	(Flowers pale greenish yellow, bright yellow in haole kalamona.)	141
Kamani	Calophyllum inophyllum	Wood for calabashes. Flowers much prized for odor.	211, 212
Kauila	Colubrina oppositifolia	Very hard wood for spears, for kapa beaters and other implements.	
Keahi	Nesoluma polynesica		
Ki or ti	Cordyline terminalis	Leaves (lai) used for wrapping of bundles, also for wrapping food to be cooked; wreath of finely combed leaves used for soothing nerves. Baked root used as confection.	66. 67

NATIVE NAME	BOTANICAL NAME	USED IN OLDEN DAYS	Page reference in Neal and Metzger "In Honolulu Gardens"
Kokio	Kokia drynariodes Kokia Rockii	(Indigenous to Molokai.) (Indigenous to Mount Hualalai.) Bark for dyeing fish-nets.	
Kokio (yellow)	Hibiscus Brackenridgei		
Kokio keokeo (white)	Hibiscus Arnottianus	(Oahu variety.)	200, 201
Kokio ula (red)	Hibiscus kokio	(Kauai and Oahu varieties.)	
Koa	Acacia koa	Wood for canoes; other wood for implements.	129, 130
Kou	Cordia subcordata	Calabashes, spittoons. Seeds edible.	265
Kukui (candle-nut)	Aleurites moluccana	Nuts for torches and for food (called inamona when cooked); oil of nuts for lamp fuel; black dye for tattooing; bark of root black dye for coloring canoes (soot of burning nuts also used for canoe paint); bark of trunk brown dye for fishnets. Milk from young twigs for sunburn, chapped lips, etc.; resin (pilali) used as glue; edible.	178, 181
Kului	Nototrichium sandwicense		

NATIVE NAME	BOTANICAL NAME	USED IN OLDEN DAYS	Page reference in Neal and Metzger "In Honolulu Gardens"
Lama	Maba sandwicensis	(Indigenous to all islands.) Seed edible; wood sacred to goddess Laka—used for sacred enclosures, houses for gods, etc.	
	Maba Hillebrandii	(Indigenous to Oahu.)	
Loulu (fan palm)	Pritchardia Martii	(Indigenous to Hawaiian islands.) Nuts edible. Fans and temporary house thatching.	41
	Pritchardia Thurstonii	(Indigenous to other South Sea islands.)	41
	Pritchardia pacifica	(Indigenous to other South Sea islands.)	40
Mahoe	Alectryon macrococcus	Fruit edible; rare tree related to lichee.	
Maile	Alyxia olivaeformis	Leis.	252, 253
Mamani	Sophora chrysophylla	Very durable wood for house posts	
Manele, a'e (soap berry)	Sapindus saponaria	(Indigenous to Hawaii.)	190
Mao or Huluhulu	Gossypium tomentosum	Native brown cotton. Leaves used for making very green dye.	204

NATIVE NAME	BOTANICAL NAME	USED IN OLDEN DAYS	Page reference in Neal and Metzger "In Honolulu Gardens"
Milo	Thespesia populnea	Wood for calabashes.	202
Naio (false sandalwood)	Myoporum sandwicense	Dried wood (aaka) has fragrance resembling true sandalwood.	
Nanu	Gardenia Brighamii	Yellow dye from fruit for kapa.	
Neneleau, neleau (Hawaiian sumach)	Rhus semialata var. sandwicensis	Wood soft and light but tough.	
Noni	Morinda citrifolia	Yellow dye from roots; red dye from bark; oil from fruit for hair; used in preparation for medicine; eaten in times of scarcity.	295
Ohe, ohe makai	Reynoldsia sandwicensis	Resin used for various purposes; light wood for making kukuluaeo, or stilts, used in game of that name.	
Ohia ai (mountain apple)	Eugenia malaccensis	Fruit edible. Wood formerly used for house posts and rafters and for coupling together double canoes—considered sacred. Used for images and for temple enclosures.	229, 230
Ohia lehua, lehua	Metrosideros polymorpha	Wood hard, durable, for spears, kapa beaters and images.	233, 234
Olona	Touchardia latifolia	Fibre plant—strongest cordage known	

NATIVE NAME	BOTANICAL NAME	USED IN OLDEN DAYS	Page reference in Neal and Metzger "In Honolulu Gardens"
Olopua, pua	Osmanthus sandwicensis	Wood very hard, close grained, and durable. Used for adze handles, etc.	
Papala kepau	Pisonia umbellifera	Viscous substance from fruit used for bird lime.	
Pili	Heteropogon contortus	House thatching and sled runs.	25
Popolo	Solanum nodiflorum	Berries edible—a pot herb.	
Pukeawe, puakeawe	Styphelia Tameiameiae	Hard wood for kapa beaters.	
Uhaloa, hialoa, or ala-ala-pa-loa	Waltheria americana	Bark of root chewed for sore throat.	
Uhiuhi	Mezoneurum kauaiense	Wood very hard, close grained, very durable, almost black, and heavier than water. Used for spears, kapa beaters, laau melomelo.	
Ulei or uulei	Osteomeles anthyllidifolia	Long branches used to hold open certain fish-nets. Fruit edible.	
Wauke (paper mulberry)	Broussonetia papyrifera	Bark used for kapa.	
Wiliwili	Erythrina monosperma	Soft light wood for canoe outriggers.	160, 161

CHAPTER 27

ANIMAL LIFE

C. H. EDMONDSON

Oceanic islands are always of intense interest to the biologist and to others as well. Isolated regions of the world, such as the Hawaiian islands, are interesting because of the many things which are not there. When we look over these islands we find that there are many forms of both plant and animal life which we might expect to find but do not find. At the same time we find other forms that are of intense interest because in some way they came to these isolated regions of the world. We have to stop to think often times and wonder where the plants and animals which we find on islands of this sort came from and how they reached these places and when they came. If we take the generally accepted view of the origin of the Hawaiian islands, that they were probably raised from the bottom of the ocean in one isolated unit or several units, unconnected with any continental land, we must consider them to have been at first masses of volcanic rock, bare of soil, bare of vegetation, and bare of animal life. That occurred ages and ages ago, we know not how long ago. Then for countless long ages of time these volcanic rocks must have been disintegrating, soil must have been forming, and from some source came the first organic life on these islands.

THE BEGINNING OF LIFE ON OCEANIC ISLANDS

We must draw an imaginary picture of the source of the first plant life of Hawaii. Doubtless plants came first and animal life later. Perhaps some bird winging its way across the ocean found a haven of rest on these islands, these bare lifeless islands. Seeds of one kind or another, attached to that bird, may have gotten a foothold in the soil. Or perhaps a drifting log was thrown on the island by a wave, and imbedded in such a log may have been seeds of plants which then gained a foothold in the soil. All such pictures are but guesses. We have no idea how the first plants or the first animals actually arrived on Hawaii. We can only imagine that seeds may have come attached to birds flying through the air or may have come as drifting things on the surface of the ocean, or may have been blown by strong winds from some other source. That is prehistoric, that is pre-human, natural history.

SOURCES OF INFORMATION ABOUT ANIMAL LIFE IN OLD HAWAII

There are a number of ways by which we can guess fairly accurately as to what was present on Hawaii 10,000 years ago. For one thing, we can make more or less accurate guesses by making a careful analysis of the plants and animals found in Hawaii today. We can look back and determine with some accuracy what their ancestors were, and to some extent how long they have been in the islands. We also study the records of those who visited Hawaii in very early times. When Captain Cook visited Hawaii in 1778 the animals mentioned in his official report to the British government were the rat, the mouse, the dog, the bat, the hog, birds of many kinds, lizards, insects, land snails, and chickens. We can believe that the early Hawaiians, as they came to Oahu and the other islands, brought with them certain forms of animal life. There is no doubt that the dog and the pig at least, and probably the chicken, were brought by the early Hawaiians. These animals were very close to the life of the Polynesian people and it is not probable that they would start out from their original home in the South Seas without these animals. Still another source of information about the plant and animal life which existed here is the fossil remains of that life. There are many fossils in the raised beaches and reefs around the islands. Near Waipahu there are beds of huge oysters, some six inches long, much larger than any present day oysters in Hawaii. On the Waianae side of Oahu, far from the sea in the raised reefs, the fossil remains of huge oysters, nearly nine inches in diameter, have been found. Each such fossil tells us something about the animal life which must have existed around the islands in the past. Still another source of information about the plants and animals once found here, is the old songs, stories, and legends of the people. These songs, stories, and legends are filled with mention of animals, and are proof that such animals were certainly here in early times.

One of the beliefs of the early peoples was that the spirit of a dead person entered into an animal. These spirits, or aumakuas, became helpers of the people. Some of these aumakuas were not as good or as helpful as others, but nevertheless they were aumakuas. Miss Beckwith has written an interesting article on the aumakua of the shark. The shark was considered one of these helpers and almost every community along the sea coast had its aumakua shark, a friendly helper held in reverence by the people. Some of the important gods or aumakuas were the shark, the eel, and the limpet. The shark and the limpet were supposed to be friendly aumakuas who stilled the waves at sea and assisted the fishermen in various ways. Owls were aumakuas in various regions, especially in Kona. The cowrie and the squid were considered among the important aumakuas; Mr. Emerson lists many lesser animals which were held in respect.

The dog was considered to be fairly good in certain cases, but nevertheless he was considered a thief. The pig, though a mischief maker, was held in reverence, for the pig was considered an animal which could identify royalty and could point out chiefs and kings even if they were disguised. The rat was considered a good aumakua, generally speaking, because one of the mythological characters in ancient times tied up all the food of the earth in a large bag and hung it up in the heavens. It was the rat who gnawed the rope and let the food drop to earth again, so for this reason, the rat was thought to be a good aumakua. The rat has always been an outstanding mammal in Hawaiian history, both legendary and recent. Some of the curious and the most interesting legends surround this little animal which the Hawaiians must have known long before they came to Hawaii itself.

In Fornander's Folklore there are some interesting stories about the history of the rat in connection with the legendary Hawaiian people. One of these is the story of Mainele. Mainele was a famous rat shooter. All of the legends seem to indicate that rat shooting was one of the chief sports of the kings and high chiefs. One day a challenger arose saying that he could beat Mainele in rat shooting and the contest was arranged. One of the feats of Mainele was to pin ten rats on his arrow at one shot; he did this always, whether he saw the rats or not. The challenger said he could beat this, and the contest began. Mainele shot and the customary ten rats were strung on his arrow. The challenger shot, and behold, ten rats were strung on his arrow, and on its point was a bat. Mainele said, "This is a draw, no one has won," but the challenger quoted an old Hawaiian saying to the effect that the bat is the cousin of the rat; therefore, he said he won because his score was eleven rather than ten, and also because he had strung all the rats on his arrow by their whiskers. Mainele had always shot the rats through the body but this expert had strung them by their whiskers; so he was finally considered the champion. There are all sorts of legends of this type. They show us not only what animals were here in the early days, but also reveal the fact that these animals must have been here for a very long time indeed for this body of legends and folklore to have grown up about them. The aumakua association in the early Hawaiian thinking links up the animal life and the people very closely, and offers further proof of the kind and type of animal life which must have existed here since the earliest days.

MAMMALIAN LIFE SUMMARIZED

We may consider this a little more logically. In Captain Cook's time the mammalian forms of animals known to exist in Hawaii were, as we have seen, the rat, the mouse, the dog, at least one type of bat and possibly two, and the hog. These were the mammals existing at the time of Captain Cook's visit, and probably for a long time before. One of the recent mammalian immigrants to the islands is the Asiatic deer, which was introduced from Japan in 1827 or thereabouts, and which is one of the largest mammals in the islands if we except the domesticated animals. Other immigrants, which entered Hawaii earlier than the deer, are cattle, sheep, the horse, and goats. All of these were introduced by early navigators, some probably by Vancouver. About 1883 the mongoose was introduced for a very definite purpose—to kill the rats in the cane fields.

BIRD LIFE

Hawaiian birds offer the biologist one of the most interesting groups of animals anywhere in the world. There are two places in which birds have been outstanding in natural history. Hawaii is one, and the islands off the South American coast are the other. Strange to say, the development of birds in Hawaii has been somewhat similar to their development in the islands off South America. In both places very strange and peculiar modifications have taken place. The modifications which took place in Hawaii were so peculiar that some specialists did not recognize the native birds as belonging to the group to which they actually belong. This interesting group of birds are Drepanids, and include the mamo, the oo, the uu, and the iiwi, all those curious older birds of Hawaii. There were some eighteen or nineteen genera of these curious birds developed in Hawaii, and they developed probably from two forms which came from somewhere, possibly tropical America in ages gone by. These two forms, if there were but two to start with, gave rise to eighteen or nineteen genera and to some fifty different species. It is thought that the cause of this was the food habits of these birds. Those long-billed honey eaters, as they were called, fed on the honey within the lobelia blossoms and their bills became modified for dipping into this flower. Other plants developed and some birds had to become modified so that they could feed upon insects and seeds. Their bills became modified in strange ways. These modifications which took place are among the most noted in biological history. They are cited everywhere in the study of ornithology as outstanding features where food habits have certainly modified birds in very marked ways.

Besides the Drepanid birds there were other forms which were peculiar to the islands. Some of these are the Hawaiian owl, which is still present; the Hawaiian goose, which is very rare but is still found on Hawaii; the Hawaiian hawk, and many sea birds which were peculiar to this region of the world. Years ago a wingless rail was found on Laysan Island. Doubtless it had been on Laysan for a long period of time, so long that it had lost the use of its wings. This curious bird was destroyed on Laysan. Rabbits were introduced there some years ago, the vegetation was destroyed, the birds were nearly wiped out, and that island became a desolate sandy place as a result. In 1923, the Tanager expedition went there and killed every rabbit. It has been recently reported that the vegetation is coming back and this will mean the returning of some birds.

REPTILES

Among the animal life of old Hawaii were found some reptiles. At the time of Captain Cook's visit in 1778, two species of lizards were probably present. Lizards were the land reptiles about which the early Hawaiians knew something, because in their legendary records the lizard was an aumakua, sometimes beneficial, sometimes not so beneficial. There are at the present time at least seven species of lizards in Hawaii. There are four geckos—these are the little lizards which come into the houses. There are three skinks, which are the long tailed lizards found outdoors, and which run so rapidly. Recently, on the campus of The Kamehameha Schools, a legless lizard which had never been reported in Hawaii before, was found. It is a little thing like an earthworm and is a burrowing form. Three young specimens were taken from the campus. The adult has never been seen here; it is supposed to be twelve or fifteen inches long, while each of these specimens was only three inches long.

The fishing folk of ancient Hawaii knew something about sea reptiles, the turtles, of which there are two in local waters today. We know that the turtle entered into the experience and life of the fishing folk in the old days.

INSECT LIFE

Among the interesting forms of life in Hawaii are the insects. The records of Captain Cook state that there were many flies in Hawaii. Apparently in no other region visited by the Cook expedition were there so many flies as there were in Hawaii. It is known that the following insects were in the islands in 1822; butterflies, cockroaches, moths, dragonflies, and spiders. There were no mosquitoes in the islands in the early 1820's. Andrew Bloxam, who was here in 1824-1825, reported butterflies, the moth, earwigs, a cicada, and a sphinx moth. In 1832, David Malo, a very capable Hawaiian who was very observing especially in the field of ethnology and natural history, recorded that these animals were present: birds, bats, dragonflies, the wasp, the grasshopper, the spider, the louse, the earthworm, the lizard. In 1837, Jarves mentioned finding many troublesome forms of insects and animals—the mosquito, cockroaches, fleas, the scorpion, the centipede, rats, and the lizard, but no frogs, snakes, or toads. It is probable that the mosquito came in as early as 1828, perhaps from Spanish ships which touched here from Central America and Mexico.

About 1850, the raising of sugar cane began to develop to a considerable degree and with this development came insects which affected the cane in a serious way. From this time on, the economic side of the insect life began to be stressed. In 1892, the Bureau of Plant Inspection was organized. Kalakaua was perhaps the first king who did much about these injurious insects. He attempted to pass laws to restrict the importation of certain plants and also of certain injurious animals. Ever since 1892, certain plants and animals have been excluded from the islands.

CHAPTER 28

THE GEOLOGY OF THE HAWAIIAN ISLANDS

HAROLD S. PALMER

The science of geology has as its aim the giving of an orderly description and reasonable explanation of the surface features of our earth and of the structures of the rocks underlying them. Many things in this world show a balance that is maintained between opposing constructive and destructive processes. With certain other things there is no balance and one class of processes predominates. In growing animals and in growing volcanoes the constructive processes predominate; and in the old animals and volcanoes the destructive forces have the upper hand. Both constructive and destructive processes are at work modifying the Hawaiian islands. On much of the island of Hawaii destructive work has accomplished very little as yet. On other islands, notably Kauai, the destructive processes have long been dominant.

In the limited space of this chapter we shall consider the constructive work of volcanoes and of reef organisms, and the destructive work of streams and waves. The work of the other agencies is less conspicuous in Hawaii, and will be omitted.

VOLCANOES AND THEIR CONSTRUCTIVE WORK

A volcano is a place where molten matter from the interior of the earth reaches the surface. The volcanoes of most volcanic regions are not scattered about in an irregular way but are arranged along lines. Examination of a map of the Hawaiian islands shows that these volcanic islands lie in a zone. In the 350 miles of the zone from Hawaii to Niihau there are some 17 volcanic centers, but the zone extends a total length of 1,600 miles from southeast to northwest, and includes many shoals and reefs and a few rocky islets beyond Niihau. These are former volcanic islands which have been very much reduced, and, of them, only Midway Island is inhabited.

If we measure the distance from one volcano to the next, as from Kilauea to Mauna Loa or to Mauna Kea, we find that the seven distances of this kind that can be measured on the island of Hawaii average about 25 miles, and range from 21 to 30 miles. Nine such distances within the Maui-Molokai-Lanai-Kahoolawe group also average about 25 miles. There must be a reasonable explanation for this uniformity of spacing. It seems probable that the forces that have tended to bring molten matter from below have encountered a rather uniformly resistant part of the earth's crust which has broken and let the molten matter through at uniform intervals.

Not only do the Hawaiian volcanoes have a linear arrangement and a uniform spacing, but they have other characteristics in common with other volcanoes. On the flanks of many of them are scattered smaller cones, such as Diamond Head, Punchbowl, Round Top and the Salt Lake Craters on Oahu. The minor cones also tend to be arranged in lines, as is most excellently illustrated in the Koko Head region of Oahu, where a line between Koko Head at the southwest end and Rabbit Island at the northeast end contains fourteen points at which eruption has taken place. This line of vents represents a rift in the flank of the Koolau volcano which opened widely enough here and there for lava to flow out or ash to be ejected.

Though we do not know the ultimate origin of lava, we do know that volcanic eruptions can be classified into two chief types, which are known as "quiet" and "explosive" eruptions. The quiet type is usual in Hawaii. It may manifest itself by a rising of lava into the summit crater, with or without an overflow of lava. Often such eruptions continue for many months or even years, and offer not only an inducement to tourists but opportunities for the scientific study of volcanism. Other quiet eruptions manifest themselves at vents on the flank of the volcano from which the lava is discharged. Quiet eruptions yield chiefly liquid lava, but dissolved in the lava is a moderate amount of gas. When the lava comes to the surface, the pressure on it is reduced and some or much of the gas comes out of solution, just as taking the cap off a bottle of soda water relieves the pressure and allows the gas to come out of solution. As the gas escapes it makes bubbles in the liquid. If the liquid is soda water, a foam or froth is made. If the liquid is lava, it also gets full of bubbles which are preserved as pores when the lava has cooled to the solid state.

Quiet eruptions may give rise to either of two types of lava, namely pahoehoe and aa. Incidentally, it is worth noting that these two Hawaiian words have been adopted by geologists of many nations and can be found in French, German, and English books as well as in American books. These are two Hawaiian gifts to scientific language. If the lava remains so hot that it is still fluid until it gets to a place where it is ponded or to a slope so gentle that it can barely flow, and then solidfies, it makes the relatively smooth pahoehoe type of surface. It is not smooth in the sense that a concrete pavement is smooth; it is smooth merely in comparison with the indescribably rough surface of an aa flow. If the lava is still in motion as it cools past its freezing point, then the outer part of the flow cools and therefore solidifies while the interior is still hot and somewhat fluid. If there is still movement within the hard, solidified, and brittle skin, the skin will have to break. It is thus broken into countless extremely irregular fragments that range in size from the finest dust to pieces the size of a piano or bigger. Most seem to fall in size between a tennis ball and a suitcase. The writer saw much of the Hoopuloa flow of 1926, and was impressed with the remarkable quietness with which the flow advanced and brought into existence its great volume of new rock.

If the crust of the earth has once been broken through by lava at some particular point, it is most likely that later lots of lava will find the same point to be their easiest place of escape. It is for this reason that eruptions tend to occur at one place for many many centuries.

Let us next consider why the resulting pile of lava tends to have the shape of a dome or of a cone. The first time the lava comes through a vent, it will flow off in the easiest direction which is down the steepest slope and flood more or less of the surrounding region, be it sea bottom or dry land. The next discharge will be deflected into some other path, as the first has been occupied. The successive flows of lava continue to be discharged, going first in one direction and then in another until all directions from the vent are covered by lava. After this the flows pile up on the older flows, to great numbers. (The writer has estimated that a minimum of one and a quarter million flows of the volume of the Hoopuloa flow would be required to build a volcano of the size of that from which the Waianae Mountains have been carved, and that very likely three or four times as many flows were made in building this dome.) For several reasons, the flows tend to build highest at the center. Fewer flows reach the margin of the volcanic heap, for only a few are of sufficient duration and great enough volume. The briefer and less voluminous flows are restricted to the central region, favoring its greater growth upward. Also, flows tend to be thinner away from the vent and to build the margins less. The final result is a dome or cone with its highest point approximately above the original vent. In the course of time the great reservoir of lava will be exhausted and activity will then cease; or it may be that eventually the lava heap will be so high as to resist completely the lessened volcanic forces below. In this event, the activity will shift to some easier point of escape 20 to 30 miles away. Here the same process will be repeated and a second dome in the volcanic chain will be built. The Hawaiian domes are of great size. The largest one is Mauna Kea with its summit nearly 14,000 feet above sea level and its base some 16,000 feet below sea level. This great mountain, if measured from the sea bottom platform on which it stands, is some 30,000 feet high. Since the lava of Hawaii is of a relatively fluid type the resulting flows spread out to gentle slopes, and as a result the domes in general have their surfaces only 5° to 10° from horizontal.

On occasions when a volcano is developing very large amounts of gas in proportion to liquid lava, the very different, explosive type of eruption occurs. Gas is much more mobile than liquid lava and comes out through the vent with tremendous speed. The effect of the quick, explosive discharge of gas is to break the liquid lava into many bits, much as a hand sprayer atomizes a liquid insecticide. The sprayer has a little pump which compresses air that makes a fine spray of droplets as it rushes past the liquid. If such a sprayer were worked for a time in a warm place, the spray might gather to form a little pool. But if this were done at the North Pole, there would result a heap of frozen, snow-like material, because with the low temperature the droplets would freeze instantaneously. Lava melts around 2000°F. When it is sprayed up by a volcano into air with a temperature less than 100°F., the drops of lava freeze almost instantly and fall to the ground as pieces of solid lava. At first they will be loose, uncemented materials called dust, ash, cinders, or bombs, according to their size. If they become cemented together in the course of time, the resulting fairly strong rock is called "tuff" The material of Diamond Head, Punchbowl, and Koko Head is tuff. The so-called "black sand" of Tantalus and Makiki Heights is volcanic ash. The explosive eruptions of Hawaii are not very long lived and form cones of small or moderate size. The cones have steep sides; many as much as 35° from the horizontal, because the ash and other grains are very angular so that they interlock and come to rest on steep slopes instead of sliding down so as to flatten the slopes.

CONSTRUCTIVE WORK OF REEF ORGANISMS

Besides the volcanoes, whose activity has produced

the greater part of the volume of the Hawaiian islands, other constructive agents have been, and are, at work. These include streams, wind, and ice, which are of minor importance in Hawaii, and organisms, of which those forming reefs will be discussed next. These organisms thrive only in water that is warmer than 68°F., and do best in still warmer water. The waters surrounding Hawaii are not particularly warm, so that this condition for abundant reef growth is not well met here. Other conditions for flourshing growth are: (1) salty water containing dissolved lime which the plants and animals can extract to make shells, etc.; (2) clear water free of mud which might interfere with their vital processes; and (3) moving water that continually brings fresh supplies of oxygen and of the minute bits of drifting food on which these fixed creatures are dependent for nourishment. The saltiness, the clearness, and the motion of water are three conditions for vigorous reef growth that are well met in Hawaii, but the lack of abundant warmth makes the reef growth only moderate. Moreover, the water should not be more than 150 feet deep, else the light that is necessary for the plant members of the reef society cannot reach them. Many of the shores of Hawaii plunge steeply into waters much too deep for strong reef making.

Formerly all the conditions must have been more favorable, for around the shores of Oahu and on parts of the shores of some of the other islands there is an extensive body of reefs. Since then, the islands have emerged a little so that the former reefs, which were obviously built below sea level, are now above sea level. In the downtown districts of Honolulu, excavations for buildings reveal a thin surface layer of black volcanic ash and below it a considerable thickness of reef.

Reefs can be built only from sea level to 150 feet below sea level, and therefore have a very limited range in which to make rock, as compared to volcanoes which can do their constructive work above or below the surface of the sea, at whatever level the lava or ash is discharged.

DESTRUCTIVE WORK

Most people think of volcanoes as destructive things. Certainly the lava flow of 1926 was destructive in that it laid waste hundreds of acres of grazing land and wiped out the village of Hoopuloa. But from the geologic viewpoint it was constructive because it brought into existence a great body of rock where there was none before. Thus viewed, volcanoes are decidedly more constructive than destructive. However, through their very powers to build they may overdo by building a mountain too heavy for its substructure to hold up indefinitely against gravity. The Waianae mountains may be used to explain this thought. The Waianae mountains project about a mile above sea level and extend some three miles below sea level, giving a total height of about four miles at the center, though less, of course, at the margins. Thus, over a good many square miles the original floor of the ocean has had four miles of rock laid upon it. A prism of rock one inch square and four miles high would weigh about 12 tons. There are, in effect, countless closely-packed four-mile high rock prisms pressing down on the old floor with a pressure of 12 tons to the square inch. This is equivalent to 1728 tons to the square foot or to some fifty billion tons to the square mile. It is perhaps more surprising that the original sea bottom can hold up such a terrific weight than that it has in places failed, and let down part of a volcanic dome. The southwest part of the former Waianae dome has sunk in this way, and also part of the northeast flank of the Koolau dome. Parts of certain other islands have foundered or been engulfed in this way. One phase of the destructive geologic processes in Hawaii is such engulfment.

A rather similar phenomenon has occurred at the summits of Kilauea and Mauna Loa, at each of which a roughly circular central region has sunk somewhat like a cork that has been pushed a little way into a bottle. But this type of central engulfment has had much less total effect than the previously described engulfment or foundering of marginal parts of domes.

A second destructive agent is the running water of streams. When rain falls, some of it flows downward over the surface of the ground until it gathers in little depressions to make rills or tiny streams, which join together to make larger and larger streams. As they flow along, grains of dirt and sand, pebbles, and cobbles fall into the water or are loosened from the stream bed and picked up. As they are carried along in the water they constitute tools by means of which the stream may abrade and lower its bed. The banks are then exposed to the air and slowly disintegrate and decompose and fall in, and so the valley is widened. In its early stages a stream works principally to lower its bed, but later the widening processes dominate. Thus young streams occupy narrow, steep-sided, and deep valleys, which are separated by broad, smooth upland divides. As time goes on, the valleys widen and the divides become narrower, lower, and less well-defined. If the process were to go on without interference, the final product would be a plain with no conspicuous relief features and just enough slope for the water to run off. But, of course, cutting is not the only thing that streams do, for they must dispose of the material they have cut away. This load is brought eventually to the shore where it settles and builds out the shoreline unless the ocean currents are so strong as to carry the debris away. Thus the island may be enlarged in its area, but at the expense of its height. The mud flats back of Waikiki, in part, represent growth of the area of Oahu at the expense of the height of the ridges of the Koolau Range.

A third destructive action is wave erosion along the shore. When waves strike the shore they throw heavy masses of water against it and often detach blocks of rock. Returning, they hurl not only the water but also the sand, pebbles, and boulders that it carries, which wear away the shoreline and cut it back. A stream gnaws chiefly at its bed, which is a sort of ribbon extending from high up in the mountains down to the shoreline. In contrast, the target of the waves is a ribbon extending along the shoreline from a few feet above to a few below sea level. Suppose that there were so little rain on an island that the work of streams were negligible. Then the waves would gnaw away at the shoreline, removing material a little above and a little below sea level. First they would cut a narrow terrace a little below the water and, back of the terrace, a little cliff. With time the terrace would become wider and the cliff would be somewhat undercut, until the overhanging rocks would collapse, bringing the cliff farther back and supplying more tools for the waves to hurl against the shore line. Waves would be at work all around the island at this process, and would make an island girt on all sides by cliffs, though the cliffs would be highest on the windward side where the waves were strongest and most persistent. At a later stage there would be a great shoal with a central crag, as is the situation of Nihoa, 160 miles northwest of Kauai. Eventually even the central crag would disappear leaving only a shoal, which might or might not become occupied by corals and other reef-making organisms. Or perhaps the reef builders would come in earlier and build a rampart to protect the island from wave attack in large measure. The supposed lack of stream work is virtually impossible, and streams would complicate the story so briefly outlined.

SUMMARY

The Territory of Hawaii is for the most part made up of great volcanic domes that have been formed by countless quiet eruptions that poured out lava flows that cooled to solid rock bodies. These domes are gently sloping, of great height, and of considerable area. On them are superposed smaller cones of ash, cinders, and bombs thrown out during explosive eruptions to make these striking features of the landscape. The volcano, which is justly regarded by some with fear, is after all the beneficent agent that has built Hawaii. Reef organisms have added a little to some parts of the islands.

The resulting structure has been modified by foundering, and by the gnawing action of streams and waves. Varying amounts of these destructive effects are seen here and there, and many combinations of them are possible. Mauna Loa, Mauna Kea, and Kilauea have been little modified by destructive work and illustrate the culmination of volcanic construction. West Maui and Kohala are little affected on the sheltered lee side, but are trenched by deep stream-cut valleys and fronted by bold wave-cut cliffs on the windward side. East Molokai, Koolau Oahu, Waianae Oahu, and Niihau have stretches of coast whose straightness is a manifestation of the line along which a part of a volcanic dome broke off to be engulfed. Waianae Oahu and Kauai have been reduced to radiating ridges and valleys by stream trenching. Farther west, shoals, with or without reefs, and with or without central rocky islets, tell of former great volcanic domes now virtually gone.

RELATION OF GEOLOGY TO HAWAIIAN CULTURE

Many features of the culture of the old Hawaiians were more or less controlled by the volcanic nature of their home. Volcanic rocks, in general, decompose rather readily and yield soils more fertile than the average. Some volcanic rocks are of such hardness, toughness, and texture, that they may be shaped into satisfactory tools. Other volcanic rocks resist the destructive effects of heat and make good imus. Still others break up into blocks of shape and size suitable for building walls, platforms, and the like.

Volcanic islands offer a number of climatic types suitable for a variety of kinds of agriculture or natural forest growth. The temperature varies inversely with the elevation, decreasing about 3°F. for every 1,000 feet of ascent. The rainfall varies with the elevation and exposure to the rain-bringing winds. There is also variation in the soil-making processes with the variation of climate, which further favors diversity of plant products.

Coral islands, in contrast, are low and therefore uniform in climate. The soils derived from the reef rock are poorer and less varied than those derived from volcanic rocks. In consequence, the volcanic, or "high," islands offer a far more varied and therefore more favorable and more stimulating environment for human progress. In the Hawaiian islands it was, to say the least, possible to develop a distinctive and high type of culture.

The influence of the volcanic character of Hawaii on human beings was not restricted to the old days, but is still of great importance. It bears on the scenic and climatic attractions that tourists find in Hawaii, and it bears just as definitely on the somewhat prosaic everyday occupations of the resident population.

THE QUESTION OF MINERALS

The writer is very often asked, "Are there any minerals in Hawaii?" The reply starts off with the question, "What do you mean by the word 'mineral?' " If we consider a mineral to be something which is neither animal nor vegetable, there is plenty of mineral in the form of rock and soils. A second meaning is the one which the geologist uses. To him a mineral is a substance of definite chemical composition, usually crystalline, and occuring in nature. Olivine, for instance, is a mineral, for it is a natural, crystalline mixture of iron silicate and magnesium silicate, whose composition is expressed by the formula $(Mg\,Fe)_2\ SiO_4$. We have also in Hawaii the minerals, augite, magnetite, feldspar, aragonite, and a good many others. The third meaning of "mineral" is the miner's and refers to rock which contains enough of some metal so that it pays to dig and treat it to get the metal. The geologist calls such metal-rich rocks by the name of "ore." In this third sense there are no minerals in Hawaii, but in the first two senses there certainly are minerals in Hawaii.

CHAPTER 29

CAN HAWAIIAN CULTURE BE PRESERVED?

E. H. BRYAN, JR., KENNETH P. EMORY, and E. S. C. HANDY

The Hawaiians have a heritage of which they may be justly proud. Though everyone may participate in that heritage through his understanding and appreciation of it, to the Hawaiians themselves falls the chief privilege and responsibility of preserving it. Much is known about the ancient culture, but not a little still remains to be found out. And much of this great heritage has been lost from the lives of the people. Many things in the culture of the old days could be adapted into present-day life to enrich it. If a culture is really to be preserved, it must be preserved in the life of people, as well as in the cases of a museum or within the covers of a book. Research has enabled the scientist to discover and record many things which otherwise would have been forgotten completely. This, though immensely important to the preservation of the heritage of the Hawaiian people, is not the whole story of what is meant by preserving the culture.

HOW THE CULTURE OF A PEOPLE IS STUDIED

The culture of any people has scientific interest and value. Ethnology is the term given to this science concerned with the life and culture of a people. It includes a study of the food of a people—how it was cooked, what household utensils were employed, and how these were made. It includes the study of the clothing and ornamentation used by the people. Under this heading are such items as hair-dressing, personal adornment, and tattooing. Then there is the home, with its dwelling, furniture, mats, baskets, tools, and all its customs and ceremonies. Weapons and warfare play an important part in the life of a people. Transportation is important; in the Pacific it has to do mainly with canoes and navigation. On the lighter side of life we find games, sports, music, musical instruments, and the dance. In Hawaii, art passes naturally over into the subject of religion, mana, and kapu. Most of these subjects are intimately related to social organization. And, finally, we have the customs and practices connected with death and burial. Ethnology has an extensive and important content.

Persons who try to study about the life and culture of a people do so in two ways: from objects and from information. They examine the objects which the people have made, as, for instance, their food pounders, their bowls, their cloth or kapa. They study the technique of their sandals, mats, baskets, and fish lines. They compare the workmanship and efficiency of their tools, weapons, canoes, musical instruments. They admire the art of their religious images and other carving. They gather their food plants, and learn what use was made of each, and how this was done. They ask questions of persons who are well informed. They get the chanters to recite their stories, the bards to sing their songs. They ask those familiar with religious practices to describe them, and the persons skilled in arts and crafts to demonstrate these. All this they describe and record as carefully as possible, in manuscripts and printed books.

All this is hard enough in places where the culture which is being studied is still going on, or where it has but recently changed. But after the culture of a people has been changed for a long time, it becomes increasingly difficult to learn about it. Then we can only learn about it from the objects which have been preserved, or by going to another region, where the people are closely related and still retain a culture similar to that which has become lost in the first region. A study of the life and customs of these people helps the scientist to determine something of what probably existed in the other community.

The culture of Hawaii began to change about one

hundred and fifty years ago. With the coming of other races to these islands, it has been changing faster and faster ever since. There are very few persons left who know about the culture of old Hawaii from having experienced it, or even from learning about it from those who did experience it. It is almost impossible today to obtain much reliable first-hand information about this ancient culture by asking questions. For example, it is well known that the Hawaiians once had names for over a hundred stars. But today, if there is anyone who can point out and give the correct Hawaiian names for more than a dozen, we should be very glad to learn of him. The same thing is true in nearly every branch of the subject. And what is worse, the information which has been recorded about many subjects is far from adequate and in some cases very unreliable. We need to put on record as much as possible of what is known before it is too late.

The same thing is true to a lesser extent of the early history of these islands. We have fragmentary accounts by the early voyagers; a few books and articles written down by native historians; the stories of the missionaries, some of which were quite naturally colored by their own beliefs; fragmentary collections of historical documents and records in our Archives; and the results of researches made by modern historians. All of these together are but an outline of the subject. Many of the details are lacking.

THE PART YOUNG HAWAIIANS MAY PLAY IN THE RECORDING AND PRESERVATION OF THE OLD CULTURE

Young people of Hawaiian blood can help secure information which would otherwise be lost. When they attempt this, they need to have within them a very sincere respect for the traditions and the practices of their people. Many times, the lives of young people seem to be so changed in every way from the ways of their elders, that these elders hesitate to reveal the lore of the past. They would not hesitate if it were plain that the young people had pride in the traditions and customs of their people. Then the best way to secure information of this type is not to ask for it, but to listen quietly as older people talk about these things. The true meaning is revealed in this way as it never is shown in answer to questioning. Perhaps the student of ethnology may be better trained to understand the meaning of what he hears and to describe accurately what he sees, but he cannot see more than the alert and interested person, who, indeed, has more chances than the ethnologist to see and to hear. The littlest thing is of value, and may be interpreted and fitted into the larger scheme when it is reported to the scientist. There still remain in the memories of a few old kamaainas, legends, stories, family traditions, genealogies, and place names which have never been written down. If these things have been worth remembering all these years, they are certainly worth writing down. Old-timers, who have learned to remember, seldom like to write. But the interested young person who wishes to record these valuable things, will make the opportunity to do so. He may also help to preserve that which has already been written down. There is hardly a kamaaina family but has somewhere stored away its copybook of chants, meles, genealogies, and historical notes. Such things should be carefully preserved and made available to students of ethnology and history. Still another thing which any young person may do, is to help preserve specimens from the past. Sometimes these objects are carelessly used and not appreciated. They should be rescued from unsuitable use and placed where they can be studied and examined, as in the Bishop Museum.

There is probably no group in the world who could excel the old time Hawaiian fishermen in intimate knowledge of kinds and habits of fish, and means of catching them. Most of this precious knowledge has already been lost, but there are a few Hawaiians living in different localities who could pass on this knowledge if the younger generation would ask for it and show themselves worthy to receive it. Nothing is more needed than that some of the young Hawaiians, where fishing is good, should learn all they can from their elders about the science and art of Hawaiian fishing. These old methods could be used today, to the great advantage of everyone, but the Hawaiians themselves can best secure the information.

It is interesting to know that the greatest collection of Hawaiian lore was made by the young Hawaiian students of Lahainaluna many years ago. Our most valuable contributions to the study of ancient Hawaiian life came from the pens of full blooded Hawaiians, Kamakau and David Malo. Maoris of the present generation, such as Te Rangi Hiroa (P. H. Buck) and Ariputa Ngata, have awakened to the fact that if an accurate and full account of the ancient traditions and ways of life of their ancestors is to be written, they themselves had better write it. They are doing a great work and the deep insight it has given them into the lives and accomplishments of their ancestors has tremendously altered their attitude toward their ancestors and in turn is changing the view of the modern world toward all similarly situated people. Thus we see that research into an ancient culture has power to transform life in the present, both the life of the student himself, and the life of people to whom his work has significance.

A message to those of Hawaiian blood might be worded like this, "There ought always to be among you of Hawaiian blood, some persons conversant with the great traditions of Hawaii, and some of you able to speak the language perfectly. There ought always to be some of you who can chant the glorification chants, the ceremonial chants, and the chants of the hula in the very same voice that stirred your ancestors and is capable of moving the total stranger to an appreciation of the mystery and beauty of these utterances. The world will then know from whence springs the quality in modern Hawaiian singing which makes it so different from European singing and gives it its charm. When ceremonies, pageants, or festivals are staged to bring before us a refreshing glimpse of the power and grace of the first race to conquer the Pacific, there should be those among you proud of their ability to make and do things as ably as the Hawaiians of old. And above all, there should be some to carry into modern life the fine things of the past. The foreigner had something to teach your Hawaiian ancestors. But your Hawaiian ancestors, from their thousand years' experience among these islands, and out of the spiritual qualities bred in them by their history, had something, indeed much, to teach the newcomers in the Pacific. Seek after and take hold of this heritage which is your birthright and allow it to enrich and give color to your life. You and the world about you will be the happier for it."

SOCIAL VALUES OF STUDYING AND KNOWING POLYNESIAN CULTURE

In order to understand the drama of old Hawaiian life, it is necessary to know what sort of people the actors were. "Know thyself," said the ancient Greeks. This means, for one thing, know all you can about the history and characteristics of the race or races from which you receive your bodily characteristics, for this knowledge will help you to think intelligently about yourself and to adjust yourself to other members of the community in which you live. This process of adjustment is helped forward as you study about the history and characteristics of the other people of these islands with whom you are continually in contact. Consequently, it is valuable for all of us here to understand about Polynesian culture as one of the great cultures which lie behind present-day Hawaii.

Few of us perhaps realize how large a part the spirit of aloha, which is our common heritage from the Hawaiian civilization, is playing in the harmonious evolution of the social consciousness in our community of many races. The lei, with all it symbolizes in gracious affection and hospitality, we have also from the Hawaiian civilization. Like

Hawaiian music, the lei is coming to have a world-wide influence. It has even been taken up in Paris as an element in modern costume. Probably some day it will be a universal greeting for guests and for those arriving and departing on steamships, at least in all countries in which garlands of flowers can be made. But the spirit of aloha, and the custom of exchanging leis, are actually only two out of the many social graces of the old Hawaiian civilization which should be understood and preserved; for in Hawaiian etiquette, in family and communal life, there prevailed a system and code which were in many ways both very subtle and highly refined. Young Hawaiians, particularly, might well take more interest in these old attitudes and courtesies, for it is these graceful things in the art of living that make for happiness more than the material conveniences.

At the present time the world is sensing the monotony imposed upon it by the uniformity of machine made objects and the adoption everywhere of the same customs and habits. Most of these belong properly to the people who evolved them in a very small corner of the earth and under conditions which ill fit many of them to take the place of many things which they are now displacing in other parts of the globe. This culture is rich and efficient in tools and in organizing for production, but particularly in the non-material things—and here lie the greatest values in life—it is in some ways notoriously deficient. It is a mistake for any people to accept, along with the perfections, the defects in a new culture when it is possible to correct them from things in their own. Yet in reaching for the new, old and faithful treasures are often overlooked.

A small example of this great mistake is furnished by the way in which certain things are done by the Boy Scouts of Hawaii. The Boy Scout movement is aimed to teach youth resourcefulness when confronted by nature, and to give him the direct touch with nature so necessary for his sound and wholesome development.

The Boy Scout movement originated in England and reaches its high development in North America. Consequently the woodcraft taught him is primarily American Indian woodcraft, so perfectly suited to that environment. But in Hawaii, the wonderful woodcraft perfected by the Polynesians for these islands has so far been ignored in teaching the Scouts. The Hawaiian scout cooks his food over an open fire. In a country where most of the year the air is frosty or bitterly cold, and the nights very long, a blaze is necessary not only for cooking but for warmth and light. But in Hawaii warmth and light are generously given by the sun. Food cooked in the imu retains more of its flavor and requires no pots and pans to scrub and to encumber one on the march. The Boy Scout carries his pack on his back. He cannot make his knapsack and the heat of the pack is very considerable. The Hawaiian carried his burdens slung on the end of a pole, a way much better suited to this climate than the way used by the Scouts. And the Hawaiian could make his "knapsack," for he could weave, in a few minutes, strong baskets of coconut leaves. His canteen was a coconut, which first furnished him with a refreshing nourishing drink, and then served him as a container. The Boy Scout has to learn to make fire with an American Indian bow drill, but the Hawaiian made fire in less than a minute from a dry hau stick picked up when he neared the place where he planned to camp.

BRINGING HAWAIIAN CULTURE INTO PRESENT-DAY LIFE

There is a very great deal in the life of old Hawaii which could be taken over into life today and made use of. This, together with the effect upon the individual of his study of Polynesian culture, make up the real way of preserving this heritage.

The old-time Hawaiians had very extraordinary knowledge about the arts of fishing and planting, about the medicinal properties of certain native plants, and about diet. The knowledge of agriculture of native peoples in many parts of the world is being studied nowadays, for it is realized that the people who have inhabited given localities for many centuries have accumulated a vast amount of valuable knowledge. The old Polynesians were skillful and ingenious horticulturists. If we only knew as much about raising sweet potatoes today as was known in Hawaii two hundred years ago, we should be able to buy very much better potatoes in the markets. This is inferred from the fact that the few old Hawaiian varieties that are still raised and which can occasionally be bought are far better than imported varieties raised commercially. Similarly, the poi, tons of which are consumed in these islands every day, would be superior to that sold now if anyone would make a discriminating selection of the varieties of taro that make the richest quality of poi. This was the aim of taro raising in the old days, but today, the taros that are raised commercially are those that are the heaviest (that is, most watery), for market value is determined by weight and not by quality. The value of poi as food is shown by its use as the basis of infant's diet in the Ewa Plantation Health Project, in which Dr. Nils P. Larsen and Dr. Martha Jones are interested. The values in the old Hawaiian diet are shown in studies made by Miss Carey Miller at the University of Hawaii. However, at the present time, not only is the finest taro not available, but many people do not take advantage of poi and add it to the diet. It is superior in every way to polished rice which is such a staple food in the islands.

The arts and crafts of old Hawaii included the carving and making of bowls, weapons, featherwork, nets, baskets, and cordage. These arts and crafts are taken advantage of commercially by curio dealers at present. But they seem generally to be left out of consideration when there is talk of the possibility of developing minor industries here to give livelihood to the members of the rising generation who cannot find employment in the major industries, government service, public utilities, and shops. Hawaiian kapa is far more beautiful than that of Samoa which is sold commercially in Honolulu by all the curio dealers. Why should not the fine Hawaiian woods like koa and kou, as well as various imported woods, managed with Hawaiian skill in techniques in working and finishing, be applied increasingly and on a larger scale to houses and ships, making musical instruments, and building boats? Lauhala baskets are very useful and lauhala mats have superior comfort and durability, but neither is produced here in great amounts. Hawaiian featherwork is unparalleled for its beauty, appeal, and lasting quality, but it is becoming a lost art. The olona fiber, and the cordage made from it, are far stronger than hemp and hemp cordage, as proved by tests in the Bureau of Standards in Washington. Are there not, perhaps, commercial possibilities in olona worth investigating? When many are troubled over the problem of livelihood for Hawaiians and for the new generations of other races born in our islands, should not the possibilities of these old Hawaiian arts and crafts, created on the spot, be taken more seriously, and not regarded as mere adjuncts to the curio trade by which only a few profit?

There is a practical side to the study of the old Hawaiian system of government and society, religion, and education, which also deserves consideration. In all parts of the world governments and educators are recognizing that it is necessary to know and utilize as far as possible the traditional institutions and ways of behaving and thinking that belong to the people who have dwelt in the land for many generations. Here in Hawaii the old native land and water rights and titles underlie much of our land system. Our laws in relation to property and marriage have to take into account innumerable conventions that come down from old Hawaiian custom. The political organism of our islands, while it is patterned after the American system, is very much influenced by Hawaiian points of view and methods. It is well for all members of our community to understand these and many other elements of Hawaiian life, for they affect us all.

On the side of recreation, the contribution of Hawaiian

culture in music and dancing, in the luau, and in the spirit of festivity that prevails on public and private occasions when Hawaiians are entertainers, is recognized by everyone. Hawaiian music, like the lei, is known everywhere. The great sport of surf riding we owe to the Hawaiian people. There are other Hawaiian sports, as ulu maika or bowling, which might become popular. And there are many other elements in the old Hawaiian culture that may, and perhaps some day will, be known and understood more widely. The hula, which is understood by few, was a subtle and refined art that is capable under discriminating leadership, of being adapted to modern refined usage, and of becoming a truly beautiful art. The sacred hula was a delicate, graceful, artistic, and appropriate form of dancing.

Perhaps the most worthwhile feature of our Hawaiian heritage deserving preservation, was a certain religious and philosophic aspect of the old cultural life. It is so subtle that it is difficult to define. The Hawaiian mele with its implications and its hidden poetic meanings underlying verbal composition of great beauty, are flowers of thought which lovers of the subtler beauties of Polynesian civilization will never allow to die. They, like the grand nature myths, are permeated with extraordinary philosophic ideas which have been admired for a century by scholars all over the world. But unfortunately the art of creating, or rendering these anew, is dying. The younger Hawaiians might help to keep this great art alive, and interest themselves in the intellectual achievements and attainments of their forefathers.

The very language itself, in all but its cruder aspects, seems likely to disappear. Young Hawaiians should learn from their elders about its rich vocabulary and variety of meanings, and refuse to allow the language to be lost. The records of the old nature poetry, in myths, prayers, or meles, in the riddles and proverbial sayings, will be preserved in print or in manuscript by the Bishop Museum. But composition and rendition should continue to be living arts. They may continue to be so if those gifted with poetic and literary talents, not only of Hawaiian blood but also of other races, will learn Hawaiian speech and explore the rich treasures of its refinements and subtleties.

In all these ways, the heritage of old Hawaii can be preserved in the lives of the people of the islands.

Comments on Chapter 2

"Polynesian Migrations"

by Kenneth P. Emory

The views held by Dr. Buck on the basis of information available during his lifetime need to be modified in the light of more recent findings, especially in archaeology. It is now realized that the ancestors of the Polynesians were in their islands before the Christian era, and that they did not migrate from the continent of Asia as a Polynesian people. Apparently individuals and groups possessing cultural and physical traits which appear among the Polynesians, in the course of centuries, moved eastward from the islands adjacent to southeast Asia by various routes and at various times. Eventually the islands in western Polynesia were reached by these peoples' descendants. Here, in isolation and before settlement of eastern Polynesia, took form those characteristics of physical types, language, and culture which the Polynesians have in common and which serve to set them apart from others.

It would seem that certain traits worked their way to Polynesia through the Micronesian chain of islands, north of the equator, and certain others through the Melanesian chain, south of the equator.

The account naming Hawaii-loa as the discoverer of Hawaii, referred to by Dr. Buck in a "somewhat uncertain Hawaiian legend," has been proven not to be an ancient tradition, but one invented after the middle of the last century in an attempt to adjust to the knowledge, by then possessed by Hawaiians, of the Bible and of the outside world.

David Malo, brought up in the court of Kamehameha I, reveals in his writings that at that time it had not been remembered "who they were who first came and settled Hawaii." He added that it was thought they came from lands called Tahiti and Hawaii, because these are names of lands beyond the Hawaiian Islands, mentioned in the ancient chants. He thought that if Hawaii was not named after the Hawaii of the chants, "possibly the first men to settle on these shores were Hawaii, Maui, Oahu, Kauai, and at their deaths the islands were called by their names."

Dr. Buck's concept of Polynesia being occupied by an earlier and then a later wave of migrants, the first one settling the Society Islands and then radiating out from thence, is no longer tenable in view of the knowledge we now have from archaeology. Dr. Buck's "later period" is more likely the outcome of local developments which took place once a large population had grown up as the result of an improved food base. It then became possible to mount voyages of exploration and conquest which brought about a stimulating interchange of inventions and new ideas.

That the first settlers in Hawaii were known as the Menehune was an idea entertained by Dr. Buck because this is implied in the Hawaii-loa myth in which he is said to be a descendant in the sixth generation from one named Manahune. Furthermore, at that time Dr. Buck believed the first migrants to Hawaii were from Tahiti and that the first settlers of Tahiti were known as the *manahune,* a term applied in historic times to the lowest class of people in Tahiti. It is quite likely that chiefs coming from Tahiti would have *manahune* in their employ, and that through intermarriage their identity was lost and the term somehow shifted to the night-working dwarfs of popular Hawaiian and Polynesian myth. To them were attributed heiaus and fishponds whose true history has been lost. Some of the services indeed might have been built by Tahitians of the *manahune* class brought to Hawaii by voyaging chiefs.

Through the excavation of the floors of natural shelters and house sites on the island of Hawaii it has been found that in the beginning of their occupation, forms of fishhooks, ornaments, and other artifacts resembled those which have been recently unearthed deep in the floors of occupation sites in the Marquesas Islands; whereas later forms on Hawaii match later forms in the Society Islands. This has raised the possibility that the Hawaiian Islands were first populated by people from the Marquesas and later received migrants from Tahiti.

Comments on Chapter 7

"The History of Land Ownership in Hawaii"

by Marian Kelly

Since this chapter was written there has been further research made into the documents concerned with land tenure and a very informative chapter written by the well-known Hawaiian historian, Professor Ralph S. Kuykendall, in his book entitled, *The Hawaiian Kingdom*, 1778-1854. Chapter Five, "The Land Revolution" (pp. 269-98), discusses the meaning of the Mahele (pp. 287-88), the Kuleana Grant (pp. 291-94), and the right of land ownership granted to foreigners (pp. 294-98).

The Mahele of 1848. Strictly speaking, this refers only to the division of the land of the Hawaiian Islands between Kamehameha III and the Hawaiian chiefs which took place between January 27, 1848 and March 7, 1848. In this division of land each relinquished any claim he may have had in the lands of the others and in exchange received clear title to his own land. A second step in this land division was the setting aside of part of the King's lands as "Crown Lands," for his own personal use, and part as government lands. By the summer of 1850, many of the chiefs had also given a portion of their lands to the government.

The Kuleana Grant of 1849. This refers to four resolutions adopted by the privy council of the Hawaiian government on December 21, 1849, and passed by the legislature on August 6, 1850, in which the commoners could make claims for ownership title to the lands they cultivated and to their houselots, providing these were not in Honolulu, Lahaina, or Hilo. The average size of a kuleana award was between two and three acres.

The results of the divisions of land under the Mahele of 1848 and the Kuleana Grant of 1849 were approximately as follows:

	Acres
Crown lands reserved for the king's use	984,000
Lands granted to 245 chiefs	1,619,000
Government lands	1,495,000

Lands granted to 9,337 commoners	28,000
Total	4,126,000

Land ownership granted to foreigners. A law passed on July 10, 1850 gave aliens who resided in Hawaii the right to acquire and hold land in fee simple and to dispose of it to any person living in Hawaii, whether Hawaiian subject or alien.

Comments on Chapter 22

"Navigation" in ANCIENT HAWAIIAN CIVILIZATION

by Kenneth P. Emory

Since the Hawaiians possessed all the domesticated plants and animals known in Polynesia, it is likely that soon after discovery and first settlement deliberate return voyages were made from the Hawaiian Islands to the homeland to secure plants and animals (the dog, pig, fowl) which had not been brought on the first voyage, or which failed to survive it.

For the hardy and venturesome Polynesians of that time, the motivation to return to loved ones or to have news of them, and to announce the marvels of the new land would have been, we can safely assume, powerful indeed. They knew they had only to keep sailing south and they would eventually find their way to Tahiti; and on the return, to sail north, and they would come to the Hawaiian chain. Hawaiian tradition definitely tells of voyages back and forth. In the face of the evidence through archaeology that the rat, dog, and pig were certainly here by a thousand years ago, we must not underestimate the feasibility of return voyages between central East Polynesia and Hawaii considering the knowledge, skills, and daring of the Polynesians.

The concept which appeared in recent renderings of Maori tradition of a fleet of canoes arriving with migrants proves upon investigation to be without solid foundation. For the settlers of New Zealand it would be extremely difficult to return to East Polynesia. It is altogether likely that a number of canoes arrived from East Polynesia, over a period of time, introducing the people and culture later found there by the European discoverers.

ABOUT THE AUTHORS

E. S. Craighill Handy, Ph.D., is an ethnologist and has been with Bernice P. Bishop Museum since 1920. After making two expeditions to Tahiti and the Marquesas, Dr. Handy has, since 1930, actively concerned himself with Hawaiian ethnology, particularly with the fundamental aspects of Hawaiian culture and natural history. Field trips throughout Hawaii and the central South Pacific have given him practical experience in these studies. From 1935 to 1937 he served as Bishop Museum Visiting Professor at Yale. After World War II, he continued field research, particularly in the Ka'u area of Hawaii, where his collaborator, Mary Kawena Pukui was born, but also in especially chosen localities of ecological interest on Oahu, Maui and Kauai. The results of these studies will be presented in bulletins of the Bishop Museum entitled *The Hawaiian Planter,* and *Native Hawaiian Therapeutics.* A description of the *Hawaiian Family* was published in a special publication of The Polynesian Society in Wellington, New Zealand in 1958.

Edwin H. Bryan, Jr., is Curator of Collections, Bernice P. Bishop Museum. Close associations, with the Museum's collection and with distinguished scientists working upon them, has given Dr. Bryan a good opportunity to view many aspects of Hawaiian ethnology and natural history. Field trips throughout Hawaii and the Central Pacific have given him practical experience in these studies. During World War II, Dr. Bryan served with the United States Army Intelligence. Following the war he served with various reconstruction agencies. Utilizing the knowledge and materials obtained during this period he established the Pacific Science Information Center and became its manager. He is the author of seven books and over three hundred scientific and popular articles.

Mrs. Lahilahi Webb* was Guide to the Exhibits, Bernice P Bishop Museum. A friend, companion, and nurse to the late Queen Liliuokalani, Mrs. Webb lived an active life in surround-

*Deceased

ings especially favorable for acquiring a knowledge of Hawaiian history, lore, and culture. She has answered the questions of many thousands of visitors to the Museum.

Peter H. Buck,* M.D. (Te Rangi Hiroa) was an ethnologist and later Director (1936-51) of the Bernice P. Bishop Museum. Dr. Buck was a distinguished Maori. Humanitarian impulses led him into the field of medicine. He served during World War I as a major in the medical corps with Maori troops. As a medical officer in New Zealand, he found that a knowledge of native culture was essential as a direct means of serving his people. He received the Rivers Medal from the Royal Anthropological Institute of London in 1936. He was a life member of the Polynesian Society and a Fellow and life member of the Royal Society, both of New Zealand. In 1946 he was knighted a Knight Commander of St. Michael and St. George. He has earned other honors including degrees at colleges and universities in England and America, has participated in many scientific expeditions, and has authored books and articles of scientific importance.

Kenneth P. Emory is an anthropologist who has been with the Bernice P. Bishop Museum since 1920. He has written reports on the archaeology of Haleakala, Lanai, Nihoa, Necker, and on important sites of Oahu and Hawaii. Since writing the chapters in this book he has been on successive expeditions into many other islands of Polynesia and to two Polynesian-inhabited islands in Micronesia: Kapingamarangi and Nukuoro. He has published reports on the research carried out in those areas. He is now directing an extensive archaeological program of research in several primary areas of Polynesia in an effort to determine the origins of the Polynesian people and their culture, and in particular the last homeland or homelands of the Hawaiians.

Albert F. Judd* was the President of the Board of Trustees, Bernice P. Bishop Museum. The eldest son of the distinguished advisor of Hawaiian royalty, he was familiar with many aspects of Hawaii, its people and natural history. His extensive knowledge of Hawaiian and ornamental plants is shown by the valuable arboretum which he assembled on the new Kamehameha School grounds. Mr. Judd made several scientific expeditions to

*Deceased

Samoa on behalf of the Bishop Museum. He was a Trustee of the Bernice P. Bishop Estate and chairman of the Committee of the Frederic Duclos Barstow Foundation.

Huc M. Luquiens* was professor of art at the University of Hawaii. His interest in ancient Hawaiian culture from the standpoint of art has expressed itself in his valuable monograph on Hawaiian art.

John H. Wise* in the years following graduation from Oberlin College, became a recognized authority on Hawaiian language and lore. He was co-author of a textbook in Hawaiian language and was a general consultant concerning Hawaiian landholdings, water rights, and customs. He served as Territorial senator on special missions to Washington D. C., and for many years served on the faculty of the Kamehameha Schools.

Thomas Maunupau* was the son of the Chief of Kalakaua's fisheries. He was in the office of the Territorial Bureau of Conveyances and come to be regarded as an expert on fishing rights and land matters.

Reverend Henry P. Judd* served in many church-related capacities in Hawaii notably as Secretary of the Hawaiian Evangelical Association. He also was considered an authority on the Hawaiian language and published a textbook which has been issued in many editions. He also was author of many Bishop Museum publications on the Hawaiian language.

Jane Lathrop Winne taught music as a member of the faculty of Punahou School from 1916-43. During these years she was one of the outstanding researchists in the music of ancient Hawaii and also accomplished much original work in that area.

Edith Rice Plews and Juliet Rice Wichman are the granddaughters of the late Honorable William Hyde Rice of Kauai. From their grandfather, who was a sincere student of things Hawaiian, and from many old Hawaiian friends and *kamaainas,* they have gathered a very valuable and authoritative fund of knowledge, especially in their respective fields of poetry and agriculture, and have generously made their findings available to modern students through their numerous publications.

Nils P. Larsen* was medical director of The Queen's Hospital

*Deceased

in Honolulu. He was editor of the Queen's Hospital Bulletin and author of many important studies, particularly in the fields of asthma and pneumonia. He was largely responsible for the Class A rating of the Queen s Hospital by the American Medical Association. He formerly instructed in medicine at Cornell University. In Hawaii, he has cooperated with and supported a wide range of medical studies, including studies of ancient Hawaiian medicine and food. He has served in numerous leadership capacities in Honolulu community activities.

Charles H. Edmondson, Ph.D., a distinguished scientist, has recently retired as professor of Zoology at the University of Hawaii, as Director of the Beach Laboratory of the University of Hawaii at Waikiki, and as Marine Zoologist of the Bernice P. Bishop Museum. He has carried on extensive research of the growth of corals and life on the coral reef, a popular account of which was published by the Bishop Museum. He is the author of many publications of the Museum and the University.

Harold S. Palmer,* Ph.D., was professor of geology at the University of Hawaii. He was the author of several studies in the geology of these islands and served as engineering and geologic consultant in water matters.

*Deceased

INDEX AND GLOSSARY

(A great many Hawaiian words are used throughout this book. The meaning of nearly all is made clear by the context. A few others are included here and defined.)

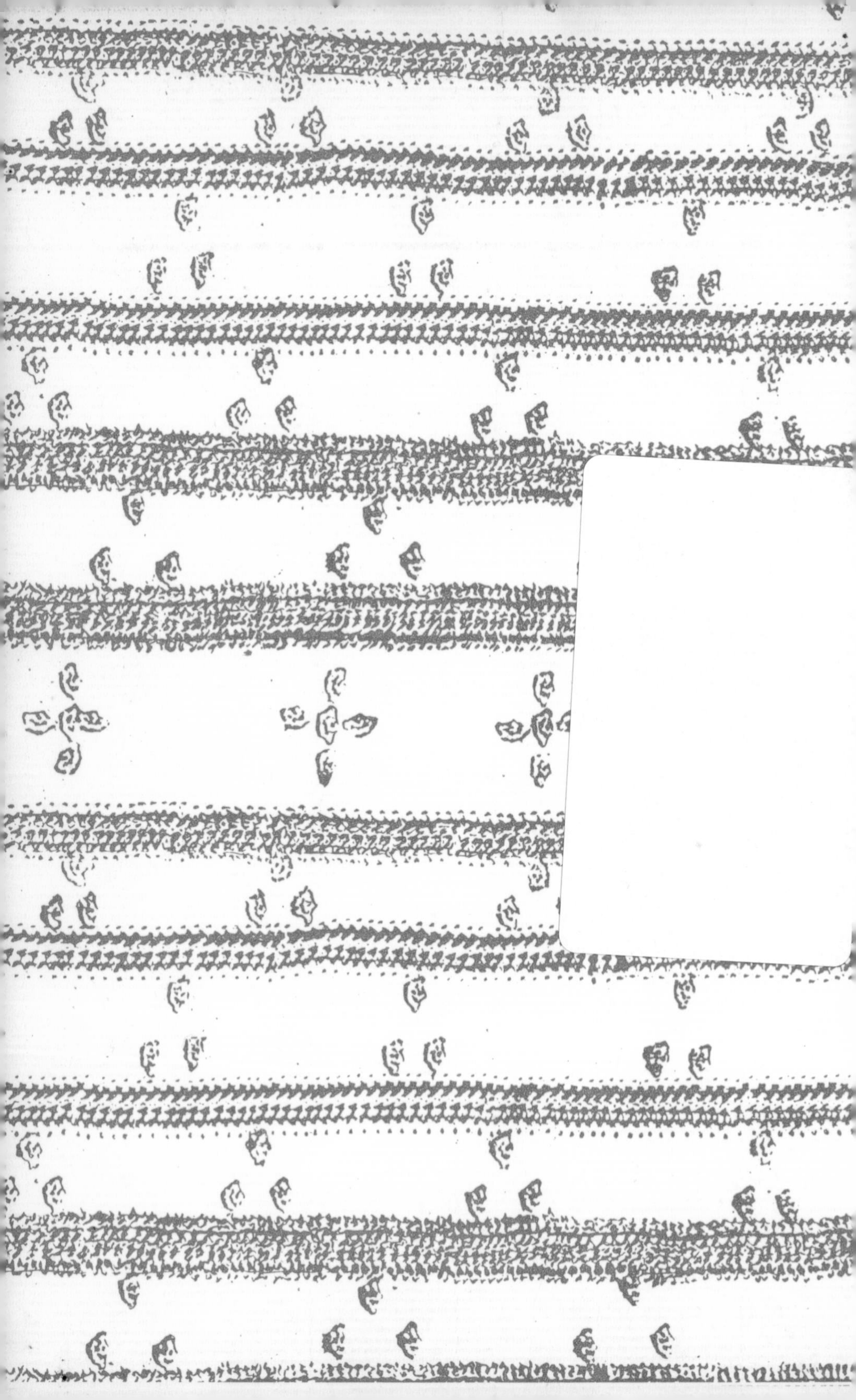